READING TORAH,

THE KEY TO THE GOSPELS

Peter van 't Riet

READING TORAH, THE KEY TO THE GOSPELS

Introduction to the Jewish Character of the Gospels

Folianti

Original title in Dutch: Zonder Tora leest niemand wel
© Folianti, Zwolle, The Netherlands 2010 (2nd revised printed edition)
Translated into English by Peter van 't Riet and Dick Broeren Sr

© Folianti 2018 (paperback edition)
ISBN/EAN: 978-90-76783-48-2
NUR-code: 703 (Bible Sciences)

CONTENT

PREFACE..7

1   ADDRESSED THEM IN HEBREW..9

    1.1 THE LANGUAGES OF THE BIBLE 9
    1.2 HEBREW, A LANGUAGE OF VERBS................................12
    1.3 HEBREW, A LANGUAGE OF CONSONANTS.....................15
    1.4 THE PROBLEM OF TRANSLATING HEBREW 18
    1.5 LIVING WITH THE SCRIPTURES................................23

2   YOU HAVE HEARD THAT IT WAS SAID 30

    2.1 TANAKH..30
    2.2 THE APOCRYPHAL BOOKS................................32
    2.3 THE ORAL TORAH................................34
    2.4 THE TARGUM 44
    2.5 THE SEPTUAGINT AND WHAT CAME AFTER IT.............46

3   AND WALKING IN ALL THE COMMANDMENTS AND
    ORDINANCES OF THE LORD 54

    3.1 THE PHYLACTERIES 54
    3.2 THE TASSELS................................55
    3.3 THE SHEMA YISRAEL PRAYER 56
    3.4 THE DAILY PRAYERS 58
    3.5 THE DAILY MEALS 64
    3.6 THE SEDER MEAL................................66
    3.7 THE SABBATH................................73
    3.8 THE CIRCUMCISION................................78
    3.9 THE NAZIRITESHIP AND THE TEMPLE SERVICE 79
    3.10   FINAL CONCLUSIONS 80

4   TO WRITE AN ORDERLY ACCOUNT FOR YOU...................81

    4.1 THE HARMONIZED GOSPELS 81
    4.2 MATTHEW AND LUKE: TWO DIFFERENT VISIONS 85

4.3 THE GOSPELS AS MIDRASH.. 91

4.4 JESUS AND MOSES IN MATTHEW... 97

4.5 FEATURES OF MIDRASH IN THE GOSPELS............................... 106

4.6 ONCE AGAIN MATTHEW AND LUKE: TWO DIFFERENT VISIONS 110

4.7 MIDRASH AS THE CENTRAL IDEA 114

5 AND THE SPIRIT IMMEDIATELY DROVE HIM OUT INTO
THE WILDERNESS 116

5.1 THE DEPENDENCY OF THE GOSPELS 116

5.2 MARK: THE OLDEST VERSION (MARK 1:12-13) 123

5.3 MATTHEW: DE FIRST REWRITING (MATTHEW 4,1-11) 130

5.4 LUKE: THE SECOND REWRITING (LUKE 4,1-13) 139

5.5 FINAL REMARK 142

6 AND TOOK HIS JOURNEY INTO A FAR COUNTRY 143

6.1 THE PARTING OF THE ROADS.. 143

6.2 THE FIRST PHASE: PAUL... 144

6.3 THE SECOND PHASE: THE INTRUSION OF GENTILE IDEAS 148

6.4 THE THIRD PHASE: THE INFLUENCE OF THE GRECO-ROMAN
PHILOSOPHY.. 150

6.5 FROM ANTI-JUDAISM TO THE HOLOCAUST............................. 159

7 WHEN HE CAME TO HIMSELF 162

7.1 A NEW CHRISTIAN INTEREST IN JUDAISM.............................. 162

7.2 THE JEWISH INTEREST IN THE GOSPELS 170

7.3 ANTI-JUDAISM IN THE GOSPELS?.. 173

7.4 THE RETURN OF LOST SON (LUKE 15,11-32) 176

7.5 A NEW PERSPECTIVE 186

NOTES 192

LITERATURE 206

ABOUT THE AUTHOR 211

Preface

Many theologians and interpreters of the gospels practise, what I would like to call, a Night Watch exegesis. They stand as it were in front of Rembrandt's Night Watch without any knowledge of his time, his life and his work. Nor do they have any insight in the art of painting, not even the art of painting in Rembrandt's days. What they do know is that this masterpiece has been called the "Night Watch" for centuries on end. And this title of course opens a wide field of crooked interpretation: aren't the days we live in not as dark as the night? Or isn't it our duty to watch over all our Christian traditions?

Here we can see how our artistic persuasion is based on an alluvium of art history as, of course, the Night Watch isn't a painting of a watch at night at all. Many gospel stories are treated in the same way. The historical circumstances, the methods of literacy of the bible writers, the personality of the evangelist and his own "theological" view, the Jewish environment in and for which the stories were written, the extensive corpus of thought of the Judaism of those days, all this often doesn't play any role at all in the interpretations of many bible interpreters.

The purpose of this book is to show that knowledge of all this is an essential condition for a good understanding of the gospels. However, the size of this book forces me to restrict myself to the synoptic gospels of Mark, Matthew and Luke. The gospel of John will be left out of our discussion for the greater part, because it deviates too much from the other three, and because it is of a later date and therefore in need of a separate treatment. I wrote about it in my Dutch publication "The Gospel from the School of Lazarus".[1] The gist of my discourse is that the gospels are original Jewish writings indeed, written by Jews and for Jews. Therefore this book is a plea for a Jewish way of reading the gospels. In the chapters 1 to 5 I will introduce the rules for this way of reading by means of a large number of examples.

How to summarize such a discourse in the title of this book? Without any knowledge of Judaism nobody will understand the gospels? Everybody will agree with such a statement. The point is: what specific knowledge of Judaism is meant? Or: Without knowledge of Talmud and Midrash nobody will understand the gospels? Today many people will agree with me on this too, but one doesn't need to go beyond Strack and Billerbeck's work. Where then lies the essence of the matter? Won't it be in the Torah, in the heart and soul of Judaism, the foundation of all the Scriptures? Hence: *Reading Torah, the Key to the Gospels*.

This book, then, introduces some basic rules on how to read the gospels. Don't expect a Christian theology on a Jewish basis (if that would ever be possible). Who wants to live and believe as a Christian on the basis of a Jewish reading of the gospels will have to get through a large amount of spiritual effort.

In chapter 6 I will describe how far Christianity drifted away from its Jewish origin in the almost twenty centuries of its existence, with Auschwitz as a dramatic final result. In chapter 7 I will briefly touch on some developments in our own age. I fervently hope that the nadir of the Holocaust will appear to be a turning point in the history of Christianity. Therefore this book is also - several decades after Auschwitz - a plea against all kinds of Christian theology that consider itself able to determine the place of Christianity and Church without devoting just one word on Judaism, the noble olive-tree of which we are no more than a wild branch.

On the whole the Bible quotations are derived from the New King James Version (NKJV). In particular cases I will quote the New English Bible (NEB) or use a translation of my own to allow for a better understanding of the original languages – either Hebrew or Greek – and of the Jewish religious context. And finally, I'd like to point out that this book was written as a twin of my book "Luke, the Jew".[2]

Autumn 2018   *Peter van 't Riet*

1 Addressed them in Hebrew
The Hebrew background of the gospels

1.1 The languages of the Bible

Hebrew is the original language of Israel. For the greater part Tanakh (the Old Testament) is written in that language.[a] It is still the linguistic heart of Judaism, but nowhere in Tanakh the word 'Hebrew' is mentioned. The language of Israel is sometimes spoken of as 'Jewish' or 'Judean'. This is the case in 2 Kings 18,16. Only much later the word 'Hebrew' began to be used under the influence of Greek and Roman authors. Hebrew, however, is not the only language found in Tanakh. And even in the days of Jesus and the evangelists it was not any longer the common language of the Jews.

Returning from the Babylonian exile at the end of the sixth century BCE the Hebrew language was replaced by Aramaic, the common language then. Aramaic is a twin-language of Hebrew. Both are related like Spanish and Portuguese. Aramaic already was an international language long before the beginning of the Babylonian Exile and its function can be compared with today's English. It was also spoken in the royal court of Jerusalem (2 Kings 18,26). During and after the exile the Jews accepted this language from the Babylonians and Persians as their common language. They even began to write Hebrew in Aramaic characters very much different from the older Hebrew script (see Table 1.1). Hebrew, as the original language of Israel however, kept its religious and liturgical functions. It remained the language used in schools and synagogues. Tanakh was still written in it, although translations in Aramaic were made (the so-called Targums). Only a few parts of Tanakh were written

---

[a] The word Tanakh is an acronym of *Torah*, the five books of Moses, *Nevi'im*, the Prophets, and *Ketuvim*, the Writings.

Table 1.1

Old-Hebrew script and Aramaic square script that replaced it after the Babylonian Exile.

Old-Hebrew script	Aramaic square script	Names of the characters
𐤀	א	alef
𐤁	ב	bet
𐤂	ג	gimel
𐤃	ד	dalet
𐤄	ה	he
𐤅	ו	vav
𐤆	ז	zayin
𐤇	ח	ghet
𐤈	ט	tet
𐤉	י	yod
𐤊	כ	kaf
𐤋	ל	lamed
𐤌	מ	mem
𐤍	נ	nun
𐤎	ס	samekh
𐤏	ע	ayin
𐤐	פ	pe
𐤑	צ	tsadi
𐤒	ק	qof
𐤓	ר	resh
𐤔	ש	shin
𐤕	ת	tav

in Aramaic: Ezra 4,7 – 6,18 and 7,12-26, Jeremiah 10,11 and Daniel 2,4 – 7,28.

Jesus and his followers probably spoke Aramaic as well. Especially in the Gospel of Mark some original Aramaic expressions are found, like *Talitha cum* (Mark 5,41), *Ephphatha* (Mark 7,34) and *Abba* (Mark 14,36). Aramaic expressions can be found too in other New Testament writings like *Maranatha* in 1 Corinthians 16,22 and *Mammon*[3] in Luke 16,9. This shows that the evangelists, although writing in Greek, were thoroughly aware of and used to the Hebrew-Aramaic origin of the gospel.

The third language we meet when reading the Christian Bible is Greek. The entire New Testament is written in it. The majority of the New Testament texts, however, were not written down in a beautiful, classical Greek style. The Greek language of the gospels, the Acts and the Revelation shows many so-called Semitisms, words and expressions derived from Hebrew or Aramaic that cannot be found in the original Greek language. A nice example of a Semitism in the translation of Genesis 2,23 can be found in older Dutch Bible translations like the so-called *Statenvertaling* (1637), which can be compared with the famous King James Bible (1611). The King James Bible renders the text as follows: "She shall be called woman, because she was taken out of man". "Woman" and "man" are related like the original Hebrew words *ishshah* (woman) and *ish* (man). The Dutch language however doesn't know a linguistic relationship between these words. Woman is "vrouw" in Dutch whereas man is "man". The Dutch translators resorted to the analogy of the names given to female animals in Dutch and translated *ishshah* with "mannin", like "aap" (monkey) and "apin" (she-monkey), "leeuw" (lion) and "leeuwin" (lioness). The Semitism "mannin" however never became part of the Dutch vocabulary. If the English language hadn't known the word "woman", maybe the English translators had translated the word *ishshah* with "she-man" to render the word-play in Hebrew. For our discussion it is important to know that examples of Semitisms like this one are very common in the Greek of the gospels and it's clear that they can't all be creative inventions of the translators.[4]

What then was the situation of New Testament Greek like in the first century?

Let's start with a historical flashback. At the end of the fourth century BCE the Greek-Macedonian king Alexander the Great conquered the entire Middle East. From then on Greek became the most important language of the area. The majority of the Jews of the Diaspora, not living in the land of Israel, began to use this language for everyday speech and writing as well. As early as the third and second century BCE Greek had become so important to them that they needed a translation in Greek of the Hebrew Scriptures, i.e. Tanakh. The Greek Bible translation that emerged is the so-called Septuagint and is still used today. The Greek of the Jews in the Diaspora, however, is very much coloured by Hebrew and Aramaic. The Greek mathematician Cleomedes (c. 50 BCE) considered "Jewish Greek" an example of bad style.[5] The evangelists and the author of the Revelation too, wrote and spoke this Semitic-coloured Greek.[6] If and when we really want to understand the gospels we consequently need some basic knowledge of Hebrew in the first place and of Aramaic to a lesser extent. Most important are those characteristics of these languages that represent their thought. In the next paragraphs I will deal with three of the most important features of the Hebrew language and consequently of Hebrew thought.

1.2 Hebrew, a language of verbs

In Hebrew verbs are much more important than in most modern West-European languages. The central position of verbs in Hebrew is mainly caused by the fact that almost all Hebrew words are derived from verbs. For example, the Hebrew verb *jalad* means "give birth to" or "beget". The word for "child" in Hebrew is *jeled*. The words *jalad* and *jeled* are obviously related to each other, where "give birth to" and "child" show no similarity at all. *Jeled* could be translated with "a born one" or "a begotten person", but in general this will not make handsome English. The relationship between verbs and nouns is a common feature in Hebrew. Indeed, in English there are nouns which are derived from verbs, as in other West-European languages like German and Dutch, but they don't play such a central part as they do in Hebrew. An example of this is a word like "entrance" which is derived from "to enter". European languages, however, are inclined to substitute such words by other words that are independent of verbs. Instead of "entrance" we usually prefer words like "door", "gate", etc. Undoubtedly this tendency comes from the need for specification and objectivity. In our modern complicated societies it is important to express exactly what you mean and at first sight this only seems to enrich our language and our way of thinking. On second thoughts however it is not a question of enrichment, but of a fundamental change in language and thought. A change moreover that alienates us from Hebrew. What's the case then?

The word "entrance" still shows what people will do with it: they enter a building or a garden through it, no less and no more. But when using words like "door" and "gate" this is no longer the case. You will be able to go in through a door, but also to leave. A door could be locked permanently, so that this prevents you to go in. It's even possible to drift down a river on a door. The word "door" points at an object that generally has some material features: it is shaped as a rectangle, it is made of wood, it has hinges and a bolt etc. The most important aspect of a door is its essence: what does it look like, what materials is it made of and finally, what purpose was it originally made for? But a door remains a door, too, when it is used for quite different purposes. The word "entrance", however, shows something quite different. An entrance, in contrast, is not defined by its shape, nor by the materials it is made of. The word "entrance" doesn't indicate its essence, but its function, its "what can it be used for". Only the way it is used, is important here. An entrance could even exist as an empty space between to walls. As soon as you can't go in through it, it is no longer an entrance. And if you go from the outside to the inside the entrance immediately becomes an exit. Here we see the most important difference between nouns which are and are not derived from a verb. The clear tie with a verb accentuates its function. If there is no connection with a verb then the essence of the thing will dominate.

Applying this to the words *jeled* and "child", different images emerge.
A child is a man or woman who is not an adult yet. Defining a child we
would enumerate its characteristics: young, small, dependent, sponta-
neous etc. Where does it come from, what is its destination, how will its
surroundings treat it? These all are aspects that tell us more about the
environment of the child and less about the child itself. In Western
thought we try to understand a child to be independent of the environment in which it lives. Even if we consider dependency to be a characteristic of a child, the nature of its surroundings plays a minor role in our
concept. Many concepts in Western thinking have a static and selfful-
filling character. Therefore this way of thinking strongly describes reality
in terms of objects.

In Biblical-Hebrew thinking, however, this is completely different.
The word *jeled*, understood as "that what is born", or maybe better "that
what is being born", evokes a completely different image. In *jeled* we see
the origin of its existence, the act by which it is generated. This birth is
not a coincidence from the past but on the contrary the foundation of the
child's existence. The word *jeled* expresses therefore that a child cannot
exist without its environment. Moreover, that it cannot be understood
without its family, its parents and the community it belongs to. To consider a child as an independent object will not only wrong the child itself
but also our concept of it because, by doing so, we form an incorrect
interpretation of reality. In Hebrew such a concept of a child is fundamentally impossible. A *jeled* is conceived and born with a clear purpose:
to continue the tradition, the way of life and the faith of its parents, its
grandparents and its family. Therefore a child must be conceived every
day by its parents, by feeding, clothing, loving, rearing and educating it.
Biological conception and birth are only the first beginnings of a long
lasting process. In this sense it is even possible in Hebrew to say that the
king of Israel is conceived by God himself on the day of his accession to
the throne: "today I have begotten you" (Psalms 2,7).

Because of the important role verbs play in Hebrew, Biblical thinking
is functionalistic rather than essentialistic. The Hebrew language expresses another attitude towards reality than our modern languages. The

most important aspect of objects is not how they are but what they are used for. In our West-European languages we don't often change the names of things when using them in very different situations. In Hebrew however the same thing gets another name if used differently. This becomes very clear comparing the words "church" and "synagogue". A church as a building will always be called "church" whatever it is used for: public worship, marriage, receptions or concerts. A synagogue how-ever is called differently in Hebrew and this depends on its function. If it is used for public worship, it is called *bet ha-knesset*, which means "house of meeting". If it is used for religious education, it is called *bet ha-midrash*, meaning "house of study". And if the community gathers in it for social events, it is called *bet ha-am*, "house of the people".

For us, West-European Christians, who are strongly influenced by Greek-Roman thought, a big problem emerges from all of this: how to reach a proper understanding of the Bible.[7] The functional, dynamic character of the Hebrew language with its strong focus on actions and events, does lead to another concept of man. Especially questions like how we act, should act, are reflected upon. The central point of Biblical-Hebrew thinking is focussed on questions such as how human beings should live with God, how they should treat their neighbours, or how they should live in their environment. Not on ideas about who or what is God, or what is the essence of man. I will return to this in the last section of this chapter.

1.3 Hebrew, a language of consonants

The books of Tanakh were originally written by means of twenty-two Hebrew consonants only (see Table 1.1). To get an impression of what this means for a good understanding of the texts I will write down the text of Genesis 1,1 in English but without vowels:

N TH BGNNNG GD CRTD TH HVN ND TH RTH

Although the possible interpretations of this text are limited, it is not difficult to find several variations of meaning. For example, we could vocalize: "In the beginning God created the haven (refuge) and the ruth (this being a very oldfashioned word for pity)". Perhaps in Hebrew there are even more possibilities than in English. The overwhelming majority of Hebrew words belongs to groups that are derived from a stem of three consonants containing the basic meaning of a verb. For example, many words are derived from the verb-stem S-P-R (*Samekh-Pe-Resh*)[a], but they all share the same basic meaning of writing (the English word "cipher" is also connected with it although derived from Arabic). It just depends on how we fill in the vowels:

SoPheR   Writer ("He who writes")
SaPhaR   He writes
SePher   Book ("That what is written")

Consequently the original Hebrew text of the Bible can be read and explained in many different ways. And Jewish tradition often takes advantage of this possibility.

The rabbis frequently explore the vocalization of the Hebrew texts by replacing the accepted vocalization with other vowel-sounds. They don't hesitate to propose explanations that on first sight are far removed from the simple meaning of the text. The following interpretation of Exodus 32,16 is an example of this. The common translation of this verse is: "And the tables were the work of God and the writing was the writing of God, graven upon the tables". The word "graven" is written in Hebrew with the consonants Gh-R-V-T (*Ghet-Resh-Vav-Tav*, whereas the 'V' is only a stand-by character for the pronunciation 'u'). The most plausible vocalization therefore is *gharut* which means "graven". One rabbinical commentary of this verse states: "Don't read *gharut* ('graven') but *gherut* ("freedom")!, because he who reads Torah, is a free man".[8] In that case the translation of Exodus 32,16 would have been literally: "And the

---

[a]   In the middle of the word the *Pe* gets often the sound of the "Ph".

tables were the work of God and the writing was the writing of God, on the tables: Freedom!". This looks like a rather far-fetched rendering of the text, but it isn't, because, on the contrary, it shows a fundamental insight in the relation between God and man. In principle God's commandments don't limit human freedom, but they make it a real possibility. For a life without God, a life without his law, is a life in pseudo-freedom, a life really enslaved to its own human impulses, its own egoistic motives and the spirit of time. Here we can discover a fundamental insight in a text that looked very simple at first.

Another example of this way of reading Hebrew texts can be found in connection with Numbers 21,14 and 15. In a statement concerning the intensity of discussions around the interpretation of the Torah (the Five Books of Moses) we read: "Even father and son, teacher and pupil, should become enemies when striving for the interpretation of the Torah. However, if they don't leave until they become friends again, it is said: "*Vahebh* ('friendship') in *Suphah* ('at the end')".[9] In this way these verses which in Numbers 21 play in a context of war en enmity, get a meaning of "friendship at the end". The thought expressed by this is: however important striving for the truth and the correct interpretation of Torah may be, there is a higher purpose in the end: making peace and friendship between people. Here again we find an unexpected depth in a rather simple text.

There are many examples of this way of reading Tanakh by the rabbis. The freedom they allowed themselves in interpreting the texts feels very modern indeed. Therefore the question arises if there are any limitations to this freedom. This is a matter of course. They kept searching for interpretations that should be in line with the fundamental concepts of Torah.[10] Dependent on how successful they were, their opinions and conclusions were handed down to the next generations.

Not until the early middle ages had the Jewish Sages begun to develop and lay down in writing a vowel system consisting of small signs above and below the consonants. The text that came into being is the so-called Masoretic Text of Tanakh and is still used for translations today. Before this codified text emerged the vocalization was handed down orally from generation to generation. That means that people learned to pronounce the text in a certain way. Of course, this didn't happen in the same way in all Jewish communities. Therefore discussions about the correct pronunciation and the corresponding meaning of the text will have happened frequently. We find a vivid example of such a discussion in the Gospel of Matthew. In verse 2,6 we read: "But you, Bethlehem, in the land of Judah, are not the least <u>among the rulers</u> of Judah; For out of you shall come a Ruler Who will shepherd My people Israel.". This verse is a quotation from Micah 5,2. There, however, we read: "But you, Bethlehem Ephrathah, though you are little <u>among the thousands</u> of Judah, yet out of you shall come forth to me the one to be ruler in Israel...". The Hebrew word (*alphei*) that Matthew translated with "rulers", "princes" or "leaders" (in Greek *hegemosin*), is rendered in the Masoretic Text of Micah by "thousands" or "multitudes". The explanation for this difference is to be found in the word that is used in Hebrew. It is derived from the stem A-L-P (*Aleph-Lamed-Pe*) and means, dependent on the vocalization, "princes" ("the first ones", i.e. "rulers") or "thousands" ("multitudes"). Therefore it is possible that some persons read "the leaders" and others "the people".[11] But Matthew is rather unique with this interpretation. The Septuagint translates also with "thousands" (in Greek *chiliasin*). Matthew however couldn't use that meaning for his discourse and so he used the possibility the Hebrew text offered him, reading the word as "first ones", "princes" or "rulers". As we have seen, this freedom of interpretation was generally accepted in those days.

1.4 The problem of translating Hebrew

There are many reasons why it is not really possible to translate Hebrew properly. In this section one of these reasons will be discussed briefly. Many Hebrew words have a double meaning which cannot be translated into modern languages. In the following paragraphs three of these words will be considered in more detail.

The Hebrew word *èrèts* means "earth" as well as "land" or "country". The word can be used for specific countries or countries in general, but in a very particular sense it is a description for "the land of Israel" as well. In our modern languages we can say that this word has two different meanings: in some cases it means "earth", in other cases "country" or "land". In the Hebrew word *èrèts* however, both meanings are interconnected and interacting. Consequently, anything that happens in a country, especially in the land of Israel, is of importance for the whole world. On the other hand the well-being of the whole earth is very important for every country. In this sense the whole and the parts are and always will be interconnected. *Èrèts Yisrael* ("the land of Israel") is Gods experimental garden for the whole earth. There the world should find its example. But the reverse also holds good: the land of Israel represents the whole world with God. If God should be served by people all over the world then this should certainly be done in the land of Israel to begin with. That's why the land of Israel is connected to the Judaism of all centuries by ties that cannot be broken. These ties, reflected in the word *èrèts* can't be rendered into modern languages by any word, whatsoever.

Even more difficult is the translation of the word *davar*. This word means "word" as well as "thing", "matter" or "deed". This shows that in the Biblical-Hebrew way of thinking the difference between speaking and acting is less important than in modern thought. By speaking a word something is done and vice versa. In Hebrew the concept of truth is not the concurrence between a statement and an impersonal reality, but the concurrence between words and actions, between speaking and acting. The Hebrew word *èmèth*, often translated with "truth", should be translated with "reliability" or "trustworthiness". This shows clearly how Biblical-Hebrew thought is mainly concerned with actions of God and man.

A beautiful example of the dual character of the word *davar* can be found in the Biblical story of Ehud (Judges 3,12 to 30). Ehud, a left-handed man, was sent out by the people of Israel to bring their tribute to Eglon, king of Moab. He then fastened a short sword upon his right thigh under his clothes. No doubt Eglon's servants would search his left thigh only, the usual place to gird a sword because most people are right-handed. After Ehud had entered Eglon's chamber he said to him: "I have a *davar* of God for you" (verse 20). Current translations render "a message from God" (NKJV) or "a word from God" (NEB). And thus Eglon would have understood it, for he rose from his seat whereupon Ehud killed him with his sword. In this case the *davar* of God was actually not a word but a thing, the sword of Ehud.[12] Not only this play upon words is lost in translations, but also the fundamental connection between language and reality, between words and deeds, can't be rendered properly into any modern language.

A third Hebrew word which can't be translated with a single modern word, is the word *olam*. This word means "world" as well as "a long period of time", "a century" or even "eternity". The word *olam* expresses a completely different concept of reality compared with the way in which we experience the world and history today. In our modern thought we can look at the world without considering time and history. Moreover we can think about time and history without involving the world as a whole. In our view the world of the Roman empire was a world totally different from the world we live in today. In our experience the days of Abraham are quite different from the days of David or Jesus. In Biblical-Hebrew thought however this is not the case. All events wherever in the world and whenever in time belong to the same *olam*. Moses, Elijah and Jesus can meet (Matthew 17,3), because they live in one and the same *olam*. This word is often translated with "eternal" or "eternity". But if *olam* is looked upon as a reality beyond our time and place, an essential mistake is being made in that translation. The *olam* is no more and no less than the world in which we live in all its aspects, a world in which our ancestors lived and in which our children will live. There is no fundamental distance in time nor in space in the *olam* between a contemporary who lives far off and an ancestor who is buried nearby.

Words like *olam* demonstrate clearly that readers of the Bible shouldn't rely too much on one translation only, but should always be aware of the fact that quite different translations of the original Hebrew text could be valid as well. A good example of this can be found in Genesis 9,12. After the Flood God established a covenant between him and Noah and chose the rainbow as the sign of that covenant. This sign is described as a sign "for perpetual generations" (NKJV) or "for endless generations" (NEB). These expressions correspond with the Hebrew words *lêdoroth olam*. In both translations the aspect of time is stressed above all things. It's however completely possible to translate "for all generations of the world". The covenant of Noah is a covenant for all mankind, once and for all. As soon as one understands this, the sign of the rainbow becomes a characteristic symbol of this covenant. The rainbow will be seen not only by all generations but it also spans the whole world. When rendering the meaning of the word *olam*, one word is not enough, but we should describe it with an expression like "the world of all times".

The examples discussed in the above-mentioned paragraphs show how difficult it is to translate Hebrew into our modern languages. But this problem was already known in the first century BCE with the translator of the book *The Wisdom of Jesus Son of Sirach* also called *Ecclesiasticus* or *Ben Sira*. For Protestants this book belongs to the so-called Apocrypha of the so-called Old Testament, while for Roman-Catholics it is a so-called Deuterocanonical book.[13] Modern translations of Ben Sira are based on the Greek text that in its turn is a translation from Hebrew. This book was originally written in Hebrew in the second century BCE and translated into Greek about a century later by the grandson of the Hebrew author. The translator wrote in the preface of the Greek version:[14]

"You are asked then to read with sympathetic attention, and make allowances if, in spite of all the devote work I have put in the translation, some of the expressions appear inadequate. For it is impossible for a translator to find precise equivalents for the original Hebrew in another language. Not only with this book, but with the law, the prophets, and the rest of the writings, it makes no small difference to read them in the original."

This means that a translation can't be used properly without consulting the original text on a regular basis. This also means that the Greek of the Greek speaking Jews of those days always should be seen against the background of the Hebrew language. This does not only hold good for translations like Ben Sira and the Septuagint, but also for original Greek books of Jewish authors like the gospels. The following example will show how going back to the Hebrew language could influence the interpretation of the stories in the gospels.

In Luke 16,8 to 9 we read at the end of the parable of the so-called unjust steward some words that are remarkable, to say the least:[a]

> "And the lord commended the unjust steward, because he had done wisely: for the children of this <u>world</u> are in their generation wiser than the children of light. And I say unto you: 'Make to yourselves friends of the mammon of unrighteousness, that, when you fail, they may receive you into <u>everlasting</u> habitations."

In this text I underscored two words: "world" and "everlasting". At first sight there is no meaningful link between these words at all. Inspection of the Greek text however, shows that "world" is the translation of *aionos* while "everlasting" is also the rendering of the Greek word *aionious*. Both Greek words are translations of the Hebrew word *olam*! And if we realize that the word *mammon* is an Aramaic word for "property" and that "children of light" is a self-description of the Jewish sect of Qumran[15], then a transparent interpretation of this text will be possible. This sect lived in the desert of Judea forsaking the world (the *olam*). The members of this sect had given up all their personal possessions. Money and private property (the *mammon*) didn't play any role in their monastic communities.[16] In this story Luke introduces through Jesus an opposite view: the world of property (the *mammon*) shouldn't be avoided, but possessions should be used with as much care as is done by the children

---

[a]   In my interpretation of these verses "the lord" in verse 8 is not the rich man but "the lord Jesus".

of this world in order to make friends with it. If material and financial support for those who need it, will be accepted as a normal feature in this world, then everyone impoverished will be received in the "habitations of the world" (of the *olam*). Luke's social program is a strikingly realistic one. So the translation "everlasting habitations" is rather deceptive and had better be replaced in this case by "habitations of the world". Reading the gospels, the Hebrew background can't in fact be missed to reach a proper understanding of the texts. Exactly because strictly speaking Hebrew is a language that can hardly be translated.

1.5 Living with the Scriptures

In the previous sections I have expounded a few fundamental character-istics of Biblical Hebrew. First of all, in Hebrew-Jewish thought the whole and the parts are linked permanently. Secondly, because matters are characterized by what is done with them, it is not possible to isolate them from their surroundings and to consider them as independent objects. Thirdly, language and reality are an interrelated unity, just like space and time, world and eternity. In considering a Hebrew text, therefore, it is always possible to develop several perspectives with regard to its meaning. Moreover, Hebrew words were originally written without vowels, therefore Hebrew texts are never completely finished. Only when they are being discussed and explained they begin to live and become meaningful. All these characteristics imply that Tanakh (The Old Testament) does not have one unambiguous meaning only, that would always be the same. A rabbinical statement says that every word of the Bible has seventy different interpretations and all these seventy interpretations are equally valid with God.[17] Every generation, and all individual members of religious communities will always have to participate actively in the process of reading, rethinking, trying out, studying, interpreting, fulfilling and discussing the text of the Bible.

In Judaism this way of living with Tanakh takes place first and fore-most in religious schools where people meet each other to study together, and to experience each one his own learning process. The crux of the question is not: "What is written in the Bible?", but: "What can be found in it?". The Bible doesn't contain a doctrine established for all times. Individuals as well as communities should find their own respective ways through history in a lasting dialogue with Tanakh. Only that dialogue can show which way could be the way of God. Jesus' statement: "Seek and you will find" (Matthew 7,7) can be applied to the process of searching that way with the aid of Tanakh. He who stops seeking however, because he thinks he has found what he was looking for, won't find anything in the end. In that case the Bible will become a closed book no matter how often it is read.

Now the question arises if everybody can derive from the Bible whatever will suit him. Evidently, this is not the case in the Jewish tradition. Interpreting and explaining Tanakh is not a free and uncontrolled activity. The rabbis maintain three leading principles when interpreting the Bible. First of all there is the text itself. How does it read? Which words are used and what is the order of words? Where in Tanakh can we find comparable expressions? By means of these and other questions the text itself directs the interpretation.

The second principle emerges from tradition. How did previous generations interpret the text? Over the centuries a large body of interpretations with regard to reading the Bible was formed. Many communities lived with Tanakh during the centuries before us. Many rabbis commented upon the texts. How did they read them and in what circumstances did this happen? The present generation will and must be able to learn a lot from their ancestors.

The third principle emerges from our own circumstances. Not everything that can be found in Tanakh is useful or immediately applicable today. Many situations in which we live, are very different from those of Biblical times. Besides, today we are confronted with questions that neither Tanakh nor tradition ever asked. It is even possible that traditional interpretations will have opposite consequences in different times. In such cases Scripture and tradition should be reinterpreted.

These three principles can easily be recognised in a story in the First Book of the Maccabees that plays in the second century BCE. The story in 1 Maccabees 2,31–41 tells how the Jews who had risen against the Syrian king, were attacked on a Sabbath by the troops of the king. They were all killed because on a Sabbath they were not allowed take up arms and so refused to defend themselves. In those days the Biblical command not to do any work on the Sabbath (Exodus 20, 8–11) was interpreted by many Jews as a prohibition to defend themselves against the attacks of enemies. When this massacre was reported to Mattathias, the leader of the uprising, he and his friends said to one another: "If we all do as our brothers have done, if we refuse to fight the gentiles for our lives as well as for our laws and customs, then they will soon wipe us off the face of the earth." Therefore they decided: "If anyone comes to fight against us on the Sabbath, we will fight back, rather then all die as our brothers have done" (1 Maccabees 2, 39–41, NEB).

This story shows in the first place the importance of the texts of the Torah about the Sabbath. Secondly, the traditional interpretation of these texts plays an important part. In that tradition the prohibition to work on the Sabbath is interpreted as a prohibition to defend themselves against enemies on the Sabbath. In the first instance this traditional interpretation is maintained. Only when a catastrophe was the result, this interpretation is replaced by one that befits the new circumstances. The decision against the rule is not a decision against the Sabbath but one in favour of life. Protection of life is first and foremost a Biblical duty. Besides, the traditional prohibition to work on the Sabbath remains unchanged in all other situations.

Subsequently, this adaptation of the interpretation of the text of the Bible to actual circumstances is and remains the responsibility of the religious communities. Not even heavenly voices are paid attention to. This attitude is beautifully illustrated in a story from around the beginning of the second century CE. A hot debate is reported in the Talmud about the ritual purity of a certain oven in relation to the regulations of the Torah (the Law of Moses). Rabbi Eliezer ben Hyrcanos is alone in his opinion against all the other rabbis present in the house of study.[18] Then the story continues:[a]

> "On that day Rabbi Eliezer brought forward every imaginable argument, they didn't accept them. Said he to them: 'If the right interpretationagrees with me, let this carob-tree prove it'. Thereupon the carob-tree was torn a hundred cubits out of its place – others affirm, four hundred cubits. But they retorted: 'No proof can be brought from a carob-tree'. Again he said to them: 'If the right interpretation agrees with me, let the stream of water prove it'. Whereupon the stream of water flowed backwards. 'No proof can be brought from a stream of water,' they rejoined. Again he urged: 'If the right interpretation agrees with me, let the walls of the schoolhouse prove it'. Thereupon the walls inclined to fall. But Rabbi Joshua rebuked them, saying: 'When scholars are engaged in a dispute about the right interpretation of the Torah, what have you to interfere?' Hence they didn't fall, in honour of Rabbi Joshua, nor did they resume the upright, in honour of Rabbi Eliezer. And they are still standing thus inclined. Again Rabbi Eliezer said to them: 'If the right interpretation agrees with me, let it be proved from Heaven'. At that moment a Heavenly Voice (*bat kol*) cried out: 'Why do you dispute with Rabbi Eliezer, seeing that in all matters the right interpretation agrees with him?' But Rabbi Joshua arose and exclaimed: 'It is not in heaven' (Deuteronomy 30,12). What did he mean by this? Said Rabbi Jeremiah: 'That the Torah (the Law of Moses) had already been given [to the people of Israel] at Mount Sinai [and was no longer in heaven]. Therefore we pay no attention to a Heavenly Voice, because You [God] have long since written in the Torah at Mount Sinai: 'After the majority must one incline' (Exodus 23,2).'

---

[a] Here the Talmud uses the word *halakhah*. As that term will be introduced at first in chapter 2, I have translated it with the word "right interpretation".

Later, Rabbi Nathan met the prophet Elijah and asked him: 'What did the Holy One, Blessed be He, do in that hour?' 'He laughed,' Elijah replied, saying, 'My children have defeated Me, My children have defeated Me'."

In this story we see another important characteristic of Biblical Hebrew and Jewish thought. Abstract matters are dealt with in the form of concrete, imaginative stories. To recognize the underlying message of the story one should know and understand the language of the images used. What is told here in a concrete story can be expressed in our Western, abstract way of thinking as follows:[19] "The tradition-process of interpreting the Scriptures doesn't occur in the loneliness of a study, but within a debating community. Its authority isn't that of an outer- or superhuman power, but that of the living experience of a community in which rules and arrangements crystallized during many generations".

Therefore the Hebrew Bible as well as the rabbis show a remarkable lack of interest with regard to an abstract doctrine and theology about God, creation, man, salvation, atonement etc. God can't be known by His characteristics, but He should be acknowledged in His actions. The Creation shouldn't be studied as something from the past, but work should be done with it and in it for generation to come. Man is man only when he participates in this process and if he tries to live in accordance with the rules of conduct God offers him in Scripture. Salvation is not something that happened to you one day, but a daily act of freeing yourself from everything that prevents you from living in a Biblical way. The rabbis concentrate upon the questions what should be done in real life. Now this is the focal point in Biblical and Jewish thought about man: not fate, but the choices he makes in order to live a good life.

Here we meet with a large difference between Biblical and Jewish thought on the one hand and Greek philosophy, having strongly influenced Christianity and Western culture, on the other. This difference between Jewish thought (which still formed a natural part of the way of thought of early Christianity) and the Greek way of thinking can be seen nicely when we compare two parallel stories from the second century

CE. The first one is from the Gospel of Thomas. It shows an acting individual who makes choices in a given situation. The second parable was written by the Greek fabulist Babrios. It shows the way things happen, the freaks of fate. Using the same images two completely different ways of thinking about reality are expressed in these stories.[20]

The Gospel of Thomas, Log. 8

Babrios, Fable 4

And he said, "The man is like a wise fisherman who cast his net into the sea and drew it up from the sea full of small fish. Among them the wise fisherman found a fine large fish. He threw all the small fish back into the sea and chose the large fish without difficulty. Whoever has ears to hear, let him hear."

A fisherman drew up his net that he had thrown into the sea shortly before, and as a good ordination wanted, it was full of all kinds of delicious fishes. But the small ones flew to the bottom of the net and escaped through the wide meshes, whereas the big ones were caught and laid stretched out in the boat.

This Biblical-Jewish interest in human behaviour can also be found in the gospels and the Acts of the Apostles. Acting even precedes teaching. In Acts 1,1 we read that Luke has written his first book (the Gospel of Luke) about "all that Jesus began both *to do and teach*". In Judaism "doctrine" is the explanation of life, and stories are told to illustrate how or why things should be done. Words can only be spoken in connection with deeds. Teachings can only be kept and passed on if they are based on the way of live. Or as Luke writes in the name of Jesus:

"But he who heard and did nothing is like a man who built a house on the earth without a foundation, against which the stream beat vehemently; and immediately it fell. And the ruin of that house was great." (Luke 6,49).

The Biblical-Hebrew way of thinking in the Judaism of the first century was also the way of thinking of the evangelists. And this, of course, has important consequences for the exegesis of the gospels and the Acts of the Apostles. Although written in Greek these books breath a Hebrew-Jewish spirit which is still insufficiently recognized by Christianity. However, the growing acknowledgement of the Hebrew-Jewish origin of the New Testament is a gratifying phenomenon today. In the next chapters I will show that the linguistic aspects of the gospels are not the only ones rooted in the Judaism of the first century CE.

2 You have heard that it was said
The library of the evangelists

2.1 Tanakh

The most important collection of books the evangelists had access to, was indisputably the Hebrew Bible. Instead of the "Old Testament" I will call these writings by their Jewish name "Tanakh", because Tanakh is neither old but new every morning, nor a testament at all. Actually, the word Tanakh is an artificial word, an acronym. The consonants T, N and Kh stand for:

- Torah (Genesis up to Deuteronomy);
- Nevi'im (the Prophets);
- Ketuvim (all the remaining Scriptures)[a].

Compared with the so-called Old Testament this order of the Hebrew Bible is based on a different idea. The Hebrew Bible doesn't acknowledge a division into historical books, poetical books, wisdom books and prophetical books. The three groups mentioned contain the following books:

- **Torah** : Genesis, Exodus, Leviticus, Numbers and Deuteronomy;
- **Nevi'im** : Joshua, Judges, 1 and 2 Samuel, 1 and 2 Kings, Isaiah, Jeremiah, Ezekiel, Hosea, Joel, Amos, Obadiah, Jonah, Micah, Nahum, Habakkuk, Zephaniah, Haggai, Zechariah and Malachi;

---

[a] In general, the Hebrew character *kaf* is pronounced as "k" at the beginning of a word, but at the end as "kh", as the <u>ch</u> in the word 'lo<u>ch</u>'.

- **Ketuvim** : Psalms, Proverbs, Job, Canticles, Ruth, Lamentations, Ecclesiastes, Esther, Daniel, Ezra, Nehemiah, 1 and 2 Chronicles.

Without any doubt, the Torah is the most important one of these three groups. Until today every Sabbath worshippers read the Torah in the synagogue services according to a fixed schedule. In one year the entire Torah is read and no section is left out. The tradition of these Torah readings is very old and in the days of the evangelists it was already an established custom (e.g. Acts 13,15; 15,21). In those days not only a one-year cycle of readings existed but also a triennial one, in which the Torah was read in a period of three years.[21] In both cases the Torah was divided into fixed sections. Every Sabbath the next section was and will be read. The section of the week, called *sidra* ("order"), is followed traditionally by a reading from the Prophets, called *haftarah* ("completion"). This *haftarah* is thematically connected to the preceding reading from the Torah. Not all parts of the Prophets are used as *haftaroth* (plural). And although a generally accepted schedule for the *haftaroth* probably didn't exist in the first century, the custom to read from the Prophets following the readings from the Torah was already firmly established in those days (e.g. Luke 4,17; Acts 13,15 and 27).

The division of the Hebrew books of the Bible into three groups is also very old. For example, it's already mentioned in the book *The Wisdom of Jesus Sirah*.[a] A similar division is mentioned in the Gospel of Luke as well (Luke 24,27 and 44). In my view the Christian Churches had better turn back to the use of this original division of the Hebrew Bible, if only because it was once used by Jesus and the evangelists.

Here I will only deal briefly with the importance of Tanakh when reading the gospels, because I am going to discuss this subject extensively in chapter 4. Then it will become clear that every page, every chapter and every section of the gospels are incomprehensible without any knowledge of Tanakh. However, we should bear in mind that

---

[a]   See the quotation in section 1.4.

Tanakh in its present form didn't exist in the days of the evangelists. Certainly, the Torah had already undergone its final redaction centuries before, and discussions by the rabbis about the authority of the Books of the Prophets had already come to an end long ago, but in the days of Jesus no accordance had been reached as yet about the authority of several other books like Canticles and Esther. Moreover, many books circulating in the Jewish society of those days were never canonized because they had no or not enough authority in the eyes of the rabbis. It was only after the destruction of the temple of Jerusalem in 70 CE that the rabbis laid down the canon of Tanakh. Many books that were not incorporated into the canon did survive however, often in a Greek translation. Many of these so-called Apocryphical books also belonged to the library of the evangelists. In the next section I will pay attention to them.

2.2 The Apocryphal Books

Not only the books of Tanakh circulated widely in the Judaism of the first century CE, but also a countless number of similar books. Some of them were handed down in the Greek manuscripts of the Septuaginta. In the Christian churches they still continue to play a part as the Apocryphal or Deuterocanonical Books. Examples of these books are the Books of the Maccabees, The Wisdom of Jesus Sirah, The Wisdom of Salomo, etc. These books were written in the period between the origin of the books of Tanakh on the one hand and that of the gospels on the other. Therefore they are very important indeed for the reading and understanding of the gospels. Nevertheless I will mention here one example only, because the interested reader can find the Apocrypha in several Bible translations.[22]

Texts from the Apocryphal books can sometimes shed a clearer light on some texts from the Gospels that lie more or less buried beneath a traditional exegesis. For example, it is very instructive to compare the following two texts.

Ben Sirah 51,23 to 27 (NEB)	Matthew 11,28 to 30 (NKJV)
Come to me, you who need instruction, and lodge in my house of learning. Why do you admit to a lack of these things, yet leave your great thirst unslaked? I have made my proclamation: "Buy for yourselves without money, bend your neck to the yoke, be ready to accept discipline, you need not go far to find it". See for yourselves how little were my labours compared with the great peace [i.e. rest] I have found.	Come to me, all you who labor and are heavy laden, and I will give you rest. Take my yoke upon you and learn from me, for I am gentle and lowly in heart, and you will find rest for your souls. For my yoke is easy and my burden is light

The usual exegesis of Matthew 11,28-30 says that man, as a miserable being, should entrust himself to Jesus whereupon he may feel redeemed and free without the need for further obligations. However, we do encounter the same words and images in the text of Ben Sirah, at first sight in a quite different context. There the focus is solely on learning in the house of study, i.e. accepting instruction and gaining wisdom. If we read the words of Jesus "and learn from me" again, but now with Ben Sirah's perspective in mind, there is a striking similarity indeed. This similarity clears the way for a completely different exegesis of Jesus' words. The focus now is on learning Torah instead of trying to obtain a quiet life. In Judaism, the yoke is a symbol of the Torah and of the rules of life derived from it.[23] The text of Matthew contains an appeal to learn how to live from the Torah, led by Jesus' teachings and example. If we compare the words of Jesus "my burden is light" with the words of Ben Sirah "see for yourselves how little were my labours", then Jesus' words should be understood in a way that differs completely from its traditional interpretation. Ben Sirah wrote his words at the end of his book after he had filled 51 chapters with wisdom, interpretations of Torah and rules of life! In this way salvation and freedom should be followed by an intensive reflection on the conduct of life.

Not only the books of Tanakh and the "official" Apocrypha circulated widely in the Judaism of the first century CE, but also many writings that are still today very important as background literature for the gospels. The Apocalyptic books for example, that paint the end of the world in dramatic colours, are such writings of which many have survived. However, because it's not easy to explain in short the significance of these books for the reading and understanding of the gospels, I won't go further into the matter. The same holds true for the Dead Sea Scrolls written by the monastic sect of Qumran, the Essenes, that have been discovered since 1947. On the other hand we will sometimes return to the Apocrypha in the next chapters.

2.3 The Oral Torah

We should realize now that Tanakh and the above mentioned books were, in fact, not the only literary source and background of the Gospels. Along with the written books a very large number of oral stories and traditions circulated widely in the Judaism of those days. All this material, handed down from parents to children, and from teachers to pupils, is called "the Oral Torah". This Oral Torah together with the Written Torah (Genesis to Deuteronomy) constitute a coherent corpus. Until today the Oral Torah interprets the Written Torah, completes it and applies it to the life of everyday. For centuries one resisted within Judaism the writing down of the Oral Torah.[24] Nevertheless there were several reasons that made it important and necessary to collect and chronicle these oral traditions. From the second century CE on many rabbis worked at the codification of the Oral Torah. A tremendous amount of literature was the result of these efforts, a corpus of literature that contains many dozens of books more than Tanakh counts. For example:

- the Talmud, in the Jerusalem and the Babylonian edition,
- the Tosephta, a completion to the Talmud,
- the Midrash Rabbah, a commentary on the Bible books of the Torah, Ruth, Esther, Canticles, Ecclesiastes and Lamentations,
- the Mekhilta of Rabbi Ishmael, a commentary on Exodus,
- the Sifra, a commentary on Leviticus,
- the Sifre, a commentary on Numbers and Deuteronomy.

An comprehensive summary of this literature can be found elsewhere.[25]

Not only stories and statements of the rabbis of Antiquity and of the early Middle Ages are found in the Oral Torah, but also many older traditions from the days of Jesus and earlier. Therefore the Oral Torah is an essential source of information for the study of the gospels. She provides us with a deeper understanding of the opinions of important Jewish groups before and in the days of Jesus. And this could prevent us from looking upon the gospels as rather exceptional writings in the Judaism of those days. Many ideas in the gospels that at first sight seem to be very original, aren't that original at all, if studied more closely in relation to similar opinions in the Oral Torah. Later in this section I will give two examples.

The traditions in the Oral Torah can be divided into two groups: *halakhah* and *haggadah*. A *halakhah* is a rule of life derived from the Written Torah or from another rule of life in the Oral Torah. The word *halakhah* is derived from the Hebrew verb "to go". Therefore a *halakhah* is like a "rule of the road of God". The Oral Torah does not only contain discussions about these rules of life, but also many stories that are meant to give insight into all kind of questions living in the community. Such stories that don't focus on decisions about the rules of life, but on insight, are called *haggadah*. A *haggadah* can be told for example to get a deeper understanding or to explain a *halakhah*. In the writings of the Oral Torah *halakhah* and *haggadah* alternate permanently. This phenomenon can also be seen in the gospels where rules of life and stories interchange frequently. A good example is the story about the plucking of the heads of grain on the Sabbath in Luke 6,1-5. This story is a *haggadah*, but a *halakhah* for the Sabbath plays an important part in it. In this respect the gospels are typically Jewish writings as well.

Some stories and traditions from the Oral Torah are also called *midrash*.[26] A *midrash* is a more or less complete body of texts that can contain *halakhah* as well as *haggadah*. With some care it could be treated as a separate literary unit. I would like to stress the words "with some care", because a *midrash* is always enclosed in other *midrashim* (plural of *midrash*), that can be of great importance for its meaning. In this way every story in the gospels can also be seen as a *midrash*. However, the word *midrash* doesn't only point at a literary unit within a broader context. The word also means "teaching". A *midrash* story always intends to teach the listener or reader something. Moreover, to understand the symbolic language of the *midrashim* the reader should have at least some knowledge of the images of that language. A *midrash* always borrows a greater part of its images from Tanakh and from other stories in the Oral Torah. In the fourth chapter I will show that the language of images of the *midrash* is constructed in a way that differs completely from the language of concepts we use in our Western culture. The gospels, too, use this midrashic language of images. It is only possible to disclose the Jewish meaning of the gospels if we study them as if they were parts of the Oral Torah. I will discuss two examples in the next paragraphs, one in the field of the *halakhah* and one in that of the *haggadah*.

a.   A halakhah of Matthew

In Matthew 5,38-39 we come across a word of Jesus that, at first sight, seems to be rather radical:

> "You have heard that it was said, 'An eye for an eye and a tooth for a tooth'. But I tell you not to resist an evil person. But whoever slaps you on your right cheek, turn the other to him also."

Here Exodus 21,23-25, a text from the Torah, is quoted:

"But if any harm follows, then you shall give life for life, eye for eye, tooth for tooth, hand for hand, foot for foot, burn for burn, wound for wound, stripe for stripe."

This rule of the Torah is often referred to as the "right of retaliation". Many exegetes have interpreted this word of Jesus by Matthew as a radical break with the Torah. If, however, we study both texts in the context of the Eastern culture of those days and in the light of the Oral Torah, then a completely different interpretation of Matthew 5,38-39 could be given. Therefore we should go further back into the Torah and borrow a text of Genesis for our discussions.

In Genesis 4,23-24 in Lamech's saying a sense of justice is put into words that has been widely spread in the Middle East from Antiquity until today: the sense of justice by blood-feud. The words of Lamech are extreme indeed, but they clearly illustrate the tendency of the blood-feud to get out of control:[27]

"Then Lamech said to his wives: 'Adah and Zillah, hear my voice; wives of Lamech, listen to my speech! For I have killed a man for wounding me, even a young man for striping me. If Cain shall be avenged sevenfold, then Lamech seventy-sevenfold."

Because of this tendency several attempts are made in the Torah to limit the system of blood-feud and the quoted text of Exodus 21,23-25 is only one example of them. Moreover, this text is closely connected with the words of Lamech. After life as a general principle seven concrete examples are enumerated in Exodus: eye, tooth, hand, foot, burn, wound and stripe. Therefore, the limitation of the blood-feud is not only in force in relation to offences against life but also to all other bodily harm. The last two words of the text of Exodus, wound and stripe, are in Hebrew the same words that are used by Lamech, literally: "I have killed a man for a wound and a young man for a stripe". Therefore, Exodus 21,23-25 is a step forward with respect to Lamech's point of view. Yet two questions can be asked about this matter:

1. Why does the Torah only limit the blood-feud and why doesn't she abolish it completely?
2. Is the quoted statement by Jesus a radical break with the Torah indeed, or should we interpret it as a following step on the way of the Torah to lessen physical violence in society?

The answer to the first question can easily be given. The Torah is too realistic to want to remove all evil from the world overnight. A deep rooted sense of justice that already existed for centuries, however objectionable it may be, can only be changed into a better direction gradually and step by step. Just by mentioning the words "wound" and "stripe" of Genesis 4,23-24 in Exodus 21, 23-25 the Torah shows the direction into which the community should continue. The next generations could make further steps on that way. When the limitation of the blood-feud has become generally accepted in Israel, a further step can be made in the same direction. That step can be found in the Oral Torah.

After the rule in Exodus to diminish physical violence in the community of Israel, the next step was made by the rabbis before and in the days of Jesus with a new interpretation to the words "eye for eye and tooth for tooth". In the Oral Torah we read: "'Eye for eye' means 'financial compensation'".[28] This means: you shall pay the value of an eye for an eye and the value of a tooth for a tooth. He who has caused physical damage, is obliged to compensate the wounded person for his sufferings. In this way physical revenge is limited to a certain degree and violence is driven back again.

This example makes it quite possible to reach a completely different interpretation of Jesus' words in the Gospel of Matthew. The words "You have heard that it was said" don't refer to the Written Torah, but to the interpretation of the words "eye for eye and tooth for tooth" in the Oral Torah. Jesus didn't move away from this interpretation, but associated himself with it. In line with the limitation of violence in society, he made the next step with his words "but whoever slaps you on your right cheek, turn the other to him also". This is, however, a less radical step than many scholars would like us to believe. For we should indeed differentiate between violence that causes physical damage and violence that doesn't. Here the slap on the cheek represents the latter form of violence. The ruling of the Oral Torah in cases of physical harm is completely endorsed by Jesus. His words only mean that violence that doesn't cause any harm, shouldn't even be answered by the same kind of harmless counter-violence. This is not a radical break with the Oral Torah but a cautious extension of it. It would have been a radical break indeed if Jesus had stated: "But whoever knocks out your right eye, turn the other to him also". Such a rule of life would be absurd indeed and Jesus would have placed himself completely outside the reality of life.

Finally it should be noticed that even Jesus' rule of life with respect to "the other cheek" was not new at all in his days, but he derived it from Tanakh. In Lamentations 3,30 it is said about a person who waits for the Lord: "Let him give his cheek to the smiter, and be filled with insult". This attitude in life by which it would be better to suffer evil rather than to do it, is typical for Jesus, but certainly not only for him. Matthew shows us that Jesus in this respect again closely joined his predecessors of Tanakh.

b.   A haggadah of Matthew

What about Matthew 23,34-35? In a harsh argument of Jesus with the scribes and the Pharisees a problem appears that could easily be overlooked. Here Jesus says:

> "Therefore, indeed, I send you prophets, wise men, and scribes: some of them you will kill and crucify, and some of them you will scourge in your synagogues and persecute from city to city, that on you may come all the righteous bloodshed on the earth, from the blood of righteous Abel to the blood of Zechariah, son of Berechiah, whom you murdered between the temple and the altar."

Indeed, many questions could be asked about this saying, but I will only ask one of them for further discussion: the fact that the name of Zechariah the son of Berechiah is mentioned and the way in which he died, is remarkable for more than one reason. This Zechariah the son of Berechiah was the author of the prophetical book Zechariah (Zechariah 1,1). If the dating at the beginning of this book is correct, Zechariah lived in the year 520 BCE. In Tanakh however, nothing is said about his death or how he died. So the question arises what Matthew could have meant with his statement that this Zechariah was killed between the sanctuary and the altar. Indeed, such a murder is mentioned elsewhere in Tanakh, but there it concerns another Zechariah. In 2 Chronicles 24 (particularly the verses 20 and 21) is told how Zechariah, the son of Jehoiada, was killed in the sanctuary. He was the high-priest in the days of king Joash who lived about 830 BCE, three centuries before Zechariah the son of Berechiah. The consequence of this is that Matthew ascribed the death of a high-priest in the ninth century to a prophet in the sixth century. How to explain this?

Two explanations seem to be obvious, but both of them must be rejected. The first one supposes that Zechariah the son of Berechiah was also killed in the sanctuary between the building of the temple and the altar. This "explanation" however, is unacceptable for three reasons. First of all the killing of a prophet would have given the authors of Tanakh enough reason to write about but nowhere Tanakh mentions anything about the death of Zechariah the son of Berechiah. Secondly, the same argument holds good for a murder in the forecourt of the temple. In the third place, nowhere in Tanakh something can be found about conflicts of Zechariah the prophet with Jewish groups that could have murdered him in this way. In general it should be said that putting forward a hypothetical fact to explain an apparent contradiction in the gospels, is a method of explanation that maybe is acceptable for Western readers today, but that has nothing to do with the way in which Jewish storytellers of the beginning of the common era wrote their stories. In the fourth chapter I will return to this issue in detail.

A second explanation supposes that Matthew made a mistake. However, such conclusions are too easily made with respect to an evangelist who is usually very well informed on Tanakh, the Jewish history and the Judaism of his days. Supposing mistakes made by an evangelist as a method to explain incomprehensible or obscure texts, is really the last instrument an exegete should use. In that case he should be quite sure of the fact that no other explanation of the text is possible. But how can he be sure, in view of our limited knowledge of the circumstances in which the evangelists wrote their gospels? Therefore in such cases an interpreter would do better to acknowledge his inability to find a good explanation for some of these texts. For Matthew 23,34-35 however, a good explanation is possible that is closely connected to the Judaism of those days. Therefore we should turn to the Oral Torah.

Matthew does something with the stories of Zechariah, son of Berechiah, and Zechariah, son of Jehoiadah that happens rather frequently in the Oral Torah: he links up the two historically different Zechariahs.[29] This isn't done because the younger Zechariah could be a reincarnation of the older one, but because both of them played similar parts in two different episodes of the history of Israel. Both Zechariahs for example, guaranteed the correct course of the sacrificial service in the temple. This is completely clear for Zechariah the son of Jehoiada in 2 Chronicles 24. And what about Zechariah the son of Berechiah? He and the prophet Haggai prophesied in Jerusalem in order to have the temple rebuild after the Babylonian Exile (see Ezra 5,1 where he is called "the son of Ido" after his grandfather; cf. Zechariah 1,1). Furthermore, the Oral Torah tells about him that he was able to show the correct place to erect the altar.[30] Now the connection of both Zechariahs with the correct course of events in the temple makes it possible to 'link them up'. That's the reason why Matthew was able, in a speech about "Jerusalem, Jerusalem, killing the prophets", to let Zechariah the son of Berechiah die the death of Zechariah the son of Jehoiada. This phenomenon of linking up two historical figures I will call "identification". In the Oral Torah again, both Zechariahs are seen as one and the same person and sometimes a third Zechariah (in Isaiah 8,1) plays a part in this identification-process as well.[31] In the fourth chapter I will show that Matthew frequently links up certain personalities. Here the conclusion could be that Matthew, in 23,34-35, neither reports the historical fact of a death that could have been mentioned elsewhere, nor does he make a mistake, but indeed uses the narrative method of identification in order to bring an argument into the story. To get a better understanding of this argument of Matthew 23, we ought to consult the Oral Torah more often.

But before doing so, we should realize one thing in particular. The Oral Torah mainly contains the ideas and opinions of the Jewish group of the Pharisees. But these Pharisees are not the same Pharisees the evangelist argues with in Matthew 23. The Pharisaic movement of Matthew's days knew conservative and progressive wings. In the Oral Torah the so-called School of Shammai represents the conservative wing, whereas the so-called School of Hillel stands for the progressive Pharisees. Just this School of Hillel had ideas that were very close to the ideas of Jesus and the evangelists. And again this School of Hillel had a considerable influence on the writing down of the Oral Torah. That's the reason why the Oral Torah and the gospels show many points of agreement. In the days of Jesus however, and Matthew wrote shortly after these days, the School of Shammai was dominant in Pharisaism particularly in Jerusalem, and indeed until the destruction of Jerusalem in 70 CE. Matthew's harsh words against the Pharisees are mainly addressed to Pharisees like Shammai. Those Pharisees had close ties with the Jewish resistance movement of the Zealots who forced an uprising against the Romans in 66 CE. Matthew 23 should be read with this historical context in mind.[32]

Considering Matthew 23,34-35 again, the first question to be asked is, what the meaning could be of the murders of both Abel and Zechariah. It's quite remarkable that a striking resemblance between the two murders is found in the Oral Torah. This tells us that the place where Cain and Abel brought their offerings, was the same place where centuries later the altar of the temple in Jerusalem would be built.[33] Therefore the murder of Abel can be considered as a forerunner of the murder of Zechariah in the temple. Moreover another parallel can be drawn between both murders. Cain was banished by God (Genesis 4,11 f.). In the Oral Torah the murder of Zechariah the son of Jehoiada is seen as the direct cause of the destruction of the temple of Salomon and therefore of the Babylonian Exile, the ultimate banishment of the people of Israel from their own country. In the Oral Torah however this link (between the death of Zechariah ben Jehoiada and the destruction of the temple) is made with regard to the destruction of the *second* temple in 70 CE.[34] And the same context is to be found in Matthew 23,34-35 where Jesus refers to the possible destruction of the temple in Jerusalem. The gist of Matthew's argument is this: by persecuting Jesus and his followers the scribes and the (conservative) Pharisees also established a social and political climate that would eventually result in the revolt against the Romans and consequently in the fall of Jerusalem and the destruction of the temple. In Jesus' belief temple service and violence don't go together. Those who want to combine temple service and the use of violence in order to settle theopolitical differences of opinion within Israel, will irrevocably cause the downfall of Jerusalem to come nearer. This is the argument Matthew puts into Jesus' mouth using the images of the Oral Torah. But this isn't the whole argument yet.

A second question remains to be answered. Here the murdered Zechariah is called "the son of Berechiah" in stead of "the son of Jehoiada". Why? Indeed, this wouldn't have made any difference at all with regard to my explanation in the preceeding paragraph. However, mentioning Zechariah the son of Berechiah refers undoubtedly to another tradition in the Oral Torah. In this tradition of Pharisaic origin Haggai, Zechariah and Malachi were the last prophets.[35] With them the era of the Prophets would have come to an end. It's obvious however, that Matthew only partly agrees with this view, because elsewhere in his gospel he makes it clear that a new period of prophecy had begun with the appearance of John the Baptist. Therefore he identifies John the Baptist with the prophet Elijah (Matthew 11,14 and 17,10-13). Matthew 23,34 too, mentions the appearance of prophets and the last verses of Matthew 23 show a completely prophetical character. After exposing the injustices of the people spoken to, he confronts them with the ultimate consequences of their actions. Completely in line with the prophets however, a way is shown by which destruction can still be averted. The closing sentence of Jesus' speech reads: "for I say to you, you shall see me no more till you say, 'Blessed is he who comes in the name of the LORD!'" (Matthew 23,39). These words refer to Jesus entering Jerusalem, seated on a donkey, a king without arms (Matthew 21,1-11). Immediately afterwards he cleaned the temple resolutely and powerfully – what else should a king in Israel do? – but without bloodshed! Here it is argued that Jerusalem can only avert the catastrophe using nonviolent resistance. The 24th chapter of the Gospel of Matthew shows however that Jesus' appeal to the scribes and the conservative Pharisees had been of no avail. Matthew wrote this after 70 CE with the destruction of Jerusalem still fresh in his memory.

At the end of this section the conclusion can be made that the Oral Torah is an unlimited source of information indispensable for the interpretation of the gospels.

2.4 The Targum

In the first chapter I explained that the Jews living in the land of Israel in the days of Jesus, didn't use Hebrew but Aramaic as their common language. Many of them would have felt the need to be able to read the Hebrew books of the Bible in Aramaic or to listen to them being read in that language. In the synagogue service this need was met as follows. When the Scriptures were recited in Hebrew, the so-called *meturgeman* stood next to the reader and he translated the Bible-text verse after verse into Aramaic and commented on it if necessary.[36] These translations were assembled into the so-called *Targumim* (plural of *Targum*), collections of the various books of the Bible translated into Aramaic and completed with commentaries. Several versions of the *Targumim* have survived. Just because a *Targum* is not only a translation, but also a commentary, it is important for the study of the gospels. The *Targumim* contain traditions and opinions about the text of the Bible that already existed in the land of Israel in the days of Jesus and the evangelists.

Some of these traditions can shed a new light on several stories in the gospels.

The Targum for example comments upon the story of the death of Moses in Deuteronomy 34 as follows:[37] "The voice came from heaven and said: 'You all who have entered into the world, consider the sufferings of Moses, the master of Israel, who troubled himself not to please himself'. Therefore Moses is *the servant of the LORD*." And Deuteronomy 34,10 is rendered as follows: "But no prophet has yet resurrected in Israel, who would have known the word of the LORD". An echo of God's promise in Deuteronomy 18,15 can be heard: "The LORD your God will raise up for you a prophet like me from your midst, from your brethren. Him you shall hear." So by means of the words "suffering" and "servant of the LORD" the Targum identifies Moses with the suffering servant of the LORD in Isaiah 53. Moreover, the expected messianic prophet, who should be like Moses, is characterized as a suffering redeemer, a suffering messiah. This same messianic expectation of the coming of a suffering servant like Moses, was the basis on which Matthew had built his story about Jesus. I will return to this subject in detail in chapter 4. Here I'll give but one example of a story in the Targum from which can be concluded that Matthew identified Jesus with Moses.

The Targum on Exodus tells that the Pharaoh of Egypt felt shocked by a dream in which he had seen a balance with Egypt on the one scale and a lamb on the other one, and behold: the scales turned in favour of the lamb. Immediately he sent for his astronomers and they foretold him that a son of Israel would be born who would destroy the land of Egypt. It was this prediction that evoked the command to kill all the little boys of the Hebrews (the Israelites).[38] The same images and themes play a part in the story of the birth of Jesus as told by Matthew (Matthew 2), although he slightly changed the mutual relations, Herod plays the part of Pharaoh and the wise men from the East play the part of Pharaoh's astronomers because of their observations of the star in the East. They announce the birth of a rival king and a meeting takes place in which the king consults the wise men about their astronomical observations. The theme of the dream plays a part in both stories as well. Finally, the meeting between the king and the wise men results in the decision of the king to kill all the little boys in the town of Bethlehem.

From the above-mentioned example it's apparent that Matthew wrote his story of the birth of Jesus as a *midrash*, a didactic narrative, on the first chapters of Exodus. Matthew found the connection between Exodus and his own story for a greater part in the Targum. I will show in chapter 4 that he didn't stop at that particular story to insert his identification of Jesus with Moses into his gospel. Finally it can be concluded that for a good understanding of the gospels knowledge of the Targumim is indispensable. This conclusion underlines the Jewish character of the gospels considerably.

2.5 The Septuagint and what came after it

In the first chapter I explained that Greek was the common language of the Jews of the Diaspora at the beginning of the Christian Era and that they read Tanakh in a Greek translation, the so-called Septuagint. The origin and the use of this translation however, were not a matter of course, and certainly not for the Aramaic speaking Jews. Jewish scholars in those days discussed rather intensively about the question which religious texts should or should not be translated into Greek. Even more important was the answer to the question whether the Hebrew texts could be translated properly into Greek. Could Hebrew be replaced by Greek without significant loss of meaning? In the end one agreed upon a Greek translation, but a Greek translation only, because other languages were considered to be less suitable.[39]

Not long after the publication of the Septuagint the Greek-speaking Jews felt the need to authorize this Greek translation of Tanakh. In the Letter of Aristeas, written about 100 BCE, is told that the Egyptian king Ptolomy II Philadelphos (284 – 247 BCE) ordered 72 scholars from Jerusalem to translate the Torah into Greek. Because of their inspired co-operation this resulted in an identical translation. The Oral Torah too, knows this tradition although in a slightly different form. There we are told that King Ptolomy ordered the 72 scholars to translate the Torah each in his own house. God is supposed to have inspired them with the same thoughts so that all their individual translations turned out to be identical.[40]

Yet the Septuagint was not so perfect as could be concluded from the above-mentioned traditions. Already in the preface of the Greek translation of the *The Wisdom of Jesus Sirah* (see section 1.4) harsh criticism can be heard with regard to the quality of the Septuagint. It's quite understandable therefore that numerous attempts were made in antiquity to make better translations of the Tanakh in Greek.[41] However these translations have never become as popular as the books of the Septuagint. As long as the Septuagint was read by Jews against the background of the Hebrew original, this was no problem at all. One could, to a certain extent, easily go back to the original text.

The evangelists quoted the Septuagint quite extensively as well, even when they, as a matter of fact, borrowed their argumentation from Tanakh. Nevertheless, it cannot be concluded that they were satisfied with the quality of the Septuagint in all respects. There are examples of quotations they didn't borrow from the Septuagint but directly from Tanakh, of course in their own translation, because thus they were more in agreement with the Hebrew language.[42] The evangelists found themselves to be in exactly the same situation as many theologians are today. They used the available Bible-translations not because they admired them, but because their readers and audience were used to them. A good exegete will have to say again and again: "The translation reads like this, but the original text reads like that". The original text here is of course the Hebrew text of the Bible. The use of the Septuagint by the evangelists was indeed functional, because it was the most wide-spread translation of those days. Unfortunately this situation changed in the Christian Church later on.

From the end of the second century CE the tradition of the Letter of Aristeas was adopted by the Christian church and declared to be a miracle in order to secure the inspired character of the Septuagint. Although the Letter of Aristeas only mentioned the translation of the Torah, its tradition was now extended to the Septuagint as a whole.[43] Consequently, the "Word of God" could be studied now without paying any attention at all to the original Hebrew Bible. In the next centuries several translations into Latin appeared. One of them, the Vulgate, acquired the same inspired character in the Western Church as the Septuagint. In 1546 the Vulgate was declared normative, which means that it became the norm for all decisions made on Biblical ground. This development caused Christianity to move far away from her Jewish-Hebrew origin indeed. Greek and Latin do not only differ very much from Hebrew and Aramaic, but they represent a completely different way of thinking. In the Christian Church this way of thinking was expressed in Greek and Latin for centuries. No attention was paid to the original Hebrew words, they were only looked at from the Greco-Latin world of thought. A couple of examples will show how a shift of meaning took place in understanding the Bible, a phenomenon that even today makes it difficult to grasp the Biblical text completely in its original sense. This change of meaning of five arbitrarily chosen words is an illustration that could easily be extended with many other examples.

In the Netherlands the words "Omnipotence" and "God Almighty" have been influenced strongly by the 13th Article of the Dutch Creed and the 9th and 10th Sundays of the Catechism of Heidelberg (both written in the 17th century). The meaning these writings give of the idea of omnipotence, is completely wrong in my eyes. In this case these writings both refer to Matthew 10,29. But talking about "the birds of heaven" they added something to the text that changed its meaning completely: "And no one of these will fall onto earth without *the will of your Father*". The original text however reads: "And no one of these will fall onto earth *without your Father*". The matter in question is not his will, but his presence and his concern. The incorrect idea that the omnipotence of God means that all things happening on the earth, even in their smallest details, reflect the will of God, is based on the Greek and Latin translations of an originally Hebrew word that has indeed a completely different meaning. That word is the word *shaddai*, which means "great", "elevated" or "exalted". Tanakh then speaks about God as an *eel shaddai*, a "great God" or an "exalted God".[44] This name of God means that his jurisdiction is not limited to a certain country or a certain region like that of the gods of the gentiles. Therefore the name *shaddai* has two sides. In the first place, the God of Israel reigns over all other gods and therefore there is no reason to serve *them* as gods. Secondly, He is he Exalted One, which means that He is not bound to one specific place on the earth at all. Wherever the faithful are or go to, they will and should be able to serve him.

The translators of the Septuagint rendered the word *shaddai* with the Greek word *pantokratoor*. This word indeed means the "Omnipotent" or the "God Almighty". *Pantokratoor* expresses more or less both sides of *shaddai*: God's omnipresence and his jurisdiction over the whole world. As long as the Jewish reader of the Septuagint heard the echo of the original meaning of the word *shaddai* in the word *pantokratoor* nothing could go wrong. When however in later centuries the Christians embraced the Septuagint, ignoring the Hebrew way of thinking in Tanakh, the word *pantokratoor* was charged with a meaning borrowed from Greek ideas about the divine world. In that world the gods acted as autocrats, as deciders on the fate of men, as driving powers of nature and history, as managers of wars and natural disasters, illness and death. The attributes earlier ascribed to the gentile gods were now ascribed to the God of the Bible. At a very early stage already the Christian Church understood the Greek way of thinking better than the Hebrew one.[45] In Matthew 10,29 we don't meet God as a decider of all things that happen in the world, but as an omnipresent, concerned Father of his creatures. A father, however, who can't prevent every calamity.

A second example of a shift of meaning can be found in the area of the sacrificial service. The ideas about the sacrificial service, closely connected with the ideas about God, are expressed in quite other terms in Hebrew than they are in Greek and Latin. One of the Greek words the New Testament uses for bringing sacrifices is *prosphero* that means "to bring" or "to offer". The Latin word for offering is *offero* from which the English word "offer" is derived. This Latin word also means "to offer", "to give". All these words stress the gift, the offered goods, that are meant to appease the omnipotent gods. An important Hebrew word for sacrifice however is *korban* (Mark 7,11). It is derived from the verb *kareev* that means "to approach", "to come near". This word doesn't stress the gift, the offered goods, but the person who approaches God to meet him. Moreover, the sacrificial gift is no more than something to intensify the relation with God and not meant to repair it by trying to satisfy him.[46] Not the sacrificial gift is the most important element in the sacrificial service of Israel, but the sacrificial action of the offerer. Not regaining God's favour by means of a gift, but enjoying the relation with Him or restoring this relation by the sacrificer coming to the service, is what it is about. However, this goal of enjoying or restoring the relation with God can also be achieved in a completely different way. The prophets make it clear that performing righteousness is even more effective than sacrificial services (Amos 5,21-24). To sacrifice in righteousness is the ideal of Tanakh (Malachi 3,3). Moreover, enjoying or restoring the relation with God is possible for men even without sacrifices, for example by the service of prayers in the synagogue that has taken the place of the sacrificial service in the temple.

In the gospels the same ideas about the sacrificial service can also be found, be it implicitly. Let us consider for example the story of the healing of a leper. Lepers were, because of the character of their illness, excluded from the sacrificial service. If they should recover, they had to show themselves up to the priest who could declare them to be cured. Afterwards they had to bring a sacrifice, not to regain the favour of God, but to fully restore the relation with God as a cured and thus renewed human being. Jesus' advice to this leper is based on this idea (Mark 1,40-45; Matthew 8,1-4; Luke 5,12-16). The later Christian notion, on the other hand, that Jesus' death would replace the sacrificial service as a sacrifice to take away the wrath of God, isn't found anywhere in the gospels. This notio isn't based on the Hebrew ideas about the sacrificial service, but on gentile ideas about satisfying the gods after having transgressed their wishes. Whenever the New Testament connects Jesus' death with the sacrificial service, as is done in the Gospel of John and the Revelation to John, this only means that the goal of the sacrificial service, i.e. enjoying or restoring the relation with God, can be achieved by living like Jesus did.

Just another example is found in the Hebrew word *torah*, that got a completely different meaning by its translation into Greek and Latin.[47] Through the Greek word *nomos* and the Latin word *lex* the meaning of the word *torah* changed into "law". But a law is a set of restricting rules laid upon men, in this case by God. The word *torah* however means "education", "teaching". It is derived from the Hebrew verb with the root *Yod-Resh-He*, which means "point out", "show", "indicate", "educate". Therefore, the Torah is a manual, a study-book, full of indications and clues for life, that will thoroughly influence the lives of men and women the more they study it. The Torah indeed is the basis of thinking about life. The Oral Torah, the "oral education", elaborates the principles and indications of the Written Torah into *halakhah*, i.e. into concrete rules of life. However, when the circumstances of life change, it is possible to study Torah and renew the rules. Acting well, guided by the Torah, is fulfilling the Torah. This principle will always be the basis for the relation of God with men. The Christian idea that the Torah is a law, i.e. a severe set of restricting rules that must be obeyed literally, is in complete contrast with the Hebrew meaning of the word *torah*. The same is true for the dogma that the "law" is no longer in force because Jesus has fulfilled it. But fulfilling the Torah is a task for every Jew, and a small number of principles in the Torah even holds good for all people. Jesus' fulfilling the Torah, indeed, doesn't take away men's duty to fulfil it either. Moreover, the evangelists even had the idea that the existence of heaven and earth depended on the smallest character of the Written Torah (Matthew 5,18; Luke 16,17).

A fourth example is the word "holy". By living in accordance with the Torah Israel should be able to fulfill their task to be a Holy People. The word "holy" however, *kadosh* in Hebrew, doesn't mean "devout", "excellent", "very God-fearing" or something like that. Literally it means "apart", "separated", "different from other people". The meaning of the word is not to withdraw from the world or from society in order to keep the good way of life only to themselves, but ultimately to present it to all people on earth as a source of inspiration for their own ways of life. Indeed, assimilation into the gentile society has always been a great danger for Israel. That's the reason why the word *kadosh* can be translated with "living in a different way than all other people do". Hallowing Gods Name should be understood in this way (Matthew 6,9): the God of Israel should be approached as a God who is completely different from all other gods. It's true, the Bible doesn't deny the existence of other gods, but they are not worth being served at all. In this respect the holiness of Israel should parallel the holiness of God (Leviticus 19,2). However, even when Israel lives in holiness and doesn't consort with the customs of the other people, they aren't automatically perfect.

Let us now, at the end of this section, consider the Hebrew word *emet*. This word is often translated with "truth", by way of the Greek word *alèteia* and the Latin word *veritas*. Truth is the agreement of utterances, opinions, dogmas and theories with reality. *Emet*, however, is less an attribute of utterances, but more a characteristic of divine or human actions. Therefore, it could better be translated with "reliability" or "trustworthiness". The word *emet* indicates that the words and intentions of a person are in agreement with his deeds. Learning from the Torah how to act, however, doesn't guarantee that one always acts with the proper intentions. Nevertheless it's a good thing to act consistent with the Torah. These very acts could, in the long run, evoke good intentions. This is in Judaism the ideal situation: not only should one act consistent with the Torah, but also live according to the intentions of the Torah. Everyone who achieves this goal is *emet*. This is the context of John 1,17, where the evangelist explains that Jesus had lived in total agreement with the intentions of the Torah. Therefore, John didn't create a contradiction between Moses and Jesus, as has often been suggested by scholars[48], nor did he find one of them more important than the other[49]. The evangelist merely indicates that the life of Jesus should be considered to be consistent with that of Moses as a fulfillment of the Torah.[50]

This series of examples of Hebrew words that got a completely different meaning via their translations into the Greek, Latin and Western

European languages, could be extended with many other examples. My final conclusion is that the gospels should be read using as much as possible the same "library" that the evangelists had at their disposal: Tanakh, the Apocrypha, the Oral Torah, the Targumim and the Septuagint as a translation from the Hebrew into the Greek language. In that case many doors to a better understanding of the Gospels will be opened, doors, however, that will remain closed if we continue to read the Gospels in the Greek-Roman way only.

3 And walking in all the commandments and ordinances of the LORD
Jewish life in the gospels

Jesus, his disciples and the early Christians after them, were Jews, all of them, and they lived like Jews. The gospels give many examples. The Jewish character of their way of life was so evident, that the evangelists seldom added extra information. Who reads these stories from a non-Jewish point of view, runs the risk to draw the wrong conclusions from lack of proper knowledge about the Jewish way of life. Many allegations that Jesus had broken with Judaism, result from such a lack of knowledge and information. In this chapter I will show some nine aspects of the Jewish life and demonstrate how strongly the gospels were connected to the Jewish religious practice of those days.

3.1 The phylacteries

The phylacteries or *tephillin* are small pieces of vellum with certain texts from the Torah written on it, and put into small boxes, that are fastened to the forehead and to the left arm by straps of leather. They are worn according to the commandment in Exodus 13,9 and 16 and Deuteronomy 6,8 and 11,18. The commandment given in the Torah, however, is formulated in a very general way. Therefore, such a commandment evokes the problem how to put it into practice. This opens the door to many discussions and sure enough the Jewish scholars of the first century BC discussed about the problem extensively.

Nowadays the phylacteries are only worn when Jewish men recite their prayers,[a] but in those days they were part of their daily dress. They were only taken off when work must be done or unclean places must be entered. Once this was done they were put on again as soon as

---

[a]   Men, because woman are not obliged to wear phylacteries.

possible.[51] Moreover, they were worn on workdays only and not on the Sabbath and on holy days, because the Torah describes the *tephillin* as a "sign on the hand". Wearing them as a sign isn't compulsory on holy days, because the Sabbath and the holy days are indeed signs by themselves.[52] Yet not every Jew wore the *tephillin*. Only the most religious part of the people did so. Therefore wearing phylacteries functioned also to set apart the more pious from the less.[53]

Against this background we come across the phylacteries in a discussion between Jesus and some of the Pharisees (Matthew 23,5). The subject of the discussion is not the wearing of the phylacteries itself, because this must have been a matter of course for Jesus and later for Matthew. Only *how* the phylacteries should be worn is the subject of the discussion. The text shows that there were Pharisees who made the straps of their phylacteries broader to exhibit their piety. Jesus condemned such an attitude, but he wasn't the only one who did so. The Oral Torah underlines clearly the words of Exodus 13,9: "it will be a sign *to you*". So the phylacteries are a sign for oneself and not for other people.[54] Other Pharisees also condemned the use of phylacteries for other goals than for self-reflection, just like Jesus. Here we see another example of the meaning of the Hebrew word *èmèt* (truth, in the meaning of trustworthiness, reliability or veracity), that I discussed in the last chapter. It is possible to wear phylacteries and thereby to fulfil the Torah. But whoever wears them to show off to other people, doesn't wear them with the good intentions of the Torah. He fulfils the commandement, but with the wrong motivation. Who acts in this way, isn't *èmèt*. In Matthew 23 Jesus makes high demands upon his disciples to practise Torah in truth, i.e. in *èmèt*.

3.2 The tassels

On account of Numbers 15,37-41 and Deuteronomy 22,12 the pious Jew from the first century CE wore the so-called *tsitsit* or tassels (also called "fringes") on the four corners of his garment. Today these tassels are only worn on the four corners of the *tallit*, the prayer shawl, but in those days they were attached to the daily garment. This garment, usually made of wool, was only put off at home or during work, but was put on again immediately after work and also when guests should arrive.[55] Consequently, the tassels surrounded the pious Jew during the greater part of the day to remind him of the obligations (Numbers 15,39). But again they were explicitly meant for the wearer himself: "And it shall be *to you* a tassel to look upon". In Matthew 23,5 we find an identical remark about the *tsitsit*, the tassels, as about the phylacteries. The discussion was *not* about wearing them. The wearing of tassels was for Jesus as well as for Matthew, as they both were pious Jews, a matter of course. However, according to Matthew Jesus sharply condemned only *the way* in which some of the Pharisees wore them and the motives that played a part with them. In this case, the length of the tassels was not prescribed. The protest in Matthew 23,5 was against those Pharisees and scribes who deliberately lenghtened their tassels to show off their piety to their fellow-man. They fulfilled the Torah, but with the wrong motivation. They weren't *èmèt*.

3.3 The Shema Yisrael Prayer

On account of Deuteronomy 6,7 the *Shema Yisrael* prayer was recited twice a day. This prayer was sung in the evening and in the morning "when you lie down and when you rise". In those days the prayer consisted of some introductory and final benedictions between which the following quotations from de Torah were said:

- Exodus 20,2-17 – the ten commandments;[56]
- Deuteronomy 6,4-9 – that begins with the words *Shema Yisrael*, "Hear, Israel", which gave this prayer its name;
- Deuteronomy 11,13-21;
- Numbers 15,37-41.

Comparing the last three of these texts with my explanation of the *tephillin* and the *tsitsit* in the last two sections, we'll see that the *Shema Yisrael* texts are closely related to them. One should read these four texts from the Torah after each other! They are one urgent appeal to organize one's life according to the directions and commandments God gave Israel in the Torah. The ten commandments at the beginning can be seen as representing all other commandments in the Torah.

Just this character of the *Shema Yisrael* is found back in a discussion of Jesus with a certain scribe about "the first of all commandments of the Torah" (Mark 12,28-34). The question after the first commandment, asked in this story, isn't a question about raising one special commandment above all the other ones. It's rather about what the rabbis call the *kelal gadol batorah*, i.e. "the principal motive" or "the central theme of the Torah". How could the entire Torah be summarized in a few sentences? Such pronouncements in very few words can be found repeatedly in the rabbinical literature. Jesus' words are a clear example of this practice:[57]

> "Jesus answered him, "The first of all the commandments is: 'Hear, O Israel, the LORD our God, the LORD is one. And you shall love the LORD your God with all your heart, with all your soul, with all your mind, and with all your strength.' This is the first commandment. And the second, like it, is this: 'You shall love your neighbor as yourself.' There is no other commandment greater than these." (Mark 12,29-31).

The explicit quotation of Deuteronomy 6,4-5 ("Hear, Israel etc.") echoes the whole *Shema Yisrael*-prayer in the words of Jesus. Therefore this word of Jesus could be taken as a summary of that prayer, which in turn is a summary of the Torah. The "first commandment of the Law" as formulated by Jesus, had indeed the same function as the *Shema Yisrael*-prayer has today, i.e. to remind the pious Jew time and again what the Torah is about. This also shows that Jesus' summary of the Torah can never supersede the Torah itself. It is only meant to refer to the whole of Torah and to word the principal motive of it. Only if one accepts the Torah unconditionally, as Jesus did according to Mark, only then this "first commandment" can help to establish a good relation with God and the neighbour. Furthermore, Jesus' summary of the Torah can be seen as a summary of the ten commandments that were part of the *Shema Yisrael* prayer in his days. Because the first five out of these ten are concerned with the relation between God and man, whereas the last five deal with the relation of man and his neighbour. Both relations can't exist without each other.

On account of the above-mentioned explanations about Mark 12,28-34 we can conclude that the *Shema Yisrael* prayer belonged to the daily prayers of Jesus and his first disciples. This conclusion is fully underlined by the answer the scribe gave to Jesus (Mark 12,32), and in which the words from Deuteronomy that follow on "Hear Israel", were quoted again.

3.4 *The daily prayers*

The daily life of pious Jews is surrounded by benedictions, thanksgivings and prayers. That's how it is today and that's also how is was in the first century CE. Saying one's daily prayers according to a fixed schedule was and is an established custom. This practice is often mentioned in the gospels as well. The Jewish prayers of those days are an essential background when reading the gospels. However, before discussing this background we shouldn't lose sight of two points of discussion.

First of all, there wasn't a fixed liturgy accepted by all the Jews of the first century CE. A liturgy, surrounding life as a whole, was a living matter. Every Jewish group and probably every individual Jew followed its own customs. Nevertheless, the main features of praying were the same for almost all Jews. Moreover, these features are still found in the liturgy of the synagogue today. The differences that existed in those days, were mainly about the form of the prayers, the order in which they should be said, the size of the introductory and final benedictions, and about the time of the day the periods of praying should begin and end.[58] The canonization of the liturgy that happened at the end of the first century CE, didn't essentially change the Jewish liturgical practice. Extending and adapting the liturgy has been possible ever since. In Judaism the practice of prayer not only follows the accepted liturgy, but the liturgy also follows the practice of prayer. Therefore the Siddur, the Jewish prayer-book, contains even today, although in a slightly different form and next to many later prayers, a lot of prayers that were already a common heritage of the Jewish people in the days of Jesus.

The second not unimportant point is that the gospels were not written for the Christians of the twenty-first century who know next to nothing of the Jewish prayers of those days. The evangelists wrote for Jews and gentiles who feared the God of Israel, all of them very well-informed on the Jewish life. Therefore, in cases of praying, thanksgiving and benediction, the reader only gets little or almost no information about the liturgical context in which these customs were practised. The early readers of the gospels didn't need that information, something that doesn't only hold good for the liturgy and the prayers, but also for many other areas of life. And that is the reason why many texts in the gospels can only be understood when read against the background of the Jewish practice of praying.

Let us try to follow a common weekday of a pious Jew in the first century CE, and we'll see that anyhow the next prayers play a part in it:

- The evening-prayer (Hebrew: *Arvit* or *Ma'ariv*) at the beginning of the new day after sunset. Central in this prayer is the *Shema-Yisrael*-prayer[59].
- The night-prayer (Hebrew: *Kri'at Shema Al Ha-Mitah*) that is said just before going to sleep.
- The morning-prayer (Hebrew: *Shacharit*) directly after getting up. Central in this prayer are the *Shema-Yisrael*-prayer and the *Amidah*-prayer (see later).
- The afternoon-prayer (Hebrew: *Minchah*) in the course of the afternoon. Central in this prayer is the *Amidah*-prayer, also called the "Eighteen Benedictions".

In addition to these regular prayers, there were however many other occasions in the daily life of a pious Jew when he wanted to express his relation with the LORD, blessed be He, saying benedictions and thanksgivings. In section 3.5 some examples of those blessings are given.

Of the four prayers mentioned above, some obvious examples occur in the gospels and in the Acts of the Apostles. In Matthew 14,23 Jesus retreats upon the mountain to say the evening-prayer. On many other places nightly prayers are also mentioned. This is the case in the stories about Jesus' last night in Gethsemane (Mark 14,32-42; Matthew 26,36-46; Luke 22,39-46). Psalms 91 and 3 are parts of the night-prayer as well.[60] One should read these Psalms as a background behind these stories and those about Jesus' arrest directly afterwards. Realizing that both prayers were said daily at that same moment, may lead to a deeper understanding of these gospel-stories.

An obvious example of the morning-prayer is found in Mark 1,35. The clearest example, however, of the afternoon-prayer occurs in the Acts of the Apostles. The hours of the day were counted from dawn (about six o'clock in the morning). The afternoon-prayer therefore might be said from halfway the seventh hour (about half past twelve). In Acts 10,9 we read that Peter goes to the roof of the house to say this prayer at about the sixth hour (twelve o'clock). However, the most common period to say the afternoon-prayer was from the ninth hour (three o'clock p.m.). That was when the afternoon-sacrifice was offered in the temple. This afternoon-sacrifice, called *Minchah*, has even given its name to the afternoon-prayer: the *Minchah*-prayer. Many Jews, living in Jerusalem, went to the temple to pray at that moment of the day (Acts 3,1). Moreover, also outside Jerusalem the afternoon-prayer was said preferably at the moment of the afternoon-sacrifice. A striking example is found in Acts 10,30, which doesn't concern a Jew but a Roman centurion who feared the God of Israel. This example shows that not only Jews, but also God-fearing gentiles prayed the Jewish prayers. This was probably an indirect way for them to participate in the sacrificial service from which they were excluded. The close relation between sacrifice and prayer is also demonstrated elsewhere in the gospels (Luke

1,10). The *Amidah*-prayer, to which I'll return later, was evidently connected to the sacrificial service. In those days it formed part of the morning- and the afternoon-prayer just because of the fact that these prayers were connected with the sacrifices in the morning and the afternoon.[61]

From a certain point of view we can even argue that the service of prayer was more important than the sacrificial service in the temple of Jerusalem. After all, the overwhelming majority of the Jews didn't live in Jerusalem. For their daily contact with God they couldn't go to the temple. For them the daily prayers replaced the sacrificial services, and this was already the case long before the temple was destroyed in 70 CE. Therefore, it isn't strange that, after the destruction of the temple, the prayer-service took over the sacrificial service completely. Many elements from the sacrificial service were added to the liturgy of the prayers.[62] This wasn't an essential renewal of the service of prayer. The close relation between both services, that existed already in the time of the temple, made it quite possible for the service of prayer to take the place of the sacrificial service after this had ceased. After all, the purpose of both services had always been the same: to experience and to restore the relation and the contact with God.[63] In this respect nothing changed for the majority of the Jews outside the land of Israel after the temple had been destroyed.

Finally, I would like to discuss the *Amidah*-prayer to some extent. This prayer is also known as the "Eighteen Benedictions"[64], although it is composed of nineteen benedictions today. Originally there were eighteen of them, and the prayer derived its name from that number. In the course of time a nineteenth benediction was added: the fifteenth, that can be seen as a continuation of the fourteenth.[65] Moreover, in the first century CE this prayer had not nearly the form it has today. At the end of that century the rabbis only decided which benedictions ought to be incorporated into the prayer, in what order they should be said and what form the last blessing of each benediction should have. Only in later centuries the entire prayer gradually got a more permanent form and wording. But even today it is prayed in different forms on different liturgical occasions. The *Amidah*-prayer from before the end of the first century CE knew a great diversity.[66] Here I'll only reproduce the introductory sentence of the whole prayer and the final blessings of all nineteen benedictions.[67]

O LORD, open you my lips,
and my mouth shall declare your praise.

1. Blessed are you, o LORD, the Shield of Abraham.
2. Blessed are you, o LORD, who revives the dead.
3. Blessed are you, o LORD, the holy God.
4. Blessed are you, o LORD, gracious Giver of knowledge.
5. Blessed are you, o LORD, who delights in repentance.
6. Blessed are you, o LORD, who is gracious and forgives abundantly.
7. Blessed are you, o LORD, the Redeemer of Israel.
8. Blessed are you, o LORD, who heals the sick of his people Israel.
9. Blessed are you, o LORD, who blesses the years.
10. Blessed are you, o LORD, who gathers the dispersed of his people Israel.
11. Blessed are you, o LORD, the King who loves righteousness and judgement.
12. Blessed are you, o LORD, who breaks the enemies and humbles the arrogant.
13. Blessed are you, o LORD, the stay and trust of the righteous.
14. Blessed are you, o LORD, who rebuilds Jerusalem.
15. Blessed are you, o LORD, who causes the horn of salvation to flourish.[68]
16. Blessed are you, o LORD, who hearkens unto prayer.
17. Blessed are you, o LORD, who restores his divine presence unto Zion.
18. Blessed are you, o LORD, whose Name is All-good and unto whom it is becoming to give thanks.
19. Blessed are you, o LORD, who blesses his people Israel with peace.

Table 3.1

Thematical similarities between the Song of Praise of Zechari'ah (Luke 1,68-79) and the final blessings of the Amidah-prayer (the "Eighteen Benedictions").

The Song of Praise of Zechari'ah	Benediction of *Amidah-prayer*
Blessed is the LORD God of *Israel*,	7th, 10th
for He has visited and *redeemed His people*,	15th
and has raised up a *horn of salvation* for us	(14th)
in the house of His servant David,	
as He spoke by the mouth of His holy prophets,	
who have been since the world began,	
that we should be saved from *our enemies*	12th
and from the hand of *all who hate us*,	
to perform the mercy promised to our fathers	
and to remember His holy covenant,	
the oath which He swore to our father *Abraham*:	1st
to grant us that we,	
being delivered from the hand of *our enemies*,	12th
might serve Him without fear,	
in *holiness* and *righteousness* before Him all	3rd, 11th, 13th
the days of our life.	
And you, child, will be called the prophet	
of the Highest;	
for you will go before the face of the Lord to	
prepare His ways,	
to give *knowledge* of salvation to His people	4th
by the *remission of their sins*,	5th, 6th
through the tender mercy of our God,	
with which *the Dayspring from on high* has	(17th)
visited us;	
to give light to those who sit in darkness and	
the shadow of *death*,	2nd
to guide our feet into the way of *peace*.	19th

Now it is remarkable to find a reflection of the *Amidah*-prayer in the so-called Song of Praise of Zechari'ah in the gospel of Luke (Luke 1,68-79). In table 3.1 next to the text of this Song the number of the benediction of the *Amidah*-prayer is placed which is obviously related to a sentence or to a word in the Song of Zechariah. As far as the *Amidah*-prayer is concerned, the comparison is only made with the final blessings mentioned above. If we would compare the Song of Zechariah with the whole of the *Amidah*-prayer, more similarities would turn up. All these similarities show clearly that the Song of Zechariah is a kind of re-arrangement of the *Amidah*-prayer, that was and is still said by pious Jews twice a day. These findings create new perspectives for the interpretation of the Song of Zechariah.

At the end of this section the conclusion can be made that the knowledge of the Jewish practice of prayer of those days is a matter of course for the reading of the gospels and the Acts of the Apostles. Moreover, in many cases the content of the prayers is important for understanding the gospel-stories. This should challenge Christians to study the Jewish practice of prayer more extensively. In my opinion the Christian churches should consider the *Siddur*, the Jewish prayer-book, to be more significant than they ever did in the past.

3.5 The daily meals

Discussing a subject like the daily meals we should keep in mind that in Judaism domestic life was, and is even today, equally important or maybe more important than the public services of the temple and of the synagogue. Probably, religious thought about domestic life is in no religion more reflected upon than in Judaism. These religious ideas were developed in detailed and searching discussions between the scribes. In the gospels we find a telling example of one aspect of domestic life, i.e. the washing of hands before the meal. However, the essential question here is not about hygiene, but about purity. And purity, moreover, is but the suitability to participate in the temple service. Impurity, on the contrary, is the condition of not being suitable for it.[69] At first sight this is a strange combination, for what has the suitability to participate in the temple service to do with the daily meal of a Jew living in or outside the land of Israel?

In Mark 7,1-2 and 5[70], Matthew 15,1-2 and Luke 11,37-38 the above-mentioned problem is argued about with the Pharisees. Purifying the hands before the daily meal was an important and principal issue for them. On account of Exodus 19,6 they were of the opinion that the purity rules of the temple service should be practised outside the temple by all Jews as well. In their view the daily meals should be eaten in a state of purity as if they were priests in the temple of Jerusalem. They considered the table of every Jew in his own house to be as if it were the table of the LORD in the temple of Jerusalem.[71] Therefore it was necessary to purify the hands before the daily meal, i.e. to make them suitable for the sacrificial meal. Most other Jewish groups, however, didn't agree. They considered the purity rules to belong to the temple service. In daily life they interpreted purity and impurity in terms of moral and immoral behaviour. This tendency can already be found in Tanakh[72] (cf. Psalm 51,12). Jesus' answer to the Pharisees has the same effect (Mark 7,6 f.; Matthew 15,3 f.. especially the verses 19 and 20; Luke 11,39 f.). It is even probable that the washing of the hands before the meal wasn't considered by all Pharisees to be a religious obligation. In the days of Jesus the general rule was: "The washing of the hands before the meal is a matter of one's own consideration, but the water after the meal is obligatory".[73] And it's this last practice, the washing after the meal, that is not discussed in the gospels!

The daily meal started with saying a short blessing over the bread: "Blessed are You, LORD our God, king of the universe, who brings forth bread from the earth". In this blessing, called *Ha-Motzi*, bread represents the whole meal. If there were wine, a blessing over the wine would be said as well: "Blessed are You, LORD our God, king of the universe, who creates the fruit of the vine". These blessings aren't only thanksgivings but also words of praise. After the blessing over the bread, the bread was broken and handed round.[74]

It's this practice we find several times in the gospels and in the Acts of the Apostles (Mark 14,19; 15,36; Luke 9,16; Acts 27,35). In the stories of the last supper the above-mentioned blessing over the bread plays a part as well (Mark 14,22; Matthew 26,26; Luke 22,19). It's true, this meal was not an ordinary meal, but a *Seder meal* on the eve of the first day of the Passover festival (Mark 14,12; Matthew 26,17; Luke 22,7-8). And also during these special meals the daily blessing over the bread was said.[75]

The daily meal was finished with a prayer of thanksgiving based on Deuteronomy 8,10. This prayer, the so-called "Grace after Meals", was said over a cup of wine. In those days it consisted of three benedictions:[76]

- a thanksgiving for the food of the meal;
- a thanksgiving for the covenant, the Torah and the land of Israel;
- a thanksgiving for God's help with the restoration of Jerusalem, the temple and the kingdom of the house of David.

At the end of this prayer the cup of wine over which it was said, was drained. As I will show in the next section, this prayer plays a part in some of the stories about the Last Supper.

3.6 The Seder meal

A special Jewish meal was and is still today the Seder meal at the Eve of the Passover festival. In the previous section I already mentioned that in the gospels the Last Supper of Jesus is described as a Seder meal. Only when this meal was eaten in Jerusalem, the Passover lamb was part of it. This lamb was slaughtered in the temple in the afternoon of the 14th of Nisan.[a] After that it was roasted on a spit and eaten in the evening of the 15th of Nisan[b] during the Seder meal. This meal followed a special order

---

[a]   Nisan is one of the Jewish months and falls in the spring at about the beginning of April.
[b]   The Jewish days don't begin at noon (12.00 P.M.), but at sunset (about 6.00 P.M.).

or *seder* (the Hebrew word for "order") that existed already in those days, and that is still followed by the Jews today. Now this liturgy is very important in order to understand the Last Supper-stories and the remarkable differences between the versions of Mark and Matthew on the one hand and Luke's version on the other. But first I'd like to make two remarks we should keep in mind when reading these stories.

In the stories of the Last Supper two different words are used for the same notion: blessing and thanksgiving. In Greek the verbs *eulogeoo* (to bless, to praise) and *eucharisteoo* (to thank) are used. Comparing the way in which these two words are used by the evangelists, we discover the fact that both expressions are completely interchangeable:

- "to bless" in Mark 6,4; 14,22; Matthew 14,19; 26,26; Luke 9,16; 24,30;
- "to thank" in Mark 8,6; 14,23; Matthew 15,36; 26,27; Luke 22,17 and 19; Acts 27,35.

Especially Luke's alternate use of both words is rather conspicuous.[a] Therefore, both words may refer to the blessing over the bread, the blessing over the wine and the thanksgiving after the meal. Not surprising of course, for in Judaism blessing and thanksgiving are two sides of the same case.

Secondly, the text of the Last Supper-story in the gospel of Luke, as as found in many of our translations, is not the original one. Old manuscripts show that the verses Luke 22:19b-20[77] are inserted into the original text. The pericope Luke 22:19-21 originally ran as follows:

"And he took bread, gave thanks and broke it, and gave it to them, saying: 'This is My body. But behold, the hand of my betrayer is with me on the table' " (Luke 22,19a and 21).

---

[a] Luke was also the author of the Acts of the Apostles.

The addition of the verses 19b and 20 was borrowed from 1 Corinthians 11,24-25 and it filled, probably according to later copiers, a lacuna in the text of Luke's story. This "lacuna" becomes clear if we compare the original story of Luke with those of Mark and Matthew. The Last Supper-story of Mark runs parallel to that of Matthew, so I will restrict myself to Matthew's version.

Putting the text of Matthew 26,20-30 next to the text of Luke 22,19a and 21-39, we discover that three of the most important parts of the Last Supper-story of Matthew are incorporated into Luke's story too, but in reversed order. Luke also omitted some important details from Matthew's version. Matthew composed his story as follows:

- the announcement of the deliverance[a] of Jesus by Judas with the words: "He who has dipped his hand in the dish with me" (Matthew 26,21-25);
- the blessing over the bread with the words: "Take, eat, this is my body" (Matthew 26,26);
- the thanksgiving said over a cup of wine with the words about the blood of the covenant (Matthew 26,27-29);
- the mention of the Song of Praise, here the second half of the *Hallel*,[b] after the meal (Matthew 26,30).

The parallel story of Luke, however, is quite differently composed and the first three parts of Matthew's story are reversed:

- the thanksgiving over a cup of wine lacking the words about the blood of the covenant (Luke 22,17-18);
- the thanksgiving over the bread with the words: "This is my body" (Luke 22,19a);

---

[a] In stead of with "to betray" and "betrayal" I translate the original Greek words that are used for Judas' action, more correctly with "to deliver" and "deliverance" as the NKJV does in Matthew 26:15.
[b] Psalm 115 to 118 (see later).

- the announcement of the deliverance of Jesus by Judas without the words: "He who has dipped his hand in the dish with me" (Luke 22,21-23);
- talks during the meal (Luke 22,24-39).

In addition to the reversion of the three parts of the story, we see that Luke omitted two important details from the first and the third part of his story. Furthermore, he added an extended talk during the meal and, at last, he doesn't mention the Song of Praise (the *Hallel*) at the end of it. To explain these differences it is necessary to compare these stories with the liturgy of the Seder meal.

The Seder meal is deeply rooted in Antiquity. The present order of this meal already existed for the greater part in the first century CE. With the exception of a single part and the precise wording, the present Seder is identical to the one that was celebrated by Jesus and his disciples. The Seder consists of fifteen parts, nine of which are important of our discussions.

The <u>first</u> part is the dedication of the festival. Here the usual blessing is said over the first cup of wine: "Blessed are You, LORD our God, king of the universe, creator of the fruit of the vine".

During the <u>third</u> part light vegetables (for example parsley) are dipped in a dish with salt water and eaten. First, the leader of the Seder does so. Afterwards the other participants do the same. The salt water is seen as a reminder of the tears of the Israelites in Egypt.[78]

The <u>fourth</u> part consists of the breaking of the second of the three Passover-breads. A small part of that bread, the so-called *Afikoman*, is hidden and, later after the meal, looked for and found by the children. Before breaking this bread no blessing is said, because it will not be eaten immediately.

For the <u>sixth</u> part the second cup is filled with wine, but this one will not be emptied immediately. After an opening question asked by the youngest person at the table (not necessarily a child), the leader of the meal tells the story of the exodus from Egypt. After this the first part of the Song of Praise, the so-called *Hallel*, i.e. Psalms 113 and 114, is sung.

Then, without saying the customary blessing over the wine – since this was already done in the first part of the Seder - the second cup, is emptied.

In the eighth part the usual blessing over the bread is said: "Blessed are You, LORD our God, king of the universe, who brings forth bread from the earth". The bread is broken and eaten. Now the actual meal could begin.

In the ninth part the bitter herbs, the so-called *maror*, are eaten. But first these herbs are dipped in a dish with *charoset*, a sauce of almonds, apples and wine, made to sweeten the taste of the bitter herbs.[79]

The eleventh part of the Seder is the usual meal that can last as long as one wants. During this part of the meal one can talk freely about all things possible.

The thirteenth part consists of the thanksgiving after the daily meal, the so-called Grace after Meals, with its three benedictions over (a) the food, (b) the covenant, the Torah and the land of Israel, and (c) the rebuilding of Jerusalem, the temple and the kingdom of the house of David (see section 3.5). Because of the special occasion some strophes are added. Prior to this the third cup of wine is filled, over which the prayer is said. After the prayer the cup is emptied.

In the fourteenth part of the Seder the second part of the Song of Praise, the *Hallel*, is sung (Psalms 115-118). After this the blessing over the fourth cup of wine is said and the cup is emptied.

With this background in mind we can understand the four parts of the Last Supper as rendered by Matthew as well as by Luke. In Matthew's gospel the announcement of the deliverance of Jesus by Judas is combined with the remark about the dipping of the hand in the dish. This refers to the third part of the Seder liturgy. The salt water, that plays a part in it and that symbolizes the tears of the Israelites in Egypt, is linked with the atmosphere of sadness that follows the announcement (Matthew 26,22).[a] Then we reach the eighth part of the Seder, the bles-

---

[a]   Part 9 can not be taken into consideration here because of two reasons:
   1) The place of part 9 in the Seder liturgy is after the blessing over the

sing over the bread. Next the thanksgiving over the wine, the <u>thirteenth</u> part of the Seder, i.e. the ordinary prayer of thanksgiving after the meal, the so-called Grace after Meals. This is underlined by Jesus' words about the covenant (Matthew 26,28)[a], which agree thematically with the second blessing of this Grace after Meals-prayer. At the end,Matthew mentions the Song of Praise (Matthew 26,30), the <u>fourteenth</u> part of the Seder-liturgy.

Luke's variant story can also be understood with the help of the Seder liturgy. We can even find an explanation for the details he left out. Luke starts with the blessing over the wine. Of course, nothing else could be meant here than the first cup of the meal, the <u>first</u> part of the Seder with the dedication ceremony of the festival. This is certainly not the second cup, because no blessing is said over it, nor is it the third or the fourth cup, that are only drunk after the breaking of the bread. Now it's clear why Luke left out the words about the covenant at this first cup of wine. Thematically there is no link between them as is the case with the thanksgiving after the meal in Matthew, i.e. the Grace after Meals-prayer (see for Matthew the last paragraph).

After this Luke, just like Matthew, rendered the blessing over the bread (Luke 22,19a) which was the <u>eighth</u> part of the Seder. Then Luke continued with the announcement of the deliverance of Jesus by Judas. This announcement is the introduction to the conversations during the meal. Together they are the third and the fourth part of Luke's story and linked with the <u>eleventh</u> part of the Seder-liturgy. There is no special connection here between this announcement of the deliverance and the ninth part of the Seder about the bitter herbs dipped in the sweet sauce, the *charoset*. The sweetening of the bitter taste doesn't fit in with the

---

bread that at this point is still to come; 2) in part 9 the smell of the bitter herbs is sweetened to avoid a atmosphere of sadness.

[a] It's important to observe that Jesus didn't say: "This is the blood of my covenant" (as sometimes is mistranslated), but: "This is my blood of the covenant", which implies that in Jesus' opinion he died for the old Mosaic covenant of God and Israel.

Table 3.2

The parts of the Seder that are paralleled by parts of the Last Supper-stories of Matthew on the one hand and of Luke on the other (for more information, see the text of section 3.6).

Seder	Matthew	Luke
part 1 : dedication of the festival, blessing over the *first cup of wine*		22,17-18
part 3 : the dipping of light vegetables in salt water, symbolizing the tears of the Israelites in Egypt	26,21-25	
part 8 : the blessing over the bread, breaking and eating	26,26	22,19a
part 11 : the usual meal with mutual conversations		22,21-23 22,24-39
part 13 : the thanksgiving prayer after the meal (Grace after Meals) with a blessing over the covenant, said over the *third cup of wine*	26,27-29	
part 14 : singing the second part of the Song of Praise, the *Hallel* (Psalms 115-118)	26,30	

theme of the deliverance. That's why Luke removed the image of the dipping from the words of Jesus (Luke 22,21). The sadness of the disciples isn't mentioned as well (Luke 22,23), because the salt water and the tears of the Israelites in Egypt don't play a part at this point of the Seder. I have briefly summarized all this data in table 3.2.

What's more, we can see here why the text of Luke 22,19b-20 could not possibly be a part of the original story. If so, those verses should have been connected with the third cup of wine, i.e. the thirteenth part of the Seder. But this cup is drained only after the conversations during the meal. In that case verse 20 should have been put after the verses 24 to 39. Evidently, the Christian copiers of the New Testament manuscripts who, in later centuries, inserted these verses into the original text of Luke, didn't appear to have any knowledge of the Seder whatsoever.

This all makes the question arise: what could have been the reason of the evangelists Matthew and Luke to compose their stories of the Last Supper parallel to the Seder-liturgy, but each doing this in his own way? A negative answer could easily be given, because when they wrote their stories the historical events were not normative. As true Jewish story-tellers, the liturgical background of the Seder meal was much more important to them than the historical facts. However, this is not the whole answer. The purposes Matthew and Luke had with their own composition of this story, can't be gathered from the stories themselves. Therefore we should study both gospels in their entirety. In the next chapter I will return to this. Then I will show that Matthew as well as Luke had good reasons to compose their stories about the Last Supper as they did.

3.7 The Sabbath

The Sabbath is celebrated on account of the following texts in the Torah: Genesis 2,1-3, Exodus 34,21, Leviticus 23,3, Numbers 15,32-36 en Deuteronomy 5,12-15. Remarkably, the Sabbath is the only holy day that is mentioned in all five books of the Torah. The Sabbath is explained as an effect from the creation of heaven and earth by God (Genesis 2,2-3). Without reducing the significance of the other Jewish festivals, the Sabbath is probably the most important of them all. The precepts of the Sabbath in the Written Torah, however, are very concise with respect to the way in which the Sabbath should be celebrated. And also in the rest of Tanakh very little is said about what is permitted and what is forbidden on the Sabbath (for example Isaiah 58,13; Jeremiah 17:21 f.; Nehemiah 10,31; 13,15 f.). Surprisingly however, in Judaism the commandment not to work on the Sabbath (cf. Exodus 20,8-11) was and still is today treated at great length and in great detail. The Oral Torah gives many precepts about what is and what is not permitted on the Sabbath. Moreover, not only precepts but also many discussions are handed down with all kind of different and often conflicting opinions of the rabbis. In these discussions the forty-minus-one main-actions that are forbidden on the Sabbath, play an important part[80]. The Oral Torah subtly expresses that there were many reasons for extended discussions. The precepts of the Sabbath are characterized as "mountains hanging on a hair", because they are numerous, but their proof from Scripture is marginal indeed. [81]

In spite of this all, many precepts of the Sabbath in the Oral Torah have a venerable age going back to some centuries before the beginning of the Christian Era. The celebration of the Sabbath is already found in the oldest parts of Tanakh (for example Isaiah 1,13; Hosea 2,10). Some of these old texts show the protest of the prophets against the transgression of an already existing tradition not to work on the Sabbath (Jeremiah 17,21 f.; Amos 8,5). Therefore, the way in which the rabbis of the first century CE dealt with the precept not to work on the Sabbath, is the result of a long process of thought about the Sabbaths-rest and how to practise it, that had already lasted for centuries. And this process is still going on today. Because this process is deeply rooted in the ancient days of Tanakh, we can state that the practice not to work on the Sabbath was followed by the overwhelming majority of the Jewish people in the first century CE. The problem is that we don't know exactly the opinion of each group about what was allowed and what wasn't on the Sabbath. The Oral Torah already renders many different opinions of the rabbis. But also in instances in which the Oral Torah gives no other opinions this doesn't mean that she reflects the customs of the entire Jewry. Nevertheless, the ideas about the Sabbaths-rest, held especially by greater parts of the people, would have been quite similar to those found in the Oral Torah. After all, the Oral Torah was compiled by the successors of those Pharisees who were closest to the majority of the people.[82]

From all this we may conclude that the number of texts and stories in the New Testament in which the Sabbath plays a part, is in fact very small indeed. Furthermore these texts are almost completely limited to the gospels and the Acts. In the letters of Paul we implicitly come upon the Sabbath but once in Galatians 4,10, where the addressees are summoned not to bind themselves to celebrate holy days. Also the Sabbath is once mentioned explicitly in the Deutero-Pauline Letter to the Colossians

(2,16). From this text too, we can only conclude that converted gentiles (Colossians 2,13) should not be obliged to celebrate the Sabbath as Jews do. Finally, in the non-Pauline Letter to the Hebrews the Sabbath is mentioned (Hebrews 4,9), but the celebration of it is not discussed.

All this should cause some exegetes to reconsider their opinion, exegetes who apparently deduce from some gospel-stories that Jesus transgressed the traditional celebration of the Sabbath and by doing so in fact dissolved or abolished the Sabbath.[83] However, if the evangelists had really wanted to state and motivate such a radical break with the Jewish tradition, they should have devoted many more stories and discussions to it. The information about the Sabbath in the gospels is obviously too little to base a possible abolishment of the Sabbath and its precepts on it, anyhow. Further examination will even show the opposite.

There is a large number of texts from which can be concluded that Jesus and his disciples celebrated the Sabbath in accordance with the existing Jewish tradition. Jesus only began his large-scale healings after the Sabbath had finished (Mark 1,32, read from verse 21). He instructed his disciples to pray lest they ever needed to profane the Sabbath in case they had to fly from suppression (Matthew 24,20). Many times the custom to visit the synagogue on the Sabbath is mentioned (Mark 1,21; 6,2; Matthew 12,9-10; Luke 4,16, 31-33; Acts 13,14, 44; 16,13; 18,4), as well as the reading of the Torah and the Prophets in the synagogue service in the morning of the Sabbath (Luke 4,16-17; Acts 13,27; 15,21). Furthermore, it's highly remarkable that the four evangelists are of the same tenor when they tell us that the care for Jesus' dead body had to be postponed a 24 hours' day because of the Sabbath (Mark 15,42-16,1; Matthew 28,1; Luke 23,54-24,1; John 19,42-20,1). Luke's version is the most distinct of all. Before sunset the women prepared spices and ointments (Luke 23,55-56a). Then he remarks: "On the Sabbath they rested according to the commandment" (verse 56b). After this he tells that they went to the tomb, taking the spices that they had prepared (24,1). The observation of the Sabbath evidently precedes the care for the dead body of Jesus.

In some stories the Sabbath is the subject. Most of them tell about the healing of sick people. In all these stories but one, Jesus complies with the precepts of the Sabbath as given by the Oral Torah. For it was allowed to heal non-life-threatening illnesses by speaking to the patients. Only the use of tools and materials other than spoken words and simple gestures was forbidden in those cases.[84] In the first three gospels Jesus complies with this entirely. The gestures made in these healings weren't different from those that were also allowed in common social intercourse on the Sabbath. For example:

- "took her by the hand and lifted her up" (Mark 1,31);
- "stretch out your hand" (Mark 3,5; Matthew 12,13; Luke 6,10);
- "laid his hands upon her" (Luke 13,13);
- "took him (by the hand)" (Luke 14,4).

Only in the Gospel of John we find a story about a healing on the Sabbath in which Jesus did use means other than the spoken word and simple gestures only. He spat on the ground, made clay of the spittle and anointed the man's eyes with the clay. Then the man should wash in the pool of Siloam, after which he came back seeing (John 9,6-7). But also here, by rabbinical standards, we are dealing with a disputable border-line case.[85]

The central point of all these stories is *not* the question *if* the Sabbath should be celebrated, *but how* it should be celebrated. Remarkably, the discussions about these healings, are almost always directed against the Pharisees (Mark 3,6; Matthew 12,14; Luke 6,7; 14,1; John 9,13). They were the very people who made the precept not to work on the Sabbath weigh heavily in the decision what should and what shouldn't be permitted on that day. But all Pharisees didn't think about this matter in the same way. That is illustrated by the only Sabbath-story in the gospels that is not about a healing.

It's the story about the plucking of the heads of grain on the Sabbath (Mark 2,23-28; Matthew 12,1-8; Luke 6,1-5). Luke is the only evangelist who tells us that the disciples rubbed these heads of grain in their hands

(Luke 6:1).[86] Now the Pharisees reproach Jesus that he allows his disciples to do something that was not permitted on the Sabbath. The main point here is the action itself of the plucking of the heads of grain. In the Pharisaic opinion this falls under the prohibition of harvesting on the Sabbath. We should keep in mind however, that here we are dealing with a borderline case about which discussion is possible. Let us consider Luke's addition first.

According to most Pharisees the rubbing of the heads of grain in the hands fell under the Sabbath-prohibition of threshing. But not all Pharisees agreed. Rabbi Yehudah, who, just like Jesus, came from Galilee, permitted it: "It is permitted to rub fruits (in the hands) on the Sabbath for eating, but it is forbidden to do so with a tool".[87] This shows that a *halakhah*, a Jewish ruling, for the Sabbath could be less severe in Galilee than in Pharisaic circles elsewhere. And although Mark and Matthew wrote rather generalizing about the Pharisees, Luke had a much more differentiated view upon them.[88] In Luke's version of this story it is striking that he wrote about "some of the Pharisees" (Luke 6,2). The discussion about the rubbing of the heads of grain, therefore, is mainly directed against the strictest wings of the Pharisaic movement, as is the case with the stories about the healings on the Sabbath.

No text is found in the Oral Torah that permits the plucking of the heads of grain on the Sabbath. However, it is quite possible that there were rabbis in Galilee, just like Jesus, who permitted their disciples to do so, be it under certain conditions. In that case, one of these conditions was undoubtedly that the plucking was exclusively aimed at one's own consumption on that moment only (see the above-mentioned words of Rabbi Yehudah about the rubbing of fruits), ánd the plucking and the eating should be done one head of grain after the other. The bodily strength needed for such plucking, especially when the heads were ripe, was very small indeed.[89] Here we encounter a certain tension which is characteristic for all the discussions about the precept not to work on the Sabbath. The Sabbath is indeed not only a day of rest, it is also a day of enjoyment. One way to enjoy it is by eating the fruits of the earth. The Sabbath is not only a day of rest, but also a day to enjoy eating and drinking. There are however situations in which some small efforts should be done to make enjoyment possible. Such borderline situations trigger the discussion about what is permitted and what is not. The Pharisees, and especially the more strict amongst them, are inclined to let the work-prohibition weigh heavier upon their decisions. The evangelists however maintain that Jesus in such borderline cases preferred to see the Sabbath as a day of enjoyment and happiness. The finishing words of the story: "Therefore the son of man is also Lord of the Sabbath" (Mark 2,28; Matthew 12,8; Luke 6,5) only mean that man, especially on the Sabbath, should be as God has intended him to be. Consequently, this approach throws a new light on these stories about healings on the Sabbath. For illnesses and physical defects don't belong to God's original and ultimate purpose with mankind. The Sabbath is the very day to show this, for example by healing sick people, preferably with words or with a simple gesture. In severe cases also by means of some light effort, against which only some of the Pharisees (John 9,16) make insurmountable objections.[90]

At the end of this section it can be concluded that, with respect to observing the Sabbath, there is no single reason to suppose a break between Jesus and the evangelists on the one hand and the Judaism of those days on the other hand. At this point, the gospel-stories should be explained as an attempt to deepen and to intensify the celebration of the Sabbath. The precept not to work is completely maintained. In some exceptional borderline cases only, Jesus considered the Sabbath, as the day of God's ultimate purpose with mankind, more important than the strict maintenance of the prohibition to work that was usual in certain Pharisaic circles. My conclusion is therefore that the gospels are, also at the point of the Sabbath, purely Jewish writings.

3.8 The circumcision

The aspects of Jewish life that could be discussed with respect to the gospels, are so numerous that I am obliged to limit them. Therefore I will only mention some of them in short, to begin with the circumcision.

Based on Genesis 17,10, all Jewish boys are circumcised on the eighth day after their birth as a sign of belonging to God's covenant with Israel. In the gospels and in the Acts not the slightest criticism of this custom is found. The circumcision is rather presented as a normal matter of fact (Luke 1,59; 2,21; Acts 7,8; John 7,22-23). Luke even tells that Paul circumcised the son of a Jewish woman, although his father was a Greek (Acts 16,1-3).When Paul visited James in Jerusalem, he showed, on the advice of James, that the rumours that he discouraged the Jews of the diaspora to circumcise their sons, were absolutely untrue (Acts 21,17-26). Indeed, in the first Jewish-Christian community in Jerusalem it was decided that converted gentiles were not obliged to be circumcised (Acts 15,1 and 19-20; 21,20-25). But for the Jews the circumcision remained obligatory. Even the prohibition for gentiles to be circumcised, as Paul repeatedly wrote in his own letters (for example in Galatians 5,2 f.), is not found by the evangelists, who wrote their gospels many years after Paul! Indeed, with respect to the circumcision in the gospels and in the Acts there is no break with the Judaism of those days.

3.9 The naziriteship and the temple service

The naziriteship[91] was a voluntary and temporary mode of retreat, based on Numbers 6,1-21. We find it again in the first Jewish-Christian community in Jerusalem (Acts 21,23). According to Luke, Paul had been a nazirite for some time and he had obeyed the precepts of it (Acts 18,18). Exactly in accordance with the precepts, some of the first Christian Jews redeemed the nazirite-promise in the temple by means of a sacrifice (Acts 21,26). The temple-service here is a matter of course as in other gospel stories (Matthew 5,23-24; 8,1-4; Luke 2,22-24; 22,7-8; Acts 24,17).[92] It's remarkable that the accusation that Jesus would have said : "I will destroy this temple made with hands, and within three days I will build another made without hands", is dismissed by Mark and Matthew as a false testimony (Mark 14,56-59; Matthew 26,59-61).

Only in later writings like the Gospel of John, the Revelation and the Letter to the Hebrews, the sacrificial service in the temple of Jerusalem is

JEWISH LIFE IN THE GOSPELS

no longer a matter of course. However, these writings should be read against the background of the developments in Judaism some decades after the destruction of Jerusalem and the temple in 70 CE when rebuilding the temple became a more and more unachievable notion. This is neither the place, however, to go further into this matter. At this point I can only conclude that the first three evangelists treated the temple as the House of God (see also: Mark 11,17; Matthew 21,13; Luke 19,46).

3.10 Final conclusions

The most important reason why the Jewish way of life is so prominently present in the gospels – as discussed in this chapter –, is without any doubt the loyalty of the evangelists to the Torah as the constitution of God's kingship over Israel. Everyone who reads the gospels without prejudice, can see that there is no reason at all for the idea that Jesus' fulfilment of the Torah could have changed the Torah into a writing that is no longer valid. On the contrary, the central position of the Torah is obviously underlined by Matthew and Luke (Matthew 5,17-20; Luke 16,17). And also according to Luke, the Torah remained the basis for the actions of the first Christians in the first Jewish-Christian community (Acts 15,21; 21,20, 24). In the next chapter I will show that, for the evangelists, the loyalty to the Torah wasn't a question of some single sentences in only a few stories. For Matthew and Luke particularly, the Torah was the pillar on which they built their gospel. Hence the title of this book: "Reading Torah, the key to the gospels".

4 To write an orderly account for you
The gospels as midrash

4.1 The harmonized gospels

It is of course, quite reasonable to assume that each gospel is read with the other gospels in mind. This is especially so with the Gospel of Luke. The headings the translators of the Bible put above the pericopes of Luke's gospel here and there, clearly illustrate this. In some translations we can read above Luke 6,17: "The Sermon on the Mount".[93] However, reading verse 17 accurately we see that the sermon was not delivered on a mountain but in the fields. In Luke's version, Jesus descended from a mountain first, before he delivered this sermon (compare Luke 6,12 with 6,17). Clearly, the editors of the above-mentioned translations looked at the Sermon in the Fields in Luke with the Sermon on the Mount in Matthew in mind (Matthew 5,1 to 7,27).

The same phenomenon can be observed in the story about the healing of a blind man (Luke 18,35-43). Some translators wrote above this pericope the title "The healing of Bartimaeus".[94] However, in Luke's story the name of Bartimaeus isn't found at all. That name is borrowed from the parallel story in Mark 10,46-52. Comparison shows that Luke not only left out the name of the blind man. The place and the time of the healing are quite different from Mark's version as well. In Luke's story the healing occurs *before* Jesus enters Jericho (Luke 18,35 and 19,1), in Mark's version when he *leaves* Jericho (Mark 10,46). For everyone who reads historically it is one out of two: either Bartimaeus was healed by Jesus from his blindness two times, or the blind man in Luke's story wasn't Bartimaeus but another man. Indeed, this story of Luke's is often read with the parallel story of Mark in mind.

There are more examples that show that Luke is often read as a matter of course against the background of the other gospels. Above Luke 22,39 sometimes the heading "Gethsemane" is found,[95] whereas

Luke didn't use that name at all. The same holds good for the heading "Golgotha" above Luke 23,26.[96] Other translations have "The empty grave and the angles" above Luke 24,1-12.[97] Luke, however, didn't use the word "angles" in his story, but referred to "two men" (Luke 24,4). The word "angles" used here in the translation, is borrowed from Matthew 28,2-5. There, however, only *one* angle is mentioned, whereas Luke referred to *two* men.

When the Bible is read in such a way it is completely overlooked however, that Luke could have had special intentions with all these changes with respect to Mark and Matthew. I call such reading of a book of the Bible with another one in mind a "harmonizing way of reading the Bible", in short "harmonizing Bible-reading". Based on the idea that the gospels render historical facts, the supposed blanks in one gospel are filled in by supposed facts from the other gospels. Often the images in one gospel story are interpreted as equal to those in the parallel story in another gospel. In this way the differences between the stories are harmonized as much as possible. This phenomenon is not only found in the headings the translators placed above the pericopes.

Reading the Bible in this harmonizing way is not limited to the gospels only. Consulting an arbitrarily chosen commentary on the Acts of the Apostles, we will soon discover how the interpreter fills in the supposed lacunas in the Acts with information from the letters of Paul. The reverse is also done usually. It should be kept in mind however that in this way little will remain of the uniqueness of each writing. Indeed, this "harmonizing Bible-reading" is already very old. About 170 CE the apologist Tatian wrote a gospel-harmony by editing the contents of the four gospels in the New Testament into a new writing. This work is called the *Diatessaron*, what means "out of four". However, Tatian even used a fifth apocryphal gospel.[98] This gospel harmony knew a large circulation and a lot of imitation, without any doubt because in this way the confrontation with the problematic existence of four different gospels could be avoided.[99] However, by this approach the own character of each of the four gospels is completely lost. And there is no place left for evangelists who each have their own, sometimes contradicting vision on the events they wrote about.

A very negative effect of this harmonizing way of Bible reading was that copiers of the gospel manuscripts began to change the texts into the direction of a greater harmony between the gospels. In many manuscripts and in many places words, sentences and whole pericopes were removed, changed or added to diminish the differences with the other gospels. An obvious example of this is Mark 16,9-20. Today in many translations this pericope is separated from the preceding text, because it is not found in some ancient, authoritative manuscripts, which justifies the conclusion that this piece of text didn't belong to the original Gospel of Mark. This means, however, that Mark's gospel originally ended with the open grave without mentioning further appearances of Jesus. For later copiers of the manuscripts this was obviously an unacceptable ending. From the stories about the appearances of Jesus in Matthew, Luke and John a new end was composed for the Gospel of Mark which was added to the existing text (Mark 16,9-20).[100] In this way the characteristic end of Mark's gospel was "harmonized away".

Another example of such an insertion into the original text we already met in the Last Supper-story of Luke (see section 3.6). There a complete cup of wine was added to the story to harmonize it with the parallel stories of Mark and Matthew. Furthermore, in the opening words of the Sermon on the Mount (Matthew 5,3 f.) and of the Sermon in the Fields (Luke 6,20 f.) the same can be observed. Matthew begins the Sermon with "Blessed are the poor in spirit, for theirs is the kingdom of heaven", whereas Luke has "Blessed are you poor, for yours is the kingdom of God". Influenced by Matthew 5,3 however, in many manuscripts the words "in spirit" are added to Luke 6,20. Moreover, there is another remarkable difference between Matthew and Luke. In Matthew Jesus speaks *about* the poor (of the spirit), whereas in Luke he speaks *to* the poor. In Matthew 5,3 we read: "for *theirs* is the kingdom", whereas in Luke 6,20 we read: "for *yours* is the kingdom". Influenced by Matthew, in some manuscripts the words "for yours" in Luke 6,20 are changed into "for theirs". The same pattern we see in the opening sentence of the Lord's Prayer. In Matthew we read: "Our Father in heaven, hallowed be your name" (Matthew 6,9). Luke starts shorter but more powerful: "Father, hallowed be your name" (Luke 11,2). Here too, in some manuscripts the text of Luke is adapted to that of Matthew. From these examples we conclude that, by this harmonizing way of reading, the characteristic settings of Luke's stories are lost. In his gospel and in the Acts Luke is much more involved in the life of everyday than Matthew.[101] Caused by his greater social involvement he makes Jesus speak directly to the poor. In this prayer, he doesn't experience God as a God far away in heaven, but as a God who can be addressed intimately with the single word "Father".

A final example from the recent past shows clearly how this harmonizing way of reading the Bible can lead to absurdities. We can find it in the opening sentence of the "Formulary to Administer the Holy Baptism to Children" used in the former Reformed Churches of the Netherlands in the second half of the twentieth century.[102] This formulary began with the words: "Our Lord Jesus Christ has commanded at his Ascension: 'Go therefore and make disciples of all the nations, baptizing them in the name of the Father and of the Son and of the Holy Spirit, teaching them to observe all things that I have commanded you' (Matthew 28,19)". According to Matthew Jesus spoke these words in Galilee (see Matthew 28,16). The Ascension, however, occurred in the neighbourhood of Jerusalem (see Acts 1,12). At the end of Matthew's gospel, where Jesus spoke the above-mentioned words, there is no Ascension at all! Who reads the gospels historically has to choose now between two possibilities: either Jesus ascended to heaven twice, once from the neighbourhood of Jerusalem and once from Galilee, or Jesus didn't speak these words at his Ascension. In this Formulary of Baptism the end of Matthew's gospel was wrongly read against the background of the Acts of the Apostles. It is a bitter thought that thousands of children were baptized under a formulary that shows a very bad way of reading the Bible.

Here I want to state clearly that this harmonizing way of reading the Bible frustrates the individual Bible books and thereby the Bible as a whole. In this way the evangelists are being silenced when they try to tell their own stories. The differences of views they had are thus obscured. Fortunately, also by the study of the Jewish character of the gospels, we learn to rediscover the uniqueness of each gospel today. Especially in Judaism it is quite normal that every author, every scholar and every rabbi has and delivers his own ideas about the matters of the community. Also if he differs in opinion from those who are of his way of thinking. This was the same with the four evangelists, who were all Jewish scholars.[103] By studying their books against the background of the Judaism of those days we learn more about Jesus and the early Christians, than by blotting out those differences by a harmonizing way of reading the Bible.

4.2 Matthew and Luke: two different visions

In the previous section, in the discussion about the opening sentences of the Sermon on the Mount (Matthew), the Sermon in the Fields (Luke) and the Lord's Prayer (both of them), I have already shown something of the difference in the atmosphere and the intentions with which Matthew and Luke wrote their gospels. Something similar occurs with regard to the places where both sermons were delivered and the circumstances under which this happened. As the name already shows, Matthew situated his story of the Sermon on a mountain (Matthew 5,1). Jesus withdrew more or less from the crowds, and when his disciples had come to him, he started one of the longest speeches in the gospels. So the idea is: he withdraws from the multitude to teach his disciples on a mountain. Only at the end of his teachings the crowds have also listened to him, apparently (Matthew 7,28-29). The relation of Jesus to the people, therefore, is hierarchical of nature: teacher – disciples – the people (see figure 4.1.a).
In Luke's story this is quite different. His version of this sermon is a Ser mon in the Fields, after Jesus has descended from a mountain (Luke 6,17; see for the mountain verse 12). Then it appears that Jesus didn't with-

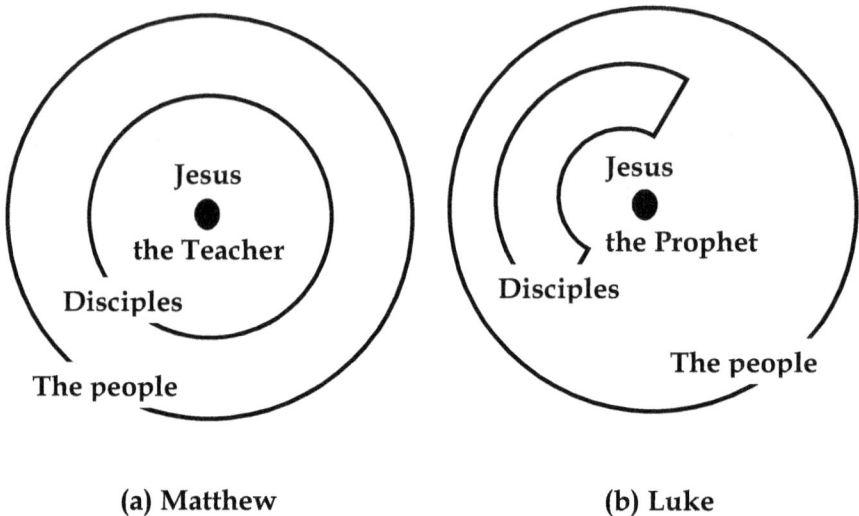

(a) Matthew   **(b) Luke**

Figure 4.1   *The relation between Jesus and the people at the Sermon on the Mount (Matthew 5,1 f.) and at the Sermon in the Fields (Luke 6,17 f.).*

draw from the crowd, but that he mingled with the people instead, and healed all who were ill (Luke 6,18-19). Only after this he began his speech that is much shorter here and that shows many differences with the Sermon on the Mount. In Luke's story Jesus' relation with the people is not hierarchical like in Matthew's one. In Luke's account of this event the disciples are only called "disciples" (Luke 6,17 and 20) and not "apostles" remarkably, although some verses before he told us that Jesus had chosen them as such (Luke 6,13). But here (verse 17 f.) they are still part of the people.

Against this background the opening sentences of both sermons get more profile as well. According to Matthew Jesus starts with the words: "Blessed are the poor in spirit" (Matthew 5,3). For him Jesus is above all a teacher. The Sermon on the Mount stresses the interpretation of the Tora. In three long chapters, Jesus teaches his disciples *halachah* (rules of life)ᵃ. In their turn, his disciples should put Jesus' teachings into practice and pass them on to the people. The "Blessed are the poor in spirit" is addressed to the disciples and urges them not to disregard those who can't keep up with the others in the study-house of Jesus. Those who can only follow the teachings with a lot of effort: "blessed they are", for it's not about the amount of knowledge one gathers, but it's about the loving intention one devotes to the study. According to Matthew, the most prominent feature of Jesus' teachings is that in the house of study the scholars shouldn't disregard the non-scholars, "for theirs is the kingdom of heaven". Without any doubt, Luke would have agreed whole-heartedly. And yet he starts his version of the sermon, a Sermon in the Fields, not with these words.

In the gospel of Luke Jesus is not the teacher who mainly teaches his disciples, as is the case in the gospel of Matthew. Comparison of both gospels shows that in Luke's gospel Jesus directs himself much more publicly towards the whole people than in Matthew's gospel.[104] In Matthew's gospel Jesus moves more within the intimate circle of his disciples, which is no problem at all for a teacher. Describing Jesus' ministry, however, Luke emphasizes the prophetic character of it a lot more. Several times he explicitly raises this matter. In Luke 7,16 we read: "A great prophet has risen up among us". In Luke 7,39 f. Jesus is tested whether he is a prophet or not. In Luke 13,33 Jesus motivates his journey to Jerusalem with the words "For it cannot be that a prophet should perish outside of Jerusalem". All these words are not found in the Gospel of Matthew.

Considering this prophetic characterization of Jesus' actions, Luke couldn't do anything else but situating the first big speech of Jesus on "a level place" amidst a multitude of people. Indeed, prophesying shouldn't be done on a mountain in the intimacy of one's own circle of disciples, but in the middle of the community on flat terrain. This also makes it clear why after four blessings (Luke 6,20b-23; Matthew gives ten blessings) Luke included four curses (Luke 6,24-26). These curses are

---

ᵃ   See section 2.3.a.

not found in Matthew. And it also explains why, according to Luke, Jesus spoke directly to the poor and the rich, to the hungry and the full. In Luke, Jesus the prophet, addresses society directly. In Matthew, Jesus the teacher addresses his disciples about society: "Blessed are <u>the poor</u> in spirit, for <u>theirs</u>…". Luke could have put these words into Jesus' mouth, but not at the beginning of the Sermon in the Fields. There he had to say: "Blessed are <u>you poor</u>, for <u>yours</u>…". Luke directly deals with the material-economic relations in the Israel of the first century CE. In the Acts of the Apostles he elaborates upon this theme in the setting of the first community in Jerusalem (Acts 4,32-35).

From the above-mentioned we may now conclude that the question after the historical facts of the events, appears to be entirely unimportant in the light of the various purposes the evangelists have had with their stories. We shouldn't ask the question: "Where precisely was Jesus, on a mountain or in the fields?", no, we should ask: "Why does Matthew tell that Jesus was on a mountain, and why does Luke tell that he was in the fields?" Jewish story-tellers never cover historical events and facts in the modern sense of the word. Stories in Tenach, in the Oral Torah and also in the gospels always reflect the views of the authors on people, events and questions of faith. The rabbis, and also the evangelists, always tell about the past with an eye on today.[105] And then, sometimes, another story should be told, a story that has little to do with what has really happened. For not the exact historical facts are important, but all that matters is how we'll pass the events on to posterity so that they can learn from it for the future. Western Christians, living in the twenty-first century, enlightened by modern science, are permanently bothered by their idea of history as a description of facts and events that can actually be traced. In such an approach, the evangelists are only reporters of facts. This modern idea of history, however, was completely strange to the rabbinic Judaism of those days. Rabbis, and also evangelists, don't register historical facts, but use and eventually adapt them to make meaningful stories. To phrase it tersely: if you want to see Jesus' suffering and death in the light of the exodus from Egypt, then you can't but tell that he was crucified at Passover, which, historically seen, is entirely improbable.

We'll be able to find a beautiful example of such an adaptation of the facts to the purpose of the story, if we compare the end of Matthew's gospel with the end of Luke's. In Matthew 28,7 and 10 we read how first the angel and then Jesus himself tell the women who had found the open grave, to go and order the disciples emphatically to go back to Galilee. Both times it is suggested that the disciples will meet Jesus in Galilee. In Matthew 28,16 we read: "Then the eleven disciples went away into Galilee, to the mountain *on which Jesus had taught them*". The Greek word that I have translated here with "taught", can be understood in two different ways. It can also mean that Jesus told them to go to this mountain. This interpretation is adhered to by the majority of the Bible translators.[106] However, in Matthew 28,7 and 10, where that "order" is worded, no mountain is mentioned. Therefore another interpretation could be more plausible: here we are dealing with the mountain on which Jesus had instructed his disciples, that is the mountain of the Sermon on the Mount (Matthew 5,1). If the disciples go back to this mountain, that is back to Jesus' teachings, they will meet him (Matthew 28,17). In other words, who wants to meet the resurrected Jesus, ought to arrange his life in accordance with the teachings of Jesus as worded in the Sermon on the Mount. To that mountain, i.e. to that Sermon, the disciples are told to go to: "Go therefore and make disciples of all the nations, teaching them to observe all things that I have commanded you" (Matthew 28,19).[a, 107] All this shows that here in this story the mountain plays a much more important part than that of a geographical entity. In the next sections I

---

[a] The sentence "baptizing them in the name of the Father and of the Son and of the Holy Spirit" can be considered as a later interpolation. The text originally ran: "Go therefore and make disciples of all the nations, teaching them to observe all things that I have commanded you". Thus the text is quoted by the church-father Eusebius (about 300 CE). The added baptism and trinity formula has no single connection with the rest of Matthew's gospel (see the endnote).

will show that, in the Gospel of Matthew, the meaning of this mountain reaches much further than is discussed so far.

At the end of Luke's gospel no trace is found of a return of the disciples to Galilee. On the contrary, in the Acts, the second book of Luke, we read that Jesus explicitly instructed his disciples not to leave Jerusalem (Acts 1,4). According to Luke, the farewell of Jesus and his disciples occurred on the Mount of Olives near Jerusalem (Acts 1,12), maybe at Bethany, on the Eastern slope of that mountain (Luke 24,50). This farewell is known as the Ascension of Jesus. Who reads the last part of the Gospel of Matthew accurately, will discover that in Matthew the Ascension isn't mentioned at all. The idea of an Ascension is even contrary to the end of Matthew: "And see, I am with you all the days unto the end of the world" (Matthew 28,20, KJV)[a]. Who lives in accordance with the Sermon on the Mount makes Jesus' presence still felt in the world (see for this idea also Matthew 25,35-46). According to Matthew, Jesus the Teacher will be present in the world, also after his death, as soon as and as long as he will have disciples who practise his teachings (see figure 4.2.a). This idea is not found in Luke, apparently. For him Jesus the Prophet, once his mission is accomplished, can ascend to heaven awaiting a next mission. *In his name*, the apostles and the other disciples will have to continue Jesus' work and to develop it (see figure 4.2.b). This means, however, that Jesus still has the possibility to exert influence over his disciples' and apostles' heads. This is most obvious in Luke's story about the conversion of Saul, when Jesus isn't seen, but his voice is heard (Acts 9,4-7). Here also Jesus maintains a direct relation to the people, in this case to Saul.

Comparing figure 4.1 with figure 4.2 we see that Matthew as well as Luke have elaborated rather consequently their own views on Jesus, the

---

[a]   In Greek the last word of the gospel is *aioonos*. In section 1.5 I explained that this word can be translated with "world" as well as with "age", "time" or "century". Many translations have the last meaning, but in my opinion the option "world" is much better because otherwise there won't be any notions of space and society, whereas the notion of time is represented twice in this sentence.

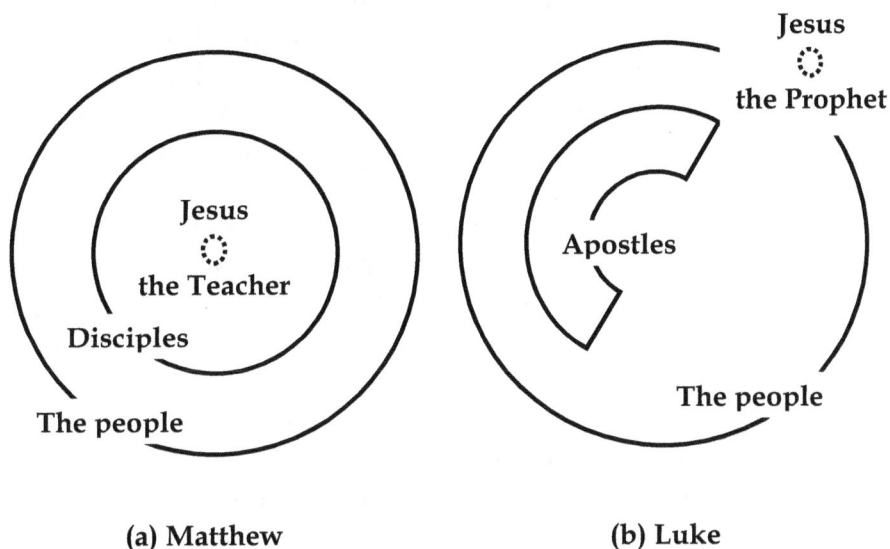

(a) Matthew   **(b) Luke**

Figure 4.2   *The relation of Jesus and the people after the Resurrection in Matthew (Matthew 28,16 f.) and after the Ascension in Luke's Acts (Acts 1,11 f.).*

disciples and the people. At first sight, this may all be about a subtle and unimportant difference. In the next section however I will show that we are dealing here with a considerable difference of opinion about the relation of Jesus to the people of Israel and about his mission in the world. Before working this out in more detail, I will first discuss the connection with stories in Tanakh as an important characteristic of the gospel-stories.

4.3 The gospels as midrash

If the comparison of two gospels already results in valuable information for the exegesis, as I have shown in the previous section, then the more so the comparison of the gospel-stories will do with stories from Tanakh. And if we see that a mountain is central in the Gospel of Matthew, the question is *not*, and especially so, *what* mountain in Galilee it may have been. The question we should ask is: what mountain in Tanakh is possibly referred to? The first mountain that appears in our mind's eye is of course the mountain in the Exodus-stories on Moses. Could the mountain in Matthew's gospel have been a reminder of the mountain Moses ascended to receive the gift of the Torah at Sinai (Exodus 19,3 f.)? And indeed, a huge number of similarities between the first chapters of Matthew's gospel and the first chapters of Exodus will be the result. This parallelism between both parts of the Bible even has a forerunner in the last chapters of Genesis. Joseph, the father of Jesus, in Matthew, (1,16 f.) seems to be quite similar to Joseph, the son of Jacob in Genesis (37,2 f.). I will deal with this parallelism first and then, in the next section I'll return to the similarity between Jesus and Moses.

The way Matthew deals with Joseph, the father of Jesus, in the first two chapters of his gospel, is obviously inspired by the image of Joseph, the son of Jacob, in Genesis. To show clearly that here we have to do with a purposeful composition of the evangelist, I am going to compare the childhood-stories about Jesus in Matthew with those in Luke. Then the following differences turn up:

- Matthew starts Jesus' pedigree with Abraham (Matthew 1,1-2). So this beginning links the Abraham-stories with those about Jesus. (Genesis 12,1 – 25,18). But Luke, on the contrary, traces the family tree of Jesus back to Adam (Luke 3,38). Matthew ignores, as it were, the stories that precede the patriarchs.
- In Matthew Joseph's father is called Jacob (Matthew 1,15-16). Here too, a clear similarity with Joseph, the son of Jacob, in Genesis is found (Genesis 30,22 f.). The comparison with Luke shows that this similarity isn't a coincidence indeed and here too Matthew composed a purposeful parallelism. For in Luke Joseph's father isn't called Jacob, but Eli (Luke 3,23-24).
- In the childhood-stories in Matthew, Joseph, the father of Jesus, is the principal person (Matthew 1,18-25; 2,13-23). It's probably here that we find the largest difference with Luke who made Mary the

most important parent (Luke 1,26-56; 2,5-7, 16-19, 33-35, 48). In Luke, Joseph only plays a minor part (Luke 1,27; 2,4-5, 16, 33, 41, 48). In Matthew it's just the other way round, for Mary's part in that story is the minor one (Matthew 1,18, 25; 2,13-14, 20-21). Joseph's principal part in the story of Matthew parallels the principal part of the other Joseph in the last chapters of Genesis (Genesis 37 etc.). And then, apparently, a number of specific similarities between both men turn up.

- In the Joseph-stories in Genesis dreams are an important motif. Joseph himself dreams twice (Genesis 37,5-11) and he is able to explain the dreams of other people (Genesis 40,5-19; 41,1-32). Also in the Joseph-stories in Matthew the dream-motif plays a prominent part, contrary to the childhood-stories in Luke in which dreams are not found at all. In Matthew Jesus' birth is announced to Joseph in a dream (Matthew 1,20-24). The wise men from the East are told in a dream that they shouldn't return to Herod (Matthew 2,12). After this, Joseph has another three dreams. Firstly in a dream he is warned to go to Egypt (Matthew 2,13). Secondly, after Herod has died, Joseph is told in a dream to return to the land of Israel (Matthew 2,19-20). And once back in Judea he is told in a third dream to travel on to Galilee (Matthew 2,22). Both Josephs are dreamers indeed!
- In Genesis Joseph is taken to Egypt (Genesis 37,28, 36). In Matthew Joseph flies to Egypt (Matthew 2,14). Also this motif of a stay in Egypt is nowhere found in Luke.
- In Genesis, Joseph has Jacob and his clan come to Egypt, thus escaping death from starvation (Genesis 41,57; 42,1-2 f.). Matthew has Jesus go to Egypt with his father Joseph and so escaping death by the sword of Herod (Matthew 2,16). Again, this motif is not found in Luke.
- In Genesis it is remarkable that Joseph strongly believes in the return of his people to the land of Israel (Genesis 50,25). The Torah and the book of Joshua explicitly mention the return of Joseph's bones together with his people to the land of Israel (Exodus 13,19;

Joshua 24,32). In Matthew Joseph also returns to the land of Israel together with the rescued Jesus (Matthew 2,21). The similarity of this return with the Exodus-story is explicitly made by Matthew quoting Hosea: "Out of Egypt I have called my son" (Matthew 2,15; Hosea 11,1).

We now understand that the childhood-stories in Matthew has stronger similarities with the Joseph-stories in Genesis, than with the childhood-stories in Luke. This means that we have here a purposeful composition of Matthew's. Matthew tells his story by means of the so-called *midrash*-method: the events told are described with certain Tanakh-stories in mind (see figure 4.3). The Hebrew word *midrash* can be defined as "a method of investigating the meaning of the Bible to answer questions of today" and "teaching the results of those investigations, for example in the form of stories".[108] Thus, a gospel-story isn't a report of historical events, but a teaching in which events from the far or the recent past are

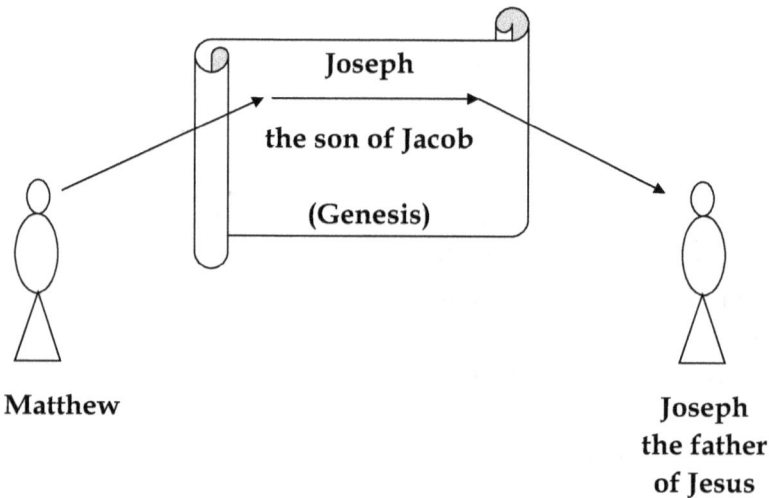

Figure 4.3 *The evangelist Matthew looks at Joseph, the father of Jesus, with in mind the Tanakh-stories in Genesis about Joseph, the son of Jacob.*

reflected upon, with the aid of ideas and themes from Tanakh. The evangelist doesn't bother about exact historical facts. With the help of Tanakh, history is transformed, as it were, into "Biblical history". In that process, an evangelist uses at least four literary tools to build up his story on stories in Tanakh:

- The same themes and images are used in the gospel-stories as well as in the corresponding Tanakh-stories.
- A person from the gospel-story is identified with a person from the corresponding Tanakh-story. In Matthew and Genesis this holds good for both Josephs. Such identifications can be supported by similarity of name, but this needn't always be the case, as we shall see in the next section.
- The gospel-story and the Tanakh-story have a strongly corresponding structure. This finds expression in the fact that related themes and images in both stories happen more or less in the same order. Obviously this is the case in the Joseph-stories in Matthew and Genesis.
- And finally there is the tool of quoting. The evangelist quotes literally from the corresponding Tanakh-stories. Or he quotes a text from another Bible-book that is related to the Tanakh-stories he uses as a parallel for his own gospel-story. This is for example the case with the quotation of Hosea 11,1 in Mathew 2,15, a quotation that is again related to the Exodus-story.

Strictly speaking, there is a fifth, very important literary tool that has not come up for discussion in the above-mentioned example of the Joseph-stories. The evangelists can also borrow themes and images from other *midrashim* in the Oral Torah, that in their days were told with the Tanakh-stories they used as background for their own gospel-stories. In the next section I will show that Matthew, writing his gospel, also used such *midrashim*.

By building up a story on the foundation of Tanakh the evangelist explains to his contemporaries what in his opinion has been the meaning of the people and the events he tells his story about. Comparison of the childhood-stories of Luke and Matthew shows that they don't resemble each other by far. This is caused by the fact that Luke has built up his stories on quite different stories in Tanakh.[109] And he has done so because in his opinion Jesus had another mission than he had in Matthew's opinion. It is not the purpose of this book to deal extensively with all the questions and problems for the exegesis that emerge here. I only hope to put the reader on the track of the evangelist as a Jewish storyteller. Once on that track, one has to go on searching to come to a proper interpretation.

As far as Matthew's identification of Joseph, the father of Jesus , with Joseph, the son of Jacob, is concerned, I'll give here a first indication of a possible meaning Matthew could have had in mind. But before doing so, however, we'll have to consult some *midrashim* in the Oral Torah first. The way in which is thought and spoken about Joseph, the son of Jacob, within these *midrashim*, has much, if not everything, to do with Matthew's argument. In the *Midrash* Joseph, the son of Jacob, is a messianic figure who wouldn't be sent to his brothers in Dothan without due consideration on his own part (Genesis 37), but who goes anyway, after making a conscious decision in spite of the hatred of his brothers.[110] Without any doubt Joseph does so, wishing to restore the relation between his father and his brothers. At the same time he knows the risk he runs. In this way Joseph became a suffering servant of the LORD, striving after the peace and the welfare of the family. Therefore, besides other messianic figures, the Oral Torah knows also a messiah, the son of Joseph. This messiah, the son of Joseph, is a suffering and in some *midrashim* even a dying messiah-figure. The words of Zechariah 12,10 are applied to him: "Yes, they will mourn for him as one mourns for his only son, and grieve for him as one grieves for a firstborn".[111] This suffering messiah, the son of Joseph, is a role model for Israel especially in situations in which taking up the suffering of the world is needed instead of running away from it, if, that is, one doesn't want to deny one's mission. As it is the task of the suffering messiah to restore and maintain the covenant of God and Israel, so it is the task of Israel to restore and maintain the tie between God and the nations of the world. The faith in the suffering messiah expresses the idea that this purpose will not be reached primarily by armed combat against persecutors and suppressors, but above all by the conscious acceptance of suffering in the tough fight to hold one's own under the enemy's yoke. Then Israel will survive the exile and will ultimately be redeemed if they fulfil their mission of being the suffering servant of the LORD (see also Isaiah 42 f.). To a certain extent one could call this a "strategy of survival".

Against the above-mentioned background it becomes clear what could have inspired Matthew to identify Joseph, the father of Jesus, with Joseph in Genesis. Through this identification he describes Jesus as a messiah, the son of Joseph, i.e. a suffering servant of the LORD. But the mission of this messianic figure is, above all, addressed to Israel. If Israel takes on this messianic way of life, it can fulfil its task with regard to the nations of the world. In a time of Roman suppression and of violent uprisings by the fanatic movement of the Zealots, this story must have been a controversial one in the Israel of those days.

4.4 Jesus and Moses in Matthew

As we already saw, Matthew identified Joseph, the father of Jesus, with Joseph, the son of Jacob, in Genesis. In this section I will show that Matthew identifies Jesus with Moses. First I will discuss the similarities with Tenach and next the similarities with the *midrashim* in the Oral Torah and the Targum.[a] In the following sections I will explain what meaning, in my opinion, should be attached to this identification.

a. Tanakh
The thematic similarities between the Gospel of Matthew and the book of Exodus are not limited to the first chapters of both books. They are found in the whole gospel even beyond the book of Exodus. Most

---

[a] See chapter 2.

obvious are the parallels in the first five chapters of Matthew. I will show fourteen, and obviously other examples could be added.

- At the beginning of Matthew's gospel the story of the birth of Jesus is told (Matthew 2,1) after an introductory story about the circumstances (Matthew 1,18-25). This is also the case with Moses: his birth is mentioned (Exodus 2,1-2) after an introductory story about the circumstances (Exodus 1).
- In both stories a king plays the part of the oppressor: Herod in Matthew (Matthew 2,1-18) and Pharao in Exodus (1,8 – 2,10).
- Both stories are about the massacre of little boys. The translation with "all children" or with "the innocent", that is sometimes found in Matthew 2,16,[112] is not correct, for in this verse as well as in Exodus 1,22 is spoken of "all boys" explicitly.
- In both stories a woman plays, in the background, an important part, crucial for the life of the principal character. Both women appear to have the same name. In Matthew it's Mary, the mother of Jesus, who gave birth to him. The name "Mary" stems from the Greek name *Mariam*, that is the transcription of the Hebrew name *Miryam* (in English *Miriam*). It was this Miriam, the sister of Moses, who rescued his life (Exodus 2,4) and who arranged an Israelitic education for him (Exodus 2,7-10a).
- Both Matthew and Exodus tell about a flight from a hostile king. Flying from Herod, Jesus is taken to Egypt by his parents. Moses flies from Pharao to Midian. Striking is the similarity between Matthew 2,13 and Exodus 2,15. In both verses the same three themes occur: killing, flying and staying in a foreign country.
- The return from the country he had fled to shows also a close resemblance with the story in Genesis. Both stories start with the remark that the hostile prince has died: "Now when Herod was dead" (Matthew 2,19) and: "Now it happened in the process of time that the king of Egypt died" (Exodus 2,23). In both cases, the return to the land of Israel takes place on the initiative of heaven. In Matthew an angle of the LORD appears to Joseph in a dream

(Matthew 2,19) and in Exodus the angle of the LORD appears to Moses "in a flame of fire from the midst of a bush" (Exodus 3,2). The words the angle speaks to Joseph: "Go to the land of Israel, for those who sought the young child's life are dead" (Matthew 2,20) are borrowed from Exodus: "Go, return to Egypt, for all the men who sought your life are dead" (Exodus 4,19). The following verses also show a large similarity. The words "Then he arose, took the young child and his mother, and came into the land of Israel" (Matthew 2,21) parallel: "Then Moses took his wife and his sons [...], and he returned to the land of Egypt" (Exodus 4,20).

Now in the next chapters of Matthew and Exodus similar themes continue to occur in rather the same order.

- The baptism of Jesus into the river Jordan (Matthew 3,13) corresponds with the Red Sea crossing of the people of Israel (Exodus 14,21 f.).
- The temptation of Jesus in the wilderness (Matthew 4,1 f.) runs parallel to the afflictions of the Israelites in the wilderness (Exodus 15,22 f.). The mention of forty days and nights (Matthew 4,2) runs parallel to the forty years Israel lived in the wilderness. In the story of Matthew Jesus' first answer to the devil (Matthew 4,4) is a quotation from Deuteronomy 8,3. If you read this verse you will see that it refers to the story of the "bread from heaven" in the wilderness (Exodus 16,2 f.). Also for the second answer of Jesus to the devil we arrive, via Deuteronomy, at Exodus again. This answer (Matthew 4,7) is a quotation from Deuteronomy 6,16. The following verse (6,17) refers to the events in Massah and Meribah (Exodus 17,1-7). Jesus' answer on the third temptation (Matthew 4,10) is a quotation from Deuteronomy 6,13. The verses Deuteronomy 6,12-14 again show a strong similarity with Exodus 20,2-5.
- Matthews story about the calling of the first disciples is without any doubt meant to introduce some structure into the group of

Jesus' disciples. In Exodus we also find a similar story about Jethro, Moses' father in law, who visited Moses and helped him to organize the people in a certain way (Exodus 18,13 f.).

- Next in both books the ascend of the mountains takes place. Jesus ascends the mountain in Galilee to deliver the Sermon on the Mount (Matthew 5,1), and Moses ascends the mountain in the Sinai-desert to receive the Torah (Exodus 19, 3, 8b, 20b; 20,21; 24,18; 34,4).

- The Sermon on the Mount, that now follows in Matthew, is no less than a commentary on the Torah (Matthew 5 – 7). Jesus starts this sermon with ten blessings: nine times "blessed are…" and one time "rejoice and be glad…" (Matthew 5,3-12). The giving of the Torah in Exodus begins with the ten commandments (Exodus 20:1-17). When putting the ten blessings and the ten commandments next to each other in the same order, some pairs show a remarkable similarity of subject:[a]

    o In the third pair "a gentle spirit" is next to "not taking the name of the LORD your God in vain".

    o In the fourth pair "those who hunger and thirst" is linked to the Sabbath as a day of rest and joyful meals.

    o In the fifth pair "those who show mercy, mercy shall be done to them" is linked to "honour your father and your mother, that your days may be long…".

    o In the seventh pair "peacemaking" is next to "not committing adultery"

    o In the ninth pair "suffering insult and persecution" is linked to "not bearing false witness".

    o And finally in the tenth pair "a rich reward in heaven" and "not longing for your neighbour's property" also are linked.

---

[a] Perhaps "mediation" of other texts in Tanakh or the midrashim from the Oral Torah could reveal still more connections.

Besides the above-mentioned thematic parallels it is remarkable as well that Matthew arranged the five lectures of Jesus to his disciples into five large text-blocks,[113] which have been divided across the whole gospel.

1. Living with the Torah (The Sermon on the Mount – Matthew 5, 6 and 7)
   This speech deals with the Torah and its application to the daily life in the days of Jesus.
2. Being a disciple (Matthew 10,5-42)
   This subject is a logical sequence to the Sermon on the Mount. After Jesus' interpretation of the Torah his disciples will have to teach his doctrine to all Israel (see e.g. verse 6).
3. The kingship of heaven (Matthew 13,3-52)
   These parables are about the kingdom of heaven. In fact, a better translation is "the kingship of heaven", because it is about acknowledging the kingship of God, taking it up and maintaining it (see the verses 44-46). This kingship doesn't descend from heaven with violence, but will work like leaven in the human society (see verse 33). Here Matthew continues the logical order of Jesus' sermons: by being a disciple of Jesus, his interpretation of the Torah should reach all Israel and in that way God's kingship will be established over his people.
4. The life of the community (Matthew 18,1 – 20,28)
   The subject of this series of lectures can be derived from the opening words: "Who then is greatest in the kingdom of heaven?" This text-block is about how people should live together under the kingship of God. Perhaps one could call this "the organisation of the community", if this sermon wouldn't have been more about the mentality needed to form a community than about the division of jobs and qualifications. And here again we find a logical continuation of the previous text-block. If Jesus' disciples want to establish the kingship of God permanently, they should live with each other in a way God wants them to do.
5. The completion of the world (Matthew 24,1 – 25,46)

This last text-block deals with the so-called "end of the age" (24,3). One had better speak about the "completion of the world".[a] This lecture has strongly apocalyptic features and is about the journey of the community through the world and through history.[b, 114] Again a logical end of the series of five text-blocks on Jesus' teachings.

After this exposition it's not difficult to imagine that Matthew, with this order of Jesus' teachings in five large text-blocks, would have liked to put a parallel along the five books of Moses (Genesis to Deuteronomy), which aren't an incoherent corpus either but form a logically ordered literary entity.

For the last two parallels between Matthew's gospel and the stories about Moses I'll deal with in this section, we'll focus our attention on the final chapters of Matthew:

- In Matthew's story of the Last Supper we read that Jesus said the following words over the cup of wine: "Drink from it, all of you. For this is my blood of the covenant[a], which is shed for many" (Matthew 26,28). Here words are quoted from Exodus 24,8 where Moses sprinkled blood on the people and said: "This is the blood of the covenant which the LORD has made with you". There it's also about a meal at the table of God (Exodus 24,11). The difference

---

[a]   Many translations render here with "the end of the *age*". The Greek text however has the word *aionos* which also means "world", as we have seen in section 1.4.

[b]   An apocalyps chiefly describes contemporary history in a "quasi-secret" language of images (see the endnote). "Quasi-secret", because generally speaking this language of images is usually well-understood within the world of Jewish ideas, but is difficult to understand for the non-Jewish world. This is caused partly by the continual and implicit references to texts of the Jewish tradition which are not or hardly known to the non-Jewish world, which consequently fails to see the connection.

between the Last Supper-stories of Matthew and Luke (see section 3.6) is caused by this parallelism between Jesus and Moses in Matthew. Luke has avoided this parallelism as much as possible and therefore he can't use the third cup of the Seder meal with the words about the blood of the covenant as in the Gospel of Matthew.

- In Matthew, the last action of Jesus takes place on a mountain (Matthew 28,16 f.). The same holds good for Moses (Deuteronomy 32,44 f.; 34,1). In both cases we hear the assignment to keep the teacher's teachings (Matthew 28,19; Deuteronomy 32,46). Both teachers in Israel died without leaving a grave: Jesus left his grave at his resurrection, whereas in the case of Moses "no one knows his grave to this day" (Deuteronomy 34,6). It becomes clear now that Matthew, at the end of his gospel, couldn't have thought of an ascension like Luke does in the Acts.[b] In Moses' case there is no question at all of an ascension at the end of his ministry: like Jesus in Matthew, he stays on earth. Their graves, i.e. the places where their lives could be commemorated, are lost to this day. Everywhere in the world the lives of Moses and Jesus should be commemorated, reflected on and followed.

With the above-mentioned fourteen parallels between Jesus and Moses, Matthew inserted into his gospel, the identification between both teachers in Israel is not yet completely dealt with. The discussed data, however, are already sufficient to conclude that this identification is the basis of Matthew's gospel. But a lot more can be said about it.

b. The Oral Torah and the Targum
In the Oral Torah there are a number of *midrashim* that can shed a new light on several aspects of Matthew's birth-story of Jesus. Joseph, the

---

[a] The NKJV renders here with "the new covenant", but the word "new" is a later interpolation into the text, omitted in more recent translations.
[b] See above in this chapter.

father of Jesus, intended to divorce Mary once it appeared that she was pregnant (Matthew 1,19). This runs parallel to a *midrash* about Amram, the father of Moses.[115] When Pharao gave the command to throw all the new-born boys of the Israelites into the Nile, Amram decided to divorce Jochebed, who would be the mother of Moses, in order to get no other children. Thanks to their daughter Miriam this plan wasn't carried out. She said to her father: "Father, your decision is worse than that of Pharao, for Pharao's decision only destroys the male children, but your decision also destroys the female children". Then Amram acknowledged his mistake and took Jochebed in again. In addition to the motive of the divorce, there is the important part Miriam played in the story of the birth of Moses as well. A part as important as that of Mary in the case of Jesus.

At another moment Miriam plays again a part of the utmost importance at the birth of Moses. One of the *midrashim* tells that the Hebrew midwives Shiphrah and Puah (Exodus 1,15) were none other than Jochebed and Miriam, who performed their jobs under a pseudo-nym.[116] This means that Miriam was the midwife at the birth of Moses! The identification of Mary or Mariam (Greek) with Miriam or Miryam (Hebrew) joins the scheme "Jesus resembles Moses" very well.

In Matthew 1,21 Joseph is told in a dream what task Jesus will have to carry out later in his life. Here too, there is a parallel in a story of that time outside Tanakh. It is handed down by the Jewish historian Flavius Josephus, who lived in the second half of the first century CE. Josephus tells that, at the birth of Moses, God appeared to Amram in a dream and let him know what task Moses would have to carry out for Israel and even for foreign nations.[117]

We also come across this dream-motive, be it in a slightly different form, in a story in the Targum.[118] There, Pharao was shocked by a dream in which he saw a balance with the land of Egypt on one scale and a lamb on the other, and the scale turned in favour of the lamb. Immediately he called his magicians, his astrologers. They predicted that a son would be born in Israel who would destroy Egypt. That eventually resulted in the command to kill all the little boys of the Hebrew (the

Israelites). Here moreover, two other motives turn up again in the story of Matthew: the magicians or astrologers, who took counsel with the prince about the child (Matthew 2,7), and the massacre of the little boys is the ultimate result (Matthew 2,16).

Finally, after all these facts a very interesting observation can be made that for a moment diverts our attention from Moses. In the past much debate had gone on about a curious detail in Matthew's birth-story, viz. the star of Bethlehem and the wise men from the East (Matthew 2,1-2). All kinds of theories circulate around this star, often illuminated by astronomical calculations. All those speculations, however, become redundant as soon as we realize that this star isn't a star from the universe, but from the *midrashim* in the Oral Torah, and from the *midrashim* around Abraham in particular.[119] The Midrash tells that in the days of Abraham Nimrod ruled the earth as a god-king. Terah, the father of Abraham, is a high official at Nimrod's court. In the evening of Abraham's birth Nimrod gives a party for the astrologers and magicians at his court. When they go home at midnight they see a special star appear in the Eastern part of the star-spangled sky. They conclude that the new-born son of Terah, the boy Abram, will grow up and be fruitful, multiply and obtain possession of the whole earth. He and his offspring will defeat great kings and inherit their countries. So far this *midrash*. There are four points of similarity between this midrash and Jesus' birth-story in Matthew:

- Both stories take place under the rule of a prince of dubious reputation;
- A child is born that will be very important for Israel;
- A star is seen in the East;
- This star is connected to the new-born child by the wise men.

Now the question arises, whether Abraham could have something to do with the birth of Jesus. This question can also be answered from the Oral Torah, because there is another *midrash*-story that runs as follows.[120] King Nimrod read in the stars that in his days someone would be born who would rise up against him and who would prove his, Nimrod's, divinity to be a lie. Then he consulted his wise men who advised him to build a big house and to assemble all the pregnant women there, guarded by watchmen. If a boy was born, he should be killed. And thus it came to pass. In this way 70.000 little boys were killed. However, the mother of Abraham contrived to hide her pregnancy and she gave birth to Abraham in secret.

It's obvious in this story that the Midrash makes an identification-link between Abraham and Moses! And on good grounds, in line with Tanakh. Both, Abraham and Moses, are exodus-figures indeed. Abraham left Ur of the Chaldeans (Genesis 11,31 f.) and travelled to the land of Canaan. Moses led the people of Israel out of Egypt and travelled with them through the wilderness to the same country. Matthew linked up with this and made a triumvirate of them: Abraham – Moses – Jesus. That is the reason why his gospel ought to be characterized as *midrash*, i.e. interpretation of contemporary events with the help of Tanakh and the Oral Torah.

4.5 Features of midrash in the gospels

The most important characteristic of the midrashim of the evangelists is undoubtedly the connection with Tanakh and the Oral Torah. Next to it there are another three aspects I will deal with briefly in this section.[121] The first of them is about the historical reliability of the gospels.

Who takes the midrash-method the evangelists use to tell their stories with, seriously, should refrain from questions like: what did happen exactly, historically seen? An example of this is the story of the massacre of the newborn boys of Bethlehem as described by Matthew. This massacre by Herod is unknown from any other historical source. Flavius Josephus, the Jewish historian and a contemporary of the evangelists, who wasn't exactly a friend of Herod's, is conspicuously silent about this,[122] although he described Herod's life in detail. If, in fact, the massacre of the boys in Bethlehem would have happened, then he and other historians would have mentioned it, without any doubt. But even the evangelists Luke and John, who wrote áfter Matthew, didn't mention it at all. Therefore we can take it for granted that Matthew's story about this massacre isn't based on historical facts, and seeing the contents of the previous section this isn't strange at all. Matthew's story is inspired by the story of the massacre of the newborn boys in Exodus 1.

Here we see an important feature of the midrash: the story-teller doesn't bother about the precise course of the historical events to express his vision on people and events in the story. The connection of the story with Tanakh and the Oral Torah is much more essential than the historicity of it. To strengthen the identification of Jesus with Moses, Matthew tells a story about a massacre of newborn boys, that didn't happen at all in his days. In this way the evangelist transforms the facts of history into "biblical history". Now, as Western readers of the twenty-first century, we get entangled into a kind of "question after the truth", the first readers of the gospels didn't bother about. We see history as an exact description of a succession of factual events in the past, and we only accept these stories as being true when they respond to this, *our* definition of history. This circumstance now makes it difficult for us to judge Bible-stories according to their own merits. We are inclined to consider a story, that only seems to be historical, as fiction, as a fantasy and consequently as a story that is of less importance for the reader. In the Judaism of the first century CE however stories were looked at quite differently. Stories are true, not because they reproduce historical facts with a certain degree of reliability, but because they present the faithful with a view, inspired by Tanakh, at their own days and circumstances. And these stories will really be true when they are reflected upon, discussed and repeated. More importantly, when their lessons are observed.

Despite this, it's not true that there should be no link whatsoever between biblical stories and the so-called historical reality. The relation between the Bible-story and the historical facts, however, differs from what a modern historian would like to see. Although if never happened historically, Matthew's story about the massacre of the new-born boys in Bethlehem characterizes King Herod, his suspicion and his cruelty perfectly. When he felt his power threatened, he didn't shrink from murder, not even on his nearest relatives.[123] The Roman emperor August once said of him: "One had better be Herod's pig than his son".[124] Indeed he had some of them executed.

A second feature of midrash is that the stories have a didactic or even polemic function. A midrash-story will always teach the reader something, or it will combat an existing opinion. Matthew's aim in the stories discussed so far, was especially to explain to the reader that Jesus was a Moses-figure and that his Jewish disciples ought to form a renewed Israel. However, we shouldn't err in this respect. It is too easy to conclude that Jesus is a second, new Moses, and that the first, the old Moses had served his turn. In that notion Jesus took Moses' place.[a, 125] Such a conclusion, however, is more inspired by later Christian theology and dogmatics, than by Matthew's gospel itself. It isn't in line at all with the midrash and with the Jewish way of thinking of those days. It is important to keep in mind the identification of Moses with Abraham in the Oral Torah for a correct interpretation of Matthew's stories. This identification doesn't mean at all that Abraham served his turn and was replaced by Moses, the "second, new Abraham". On the contrary, the significance of Abraham is completely maintained. Only Moses is considered a completion, a broadening or, if you want, an extension of Abraham. The characteristic features of the exodus, already visible in Abraham, are further worked out in Moses. That's the meaning of such identifications in the Oral Torah as well as in Matthew's gospel. The same holds good for Moses and Jesus. In the figure of Jesus Matthew elaborated upon certain traits of Moses in relation to his own days. In this way the figure of Moses isn't abolished or done away with. On the contrary, Moses remains Moses ánd the blue-print of Jesus. If we don't fully maintain the figure of Moses, Jesus would have no chance to come to life. Who brushes Moses aside, removes the essence of Jesus. Then Jesus will fall as yet under the sword of Herod.

---

[a]   This is the tenor of most publications that Christian theologians wrote about this subject (see the endnote).

Next I would like to stress a third feature of midrash: no secret is made of difference of opinion with those of the same way of thinking, but you just write another story about the things that occupy your mind. Luke did so after he had read other gospels (Luke 1:1-4). The identification of Jesus with Moses is completely or almost completely absent in his gospel. In his gospel other Tanakh-figures, he identifies Jesus with, come forward. But within the limited scope of this work it isn't possible to deal extensively with this issue. In former publications I already paid attention to these Jesus-identifications in Luke.[126] Here I'll only give a brief summary.

In the story of the Sermon in the Fields (Luke 6,17 f.) a clear identification of Jesus with the prophet Joshua occurs. At the beginning of the conquest of the land of Canaan Joshua too makes a speech in which a blessing as well as a curse play an important part (Joshua 8,33 f.). Another and more important identification in Luke is that of Jesus with Elijah. This one is clearly found in the stories about the resurrection of the only son of a widow in Nain (Luke 7,11-17), Jesus' visit to a Samaritan village (Luke 9,51-56), the following of Jesus (Luke 9,57-62), and especially in the story of Jesus' ascension (Acts 1,4-11).[a] In Matthew we will look for these identifications in vain.[127] This now, makes it understandable why Luke didn't take over Matthew's Sermon on the Mount, but had to change it into a Sermon in the Fields: for him Jesus wasn't a Moses-figure, but a Joshua-figure. And now it also becomes clear what's the matter with Jesus' farewell to his disciples in both gospels. There is no ascension in Matthew, because in his gospel Jesus is a Moses-figure. Luke on the other hand, does tell us about the ascension, because for him Jesus is an Elijah-figure. Consequently, a completely new light is thrown on the question of the historicity of the ascension.

The difference of opinion between Matthew and Luke however isn't a matter of a non-committal choice of different Tanakh-figures as a back-

---

[a]   As an exercise the reader can try to find the backgrounds of these stories in Tanakh. For an extended explanation, see the literature mentioned in the previous endnote.

ground for their stories about Jesus. There is a deeper basis for these different choices. Moses or Joshua-Elijah? That has everything to do with the ideas of both evangelists about Jesus' relation with Israel as discussed in section 4.2.

4.6 Once again Matthew and Luke: two different visions

In section 4.2 I have shown that Jesus is especially the teacher in the Gospel of Matthew. This is fully supported by the identification of Jesus with Moses, who was and is the pre-eminent teacher of Israel. Matthew's main purpose was to portray Jesus as the innovator of the interpretation of the Torah. The words: "You have heard that it was said to those of old..., but I say to you..." are characteristic for the Sermon on the Mount (Matthew 5, 6 and 7). In section 2.3 we have already come to the conclusion that this has nothing to do with a complete revolution in the interpretation of the Torah, but with an extension, a radicalization or a completion of that interpretation. The central part the disciples play in Matthew as a kind of intermediaries between Jesus and the people, fits this view exactly. The necessary condition of this renewed interpretation of the Torah is a community which is able and willing to put it into practice, and prepare it for the future. Therefore, one could take it for granted that – at least in Matthew's eyes – the group of Jesus' followers has become more or less the core of the Jewish people. They constitute, as it were, the true Israel within Israel. Nevertheless, one should be careful with this conclusion and certainly not derive any anti-Judaism from it on Matthew's side.

First of all, this opinion of Matthew's about the "true Israel within Israel" was not uncommon at all in the Judaism of those days. Other groups had the same or a cognate opinion about themselves too. For example the Essenes who lived in a monastic community in Qumran. In their writings the so-called Teacher of Righteousness plays an important part. Just like Jesus in Matthew this teacher is introduced by the Essenes as a Moses-figure.[128] The inhabitants of Qumran also saw themselves as the true Israel, the other Jews would join in with in due course. Today, nobody will think their opinions to be anti-Judaic. They only had diffe-rent ideas about Judaism than most other Jews in those days.

Secondly, we 'll have to consider the fact that Matthew's identification of Jesus with Moses plays a certain part in his often harsh polemics against the strict Pharisees. In this sense the following opening-sentence of the harsh lecture against the scribes and the Pharisees should be read as a key-text: "The scribes and the Pharisees took Moses' seat"!! (Matthew 23,2). And this now should be Jesus' seat, according to Matthew! In no other gospel the polemics against the Pharisees is more severe than in Matthew's,[129] because these strict Pharisees also considered themselves as the true representatives of Israel. In this polemics a less scrupulous practice of the Torah is not the point for Matthew. Matthew 23,3 even shows the opposite. According to Matthew Jesus was chiefly concerned about the trustworthiness of the interpretation of and the obedience to the Torah. In Matthew's eyes this trustworthiness of the strict Pharisees left much to be desired. Therefore we have to read his gospel chiefly as an internal Jewish discussion. Christians from the gentiles ought to participate only in that discussion *after* having engaged themselves with Judaism. An anti-Judaic tendency could only be imputed to Matthew's gospel if one doesn't recognize and acknowledge the essentially Jewish character of his writing.

In the third place it's clear that Matthew describes the group of Jesus' followers as a Jewish company. Even if Matthew had considered Jesus' followers as the true Israel – nowhere in his gospel however, this is explicitly found – this doesn't mean that he regarded the Jews who didn't follow Jesus, as persons who didn't belong to Israel. In the Jewry it's very common that some groups see themselves as the true representatives of Israel without excluding other Jewish groups from the people of Israel. Moreover, the lesser part of Israel also belongs to Israel. There is a permanent awareness that one's own election should serve the whole people. Just being a part of the larger whole of Judaism gives sense to the existence of every single group. By profiling yourself with respect to other Jews in discussion and polemics you can develop and strengthen the identity of your own Jewish group. This can also be seen in Matthew. Despite the harsh polemics against the Pharisees these fellow-Jews continue to be a part of Israel, and the Jewish followers of Jesus should, in some cases, follow and even surpass their example. At the beginning of the Sermon on the Mount we hear: "For I say to you, that unless your righteousness exceeds the righteousness of the scribes and Pharisees, you will by no means enter the kingdom of heaven" (Matthew 5,20). The idea that the Christian church, as the so-called new Israel, could have replaced the so-called old Israel, is completely outside the scope of Matthew's gospel. This is an insertion from the later Christian theology. Matthew holds the view that the community of the followers of Jesus ought to be more true to the Torah than the Pharisees were (Matthew 5,17-20; 23,3). And because the duty to observe the whole of the Torah holds good for Jews only, Jesus' preaching in Matthew is the basis for a Jewish "church". Characteristic of Matthew is the concentration on the *own* group and on the *own* way of life. But not all Jewish followers of Jesus' agreed with him.

The renewal of the Torah-interpretation is, according to Matthew, a unique event, accomplished by only one teacher: Jesus of Nazareth. At the end of his gospel the disciples are instructed once more to observe Jesus' interpretation of the Torah until the completion of the world. (Matthew 28,16-20). Luke however, had a completely different idea. For him Jesus wasn't in the first place the teacher, but rather a prophet. We have already seen this in section 4.2. His identification of Jesus with Elijah clearly underlines this. Therefore in his view Jesus wasn't the great renewer of the Torah-interpretation. In Luke's gospel the phrase "You have heard that it was said to those of old..., but I say to you..." is not found at all. For Luke Jesus' teachings didn't differ at all from what Moses and the Prophets had taught Israel for centuries (Luke 16,31). If there's any renewal to discern in the Gospel of Luke, it is a renewal of prophecy, not of Torah-interpretation. The prophecy that had fallen silent in Israel after the performance of Haggai, Zechariah and Malachi,[a] came to life again with Jesus (Luke 7,16). If any adaptation of the

---

[a] See section 2.3.b.

halakhah (the rules of life) should be necessary on the strength of new circumstances, this would not only be a matter of Jesus. The renewal of the *halakhah* – characteristic indeed for the rabbinical Judaism – could also be accomplished by the apostles who came after Jesus (Acts 10,1 – 11,18; 15,6-21).

A second characteristic difference between the opinions of Luke and Matthew is linked up with all this. Luke isn't concentrated on the own group as a relatively closed community of followers of Jesus, in which the own rules of life are maintained and observed as well as possible. The circle of disciples is certainly not a kind of true Israel within Israel for him. On the contrary, the community of Jesus is open to all kinds of Jews and even to God-fearing gentiles later on. We read about Samaritans (Acts 8,4 f.), a Falasha, an Ethiopian Jew (Acts 8,26 f.), Pharisees (Acts 15,5) and followers of John the Baptist (Acts 18,24 f.) who all are or will become members of the community of Jesus' followers. Jesus' focus on the whole people, we already saw in Luke,[a] has a logical continuation in the Acts. This is also expressed in the continuous appeal of the apostles and disciples to the people (cf. Acts 2,14; 3,12; 5,20, 25; 6,8; 21,40). Consequently, the sharp polemics of Matthew against the Pharisees can not or hardly be found in Luke. In his gospel Jesus' main and only adversaries were the Sadducees and the chief priests, who were the people in charge in the Jerusalem of those days.[130] In the first half of the Acts Luke describes the apostles as the leaders of a prophetic, non-violent opposition against the aristocracy of Jerusalem (Acts 4,1-31; 5,17-42; 6,8 – 7,60). They try to make the people accept Jesus' attitude in life by convincing them with arguments from Torah and the Prophets. That's why the Acts are not so much about Jesus himself as about his "name", i.e. his teachings and his action-program, his way of life (Acts 2,38; 3,6, 16; 4,10, 17, 18, 30; 5,28, 40; 8,12, 16; etc.). The prophetic program of Jesus, that Luke unfolds in his gospel, is, in the Acts, continued by Jesus' followers. Therefore, contrary to Matthew (28,20), Luke doesn't need the constant nearness of Jesus. In the beginning of the Acts Jesus can ascend

---

[a] See section 4.2.

to heaven just like Elijah. His work will certainly be continued. Moses and the Prophets, who will be read in the synagogue every week, will guarantee that after all (Acts 15,21).

As we see, reading the gospels as *midrash* uncovers two completely different patterns of community-formation in Matthew and in Luke. What is covered by "harmonizing Bible-reading", will become visible again when we are going to read the gospels as Jewish books.[131]

4.7 Midrash as the central idea

In the scientific literature the term "midrash" is used more often than not for the method of Bible-interpretation employed by the rabbis of Antiquity. This method exists of a complex set of exegetical rules that are chiefly of a linguistic and logical character. The word "midrash" is used as well for those rabbinical writings that are based on this exegetical method.[132] Understood in this way, the *midrash* will be an interesting background for the study of the gospels, but both midrash and gospels remain essentially different forms of religious literature. The scene will change dramatically however, if we are willing to understand the notion of midrash in the much broader sense I have discussed in this chapter. Not the precise linguistic and logical rules of exegesis are characteristic for the midrash (besides, these were subject to all kinds of developments), but its chief feature is its functional character: midrash as the link between Tanakh and the life of the story-teller and his audience.

Understood in this broader sense the midrash-notion doesn't only cover the rabbinical literature but the gospels as well. This notion does not only connect the gospels with the Jewish tradition, but it's also a powerful tool for the investigation of the gospels. Numerous problems exegetes are wrestling with, come to a clear solution, by using this tool. Differences between the gospels become explicable. The main lines of the individual gospels will emerge. Many dark passages will become transparent. Even all kinds of problems with the differences between the manuscripts can be solved with the midrash-approach. For all these reasons this midrash-approach, as I have described in this chapter and in

"Luke the Jew", should be placed in the centre of the study of the gospels. Only if and when we are prepared to understand the gospels as midrash-literature they will be done full justice.

5 And the spirit immediately drove him out into the wilderness
The evangelists at work

It is a precarious venture to describe the method the evangelists used in composing their gospels. An attempt has only limited sense. Much of what is put on paper, will be based rather on the fantasy of the scientific genius of the inquirer than on the real course of events many centuries ago. Nobody can look back in time and nobody of those who witnessed these events, wrote a historically reliable report. There is no end of theories about the origin of the gospels. I would have left this aspect of the gospels alone were it not that the Jewish way of Bible-reading I mentioned in the previous chapters, could throw a completely new light on the ideas that have come about in this field since the 19th century. To illustrate this I will restrict myself in this chapter as much as possible to one story: the testing of Jesus in the wilderness.[a]

5.1 The dependency of the gospels

The church-father Augustine (354 – 430 CJ) already saw that the gospels of Mark, Matthew and Luke not only showed some differences but also a great measure of similarities. This feature made him conclude that these three gospels had not come about independently. According to Augustine Mark depended on Matthew. Luke, in his turn, depended on Matthew and Mark together.[133] Thus, some kind of source-theory was drafted for the first time, i.e. a theory that states which gospels served as sources for the writing of other gospels. Such source-theories however became the vogue not earlier than in the 19th century. Since these days the solution to the problem of the mutual similarities and differences

---

[a]   For the translation "testing" instead of "temptation" see the next section.

between the first three gospels was sought in quite another direction than that of Augustine's.

A theory about the mutual dependency of Mark, Matthew and Luke should reckon with the following data. In Matthew and Luke the order of the stories is largely the same as in Mark. Moreover they frequently change Mark's wording and, in certain places, insert their own stories. From this we can conclude that Matthew as well as Luke have used Mark's gospel, writing their own gospels. Furthermore Matthew and Luke have a certain amount of text-material in common that is not found in Mark. Some examples: the testimony with regard to John the Baptist (Matthew 11,7-11; Luke 7,24-28) and the words about being wakeful (Matthew 24,45-51; Luke 12,42-46). Matthew and Luke often inserted this material into their gospels in quite different places. This made many researchers conclude that both evangelists used an identical writing that supposedly contained a collection of words of Jesus'. This hypothetical writing is generally defined with the term *Quelle* (German for "source"), abbreviated to "Q". Because of the fact that the material of this supposed source Q is found in quite different places in Matthew and Luke, it is supposed as well that both evangelists had no knowledge of each others work. In this way a source-theory emerges in which Matthew and Luke made use, independent of each other, of the same two sources: Mark and Q (see figure 5.1).[134]

However, more explanation was needed. Matthew tells stories we don't find in Luke and Luke too, has stories that are not found in Matthew. For instance the parables of the wise and the foolish maidens (Matthew 25,1-13) and the parable of the lost son (Luke 15,11-32). Now one could suppose that both evangelists had written and added those stories themselves, but within the source-theory this doesn't seem to be an option. That's why there must have been other sources: one which Matthew has drawn on without Luke knowing this source and the other way round, a source Luke could draw on without Matthew knowing of its existence. These sources were called "M" for Matthew and "L" for Luke.

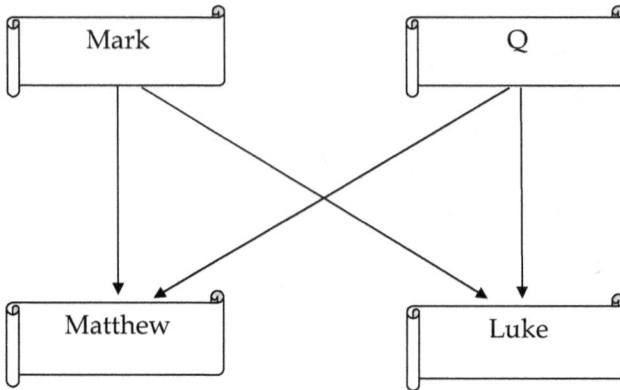

Figure 5.1   *Scheme of the most widespread source-theory of the gospels: Matthew and Luke used Mark and Q independent of each other.*

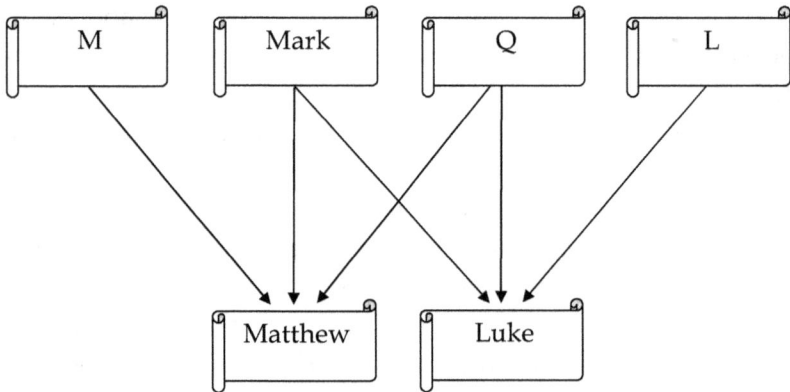

Figure 5.2   *First extension of the two-sources-theory: next to Mark and Q, Matthew and Luke each used an own source for their particular material, viz. M resp. L.*

In this way the two-sources-theory became a four-sources-theory (see figure 5.2).[135]

However, this theory didn't solve all problems yet. In spite of the fact that Matthew and Luke followed the mainlines of Mark's gospel, they quite frequently differed from Mark in detail. So a source-theory was formulated that states that Matthew and Luke didn't use the present-day gospel of Mark, but that there was another source that resembled the present-day gospel of Mark very much. Even Mark himself would have used this source that eventually is called "proto-Mark".[136] The scheme gradually grows increasingly complex (see figure 5.3).

I could go on discussing various source-theories for a long time yet: a great number of them were developed. However, I will restrict myself to one of the latest source-theories, formulated some decennia ago in circles of Jewish Bible-scholars.[137] They frequently established that Luke's gospel, of all other gospels, is most in accordance with our knowledge of the Judaism of those days as described in the Oral Torah.[138] Furthermore, they supposed that the drifting apart of Christianity and Judaism already began early in the first century CE and that it has been a continuing process since then. Small wonder that in their eyes Luke's gospel must have played a more central part in the process of the birth of the gospels. They suppose that first the gospel of Luke was written with the aid of the sources proto-Mark and Q. This gospel was still close to Judaism. The next step in this process of estrangement was the writing of the current gospel of Mark as a rewriting of proto-Mark using the gospel of Luke. The final step in this process of estrangement was made by Matthew who wrote his gospel using proto-Mark, the current gospel of Mark and Q, however without any knowledge of Luke's gospel. Who once more examines the data of the previous paragraphs will see that also this source-theory can explain them all, provided that M and L are added to it (see figure 5.4). And at the same time this demonstrates clearly the weakness of all these source-theories: many other constructions could be thought up, enabling us to explain all similarities and differences between the first three gospels.

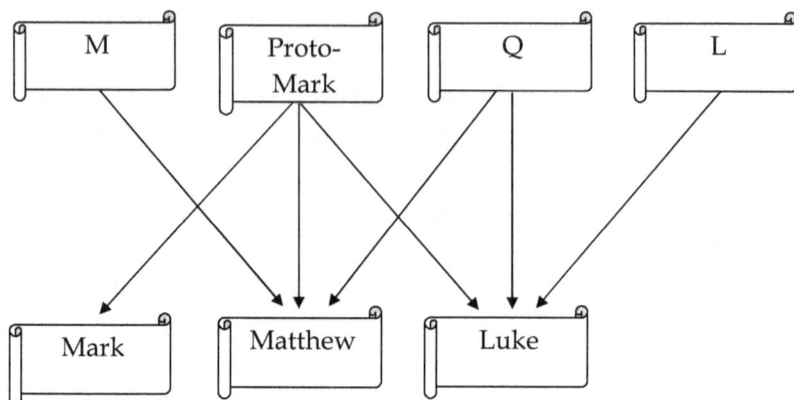

Figure 5.3   *Second extension of the two-sources-theory: the source "Mark" is replaced by "proto-Mark".*

Several fundamental objections could be brought up against source-theories in general. The origin of the gospel of Mark (figure 5.1 and 5.2) or of proto-Mark (figure 5.3 and 5.4) isn't explained by it at all. The writer of such an early gospel must have had a large amount of freedom in constructing the series of his stories, but within these selfsame source-theories the other evangelists are denied to do the same by the use of sources. A vivid example of this is found in Luke. He does follow Mark for the greater part, but it's rather remarkable though that a whole series of linking stories in Mark's gospel is not found again in his – Luke's gospel. These stories from Mark 6,45 – 8,26 should have been inserted between Luke 9,17 and 18, but they are not! This is also called "die grosse Lücke" ("the big gap"), a German expression. Of course, this too, can be explained by a source-theory: Luke used a version of proto-Mark in which these stories were missing for some reason. Or – another explanation – Luke had the disposal of a damaged text of the gospel of Mark in which, accidentally, these stories happened to be lacking.[139] That Luke could have allowed himself the freedom to remove this series of Mark's

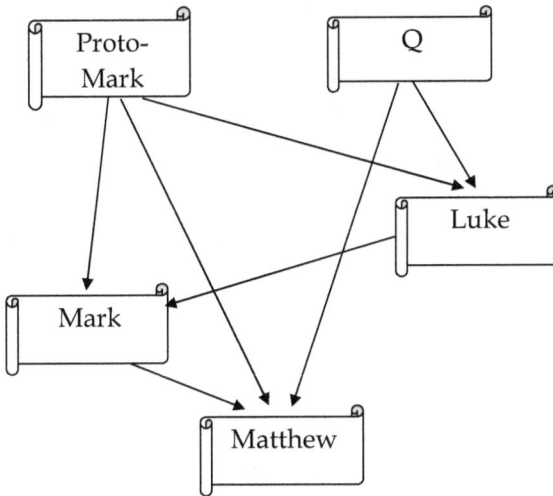

Figure 5.4   *The source-theory of the gospels developed in circles of Jewish scholars (for explanation: see the text).*

stories, is of course not accepted by a source-theory like that. Unjustly however, for closer investigation shows that Luke couldn't use these stories at all in the plan of his gospel.[140]

Moreover, the Q-source plays a very obscure part in all source-theories. Q is completely hypothetical. There is no sign whatsoever, not even with the Christian authors of the first centuries, that something like a writing Q did ever exist. In fact, the same is true for proto-Mark. The consideration behind the supposition of the existence of these sources is to maintain the historical reliability of the gospels to a certain extent. If the gospels, written decades after Jesus' death, go back to older written sources, a certain historical reliability is guaranteed. It is this wish for historicity that keeps the two-sources-theory about Mark or proto-Mark and Q alive.[141] However, the freedom with which the evangelists treated their subject - I showed several examples in the previous chapter - unsettles these source-theories in my view. Simply on the basis of similarities and differences between gospel-texts it is not possible to decide which evangelist made use of which of the other gospels.

Likewise, the source-theory doesn't clarify at all *how* an evangelist used his sources. Jewish story-tellers in the first century treated the available material with great freedom and according to their own views. If we consider the gospels to be midrash, the similarities and differences between the first three gospels should sooner be explained from the visions of the evangelists determined by Tanakh, than by copying various sources. We can take for granted that if one evangelist systematically deviates from another, he's done so consciously and with good intentions.

So I'll assume that Matthew knew Mark's gospel, but that he used the material entirely in accordance with his own view. In addition to Mark he possibly inserted other, oral traditions about Jesus in his own way. And he certainly wrote a number of stories himself, relying on the ideas found in Tanakh, to complete his series of midrash-stories. This holds good for Luke as well, considering this evangelist did not only know

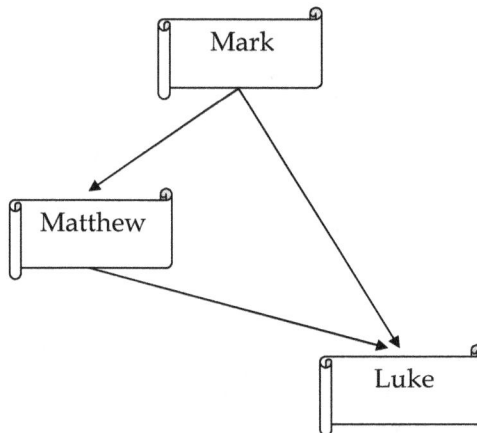

Figure 5.5   *Scheme of the simplest theory about the interdependence of the first three gospels as assumed in this book: Matthew rewrote Mark, Luke rewrote Mark by using Matthew.*

Mark's, but Matthew's gospel as well. As far as I'm concerned Q isn't needed at all.[142] Luke could easily find the material that is attributed to Q in Matthew. What's more, comparing Mark and Matthew he could see how Matthew had set about it. As seen in the previous chapter Luke's vision on Jesus differed rather thoroughly of Matthew's. Therefore, on the basis of Mark's gospel, Luke incorporated much of the extra material of Matthew's in a quite different way in his gospel (see figure 5.5). In the next sections I will describe this process in the light of the story about the testing of Jesus in the wilderness.

5.2 Mark: the oldest version (Mark 1:12-13)

The oldest and shortest version of the story about the testing[a] in the desert is found in Mark. After Jesus had been baptized by John the Baptist, and after the spirit had descended upon him like a dove, the text continues without much ado:

> "Immediately the spirit drove him into the wilderness. And he was there in the wilderness forty days, tested by satan, and was with the wild beasts; and the angels ministered to him." (Mark 1,12-13).

After this Jesus immediately went to Galilee to preach the gospel of God.

Now we should resist the temptation to read this short story as a historical announcement. Mark could have had numerous reasons to tell this story at this place, even if Jesus had never visited the desert in his life at all. The spirit, de desert, the forty days, being tested, the satan, the wild beasts, the angels serving him..., to us, western twenty-first-century Christians, these are no more than facts and circumstances, as far as we still believe in the existence of the satan and the angels. For

---

[a] Most translations use here the word "temptation". Later in this section I will substantiate why I render "test", "testing" or "trial".

Jewish storytellers and listeners in the first century however, those words were deeply rooted in Tanakh and the Oral Torah.

It isn't difficult to understand which stories in Tanakh Mark would have thought of, telling this short story. The preceding baptism in the river Jordan, the forty days-stay in the desert, the testing and after that Jesus' work in Galilee, all this reminds one very much of Israel's crossing through the Red Sea, the forty years-stay in the desert, the trials of hunger, thirst and idolatry (Exodus 16, 17 and 32), followed at the end by the entering into and the conquest of the land of Canaan. Therefore, the short story in Mark about the testing in the desert is obviously the central part of a tripartite story which parallels Israel's journey from Egypt to Canaan:

- the baptism of Jesus (Mark 1,9-11)
- forty days in the desert (Mark 1,12-13)
- preaching in Galilee (Mark 1,14-15)

- the Red Sea crossing (Exodus 14,21-31)
- forty years in the desert (e.g. Deuteronomy 29,5)
- taking possession of Canaan (Joshua 3 f.)

In this way Mark characterizes Jesus' further actions as a renewed attempt to bring the land of Israel under the kingship of God, this time without the use of violence. I'll comment briefly on some important words in Mark's story.

The spirit. Although Mark doesn't use the words "the spirit of God" or "the holy spirit", not even in Mark 1,10, he undoubtedly means by "the spirit" the spirit of God. These expressions "spirit of God", the "spirit of the LORD" or the "holy spirit" are frequently found in Tanakh. To begin with in the story of the creation of the world, before any word is spoken (Genesis 1,2). The Hebrew word for "spirit" is *ruach*, meaning "wind" of "breath". The spirit of God, the wind or breath of God, is a beautiful image of "God at work". God can't be seen, just like wind and breath, but one does observe His influence in the world.

Now we shouldn't imagine this spirit of God as one of the three persons of the "Holy Trinity". This later dogma of the Christian church is totally alien to Judaism. Actually one shouldn't think of the holy spirit as a spiritual being at all. The Bible very often doesn't speak of "*the* holy spirit", but of "holy spirit" without the definite article. It's not about a person, but about a *phenomenon* that is linked with the actions of God. The expression "holy spirit" is a form of metaphorical language for God's influence on the creation and especially on people. But how this influence works, isn't rendered at all by the simple expression "holy spirit". Sometimes it is the wind of God 'hovering over the face of the waters' (Genesis 1,2). In other cases it is the breath of God's nose (Exodus 15,8 and 10; the word *ruach* in these verses is translated with "breath"). Sometimes it is a huge wind thrown by God upon the see (Jona 1:4). But it can also be a descending dove (Mark 1,10).[143] And if the spirit of God descends upon people, even the difference between the spirit of God and the soul of the people disappears completely. A midrash-story in the Oral Torah tells that the soul of man was created on the first day, for the soul of man is nothing else but the spirit of God, hovering 'over the face of the waters' (Genesis 1,2).[144] Indeed, if man has been created in the image of God (Genesis 1,26-27) and if God has breathed the breath of life into his nostrils (Genesis 2,7), then this must be so. Quite in line with the Oral Torah, with regard to the expression "holy spirit" or "spirit of God" we'd better think of divine inspiration than of a divine person. In the Oral Torah the expression "holy spirit" is often a synonym of "prophetic inspiration coming from God".[145] A man moved by the spirit of God, is driven by motives coming from God, especially when studying Tanakh intensively.

If Mark writes here about the spirit that drove Jesus into the desert, then Tanakh had already been heard with the words of Jesaja: "The voice of one crying: 'Prepare in the wilderness the way of the LORD; make straight in the desert a highway for our God'" (Mark 1,3; Jesaja 40,3).[146] Without a doubt Mark was of the opinion that this God-inspired word of the prophet, had inspired Jesus. And so, according to Mark, the spirit drove Jesus to the desert.

The desert. The desert is, to begin with, the place where one prepares oneself for a later task. Indeed, the former slave-nation Israel had to stay forty years in the desert to overcome their slave-mentality and to prepare themselves for a free and independent national existence in the land of Canaan. The prophet Hosea describes this stay in the desert as a time of betrothal between God and Israel, a period that is a model as well for Israel's return to God after later periods of apostasy (Hosea 2,13-22). There, in the desert, both parties learn to know each other in all their weaknesses and all their strengths. Therefore, the time in the desert is also and especially a time of learning, in which the Torah is taught to Israel. And tests, trials even, are part of the learning process.

The desert is, in line with this meaning, also a place to which one flees in times of danger, persecution and suppression (1 Kings 19; 1 Maccabees 2,29; etc.). Even then the flight into the desert is only mentioned because the stay in the desert is seen as the preparation to the return to the inhabited land in order to fight evil and suppression. At the beginning of the Christian era the Essenic community also wanted to prepare "the way of the LORD" in the desert as a fulfilment of Jesaja 40,3. A conspicuous similarity with Mark 1,3f indeed. The Essenes, however, stayed in the desert, awaiting the kingdom of God in Israel, whereas Mark makes Jesus leave the desert after forty days to proclaim the coming of God's kingdom in Galilee (Mark 1,15). Here we can discern an anti-Essenic, polemical undertone in Mark's story.

The desert, however, played an important part as well in another movement in the Judaism of those days: the movement of the religiously inspired freedom-fighters of the Zealots. For them the desert was the place of preparation for the violent clash with the Roman occupier. In those days many of them expected the messiah to begin his actions in the desert in order to liberate the country from the Romans by force of arms (see e.g. Matthew 24,26; Acts 21,38). In Mark's story there is a clear polemical undertone against these Zealots as well. For the question is: what spirit drove Jesus into the desert? The "spirit like a dove", the bird of peace par excellence! (Mark 1,10). In the desert he prepared himself for his task to proclaim the coming of God's kingdom in a non-violent way. This preparation is hardly possible without learning to endure trials, for such a task is a heavy one in a time dominated by violence.

He was tested. We shouldn't associate this word with temptation, but with testing or trial. The difference between both words are the underlying motives. Temptation aims to overthrow the tempted one. The Greek verb *peirazoo*, that is used here, however means first and foremost "to test, to try". This is wholly in line with the desert as a place of learning. Being tested is about determining if someone is capable of a future task. Moreover, the test itself can be a learning experience that renders a person more able for the later task awaiting him. Especially if the test lies in the sphere of religiously inspired action. In that case the test is always about making choices. Who stands such a test, is better equipped. Learning to make the good choice in such a test makes man a better person (a person more 'tov') in accordance with the model of Genesis 1.[a]

The Oral Torah asserts us that God only tests the righteous, not the impious. The righteous indeed is able to stand the test. Thereby elevation is their part[147], i.e. they will become more important to the religious community. In Tanakh trials that originate with God or that occur with his approval, are only told with regard to the righteous ones, like Abraham and Job. The Oral Torah also tells that nobody will be raised to rule by God without being tested and tried by him. The three patriarchs as well as Joseph and the tribe of Levi are mentioned as examples.[148] An observation indeed, from which can be gathered that many rulers in our world were never raised to rule by God. Against this background the trial of Jesus in the desert suits Mark's story completely. In his eyes, Jesus was a righteous one, and passing the test made him suited to the task as a teacher of the people that was awaiting him.

The satan. Many people think of the satan as the representative of the absolute evil: a power independent of God that fights against him, but will be conquered by him at the end of time. This way of thinking is anything but biblical. The biblical point of view is that all powers in the uni-

---

[a]   The Hebrew word *tov* means "good". It is used seven times in Genesis 1.

verse are subordinated to God and are able at the most to use their influence within limits settled by him. This also holds good for all those cases when the satan is mentioned. This can clearly be seen in the book of Job. The satan indeed got in control of Job's properties, but not of his life (Job 1,12). Furthermore, nowhere in Tanakh is the word "satan" the proper name of a being or of an evil spirit who rivals God in power.[149] The word "satan" is always a class-name. It indicates a certain function someone or something has. That satanic function can vary from adversary via accusation to being tested. Often the word "satan" is translated with "adversary" when it is just about a human being (e.g. 1 King 11,14). In other cases it is translated into "accuser". Then it is about a function in a session of a court (e.g. Psalms 109,6). Sometimes a snake fulfils the function of the satan, as in the paradise-story, however the word "satan" is not used there (Genesis 3). Sometimes someone's lust for power is a satan to him (1 Chronicles 21,1 f.). Nevertheless, the function of the satan isn't always an evil or negative one. Even the angel of the LORD can be a satan. In Numbers 22,22 we read: "and the angel of the LORD took his stand in the way as his *satan* (adversary)", after which the story about Balaam's ass follows. Here the satan plays a positive part on behalf of God. Elsewhere the satan is the prosecutor in the court of the LORD (Zechariah 3,1 f.). In the story about Job the satan is even reckoned to the sons of God (Job 1,6). There his task is to try Job's loyalty to the LORD, maybe one should say to test it.

Against this background there is no reason to see Jesus' meeting the satan in the desert as a fight with God's greatest enemy. It is rather about the testing of a righteous one for the benefit of the cause of God. In this way Mark included Jesus in the array of Tanakh-figures who ever passed satan's test successfully. Job belongs to it. Also Abraham, who was, on account of the Oral Torah, accompanied by the satan on his way to Moriah to sacrifice Isaac (Genesis 22).[150] The test in the desert has a clear function in the context of Jesus' relation to God. The satan is the testing side of God. The very first 'exegesis' we have of this story from Mark's, shows that this is the correct explanation. When Matthew rewrites this story for his own gospel, he writes: "Then Jesus was led up by the spirit into the wilderness to be tested by the devil (i.e. the satan)" (Matthew 4,1). The testing of the righteous occurs on the initiative of God and is an instrument to prepare them for their task in the world.

Wild beasts. The wild beasts are already mentioned in the story of the creation. They are created on the same day as man (Genesis 1,24). Here Mark conspicuously uses the same word as the Septuagint does in the story of the creation. Elsewhere in Tanakh the wild beasts appear to have a clear function in the relation of God with men. The snakes indeed scourged Israel in the desert after they had indicated they'd rather to return to Egypt (Numbers 21,4-6). It's told elsewhere that God protected Israel against snakes and scorpions (Deuteronomy 8,15). In the prophets we also read about all kind of desert-beasts: hyanas, owls, ostriches, wild dogs, jackals, the arrow snake and the kite (Isaiah 13,21-22; 34,15). The very beasts from the wilderness will threaten the inhabitants of Jerusalem when they break God's justice: the lion, the wolf and the leopard (Jeremiah 11,6-8). But exactly these threatening wild beasts play an important part in Isaiah's vision of the messianic realm of peace: the wolf, the leopard, the young lion, the bear, the lion, the asp and the adder (Isaiah 11,6-8). Of course, we shouldn't read this vision as a prophecy on a complete change of nature. Isaiah's own interpretation of this vision in the next verses (Isaiah 11,9-10), points into an entirely different direction. It is about the nations who will seek the root of Jesse, that will be a banner to the people, a *nes ammim* (Isaiah 11,9). The big wild beasts in Isaiah's vision are the big war-seeking nations (cf. Daniel 8). The small tame animals are the little nations who - with great difficulty - hold their own in this violent world. Once all of them shall live in peace together around the holy mountain of the LORD. Mark evokes this image with the words: "and he was with the wild beasts". Who bears the testing in the desert, will be able to bring God's realm upon the earth.

And the angels ministered to him. Small wonder!

5.3 Matthew: de first rewriting (Matthew 4,1-11)

Writing his gospel, and using Mark's, Matthew can use the story about the test in the desert extremely well within the scope of his identification of Jesus with Moses. After the story about Jesus' baptism by John the Baptist (Matthew 3,13-17) that parallels the story of crossing the Red Sea in Exodus, the desert-story is a perfect parallel of the story of Israel's journey through the desert, in which Moses plays such an eminent part. This parallel with Exodus was, as we have seen already, the basis for Mark's story too, and Matthew could simply take it over. Mark's story about the test in the desert is however very brief and offers Matthew every opportunity for an extension. Moreover, the stories about Israel's journey through the desert contain rich material to link up with the theme of the testing. And this now is the weaker point of Mark's story. Nothing specifically is told about the tests. That's probably the reason why Matthew decided to add three elaborated tests to the story. Why three? Very probably for literary reasons. A division into three parts enables a clear climax without complicating the structure of the story too much. It is the form of the classical drama, but many gospel-stories are structured in this way as well: an introduction, three scenes and an epilogue.[151] Now Matthew's story is structured as follows:

- introducing observation (Matthew 4,1),
- the first test (Matthew 4,2-4),
- the second test (Matthew 4,5-7),
- the third test (Matthew 4,8-10),
- final observation (Matthew 4,11).

It isn't difficult to find stories in the book of Exodus that fit in with the three tests. Immediately after the crossing of the Red Sea we read about the Israelites grumbling because of the poor food (Exodus 16,2 f.) and quarrelling with Moses because of the lack of water (Exodus 17,2 f.). Further down in Exodus the worship of the golden calf is described (Exodus

32,1 f.). However, to be able to link up with these stories, Matthew has even more material at his disposal. The book of Deuteronomy reflects upon these stories in words Matthew can use. For the first test he can link up with Deuteronomy 8,1-3. He causes a discussion to take place between the tester and Jesus and he makes Jesus answer with the last word of these Torah-verses: "Man shall not live by bread alone, but by every word that proceeds from the mouth of God". (Deuteronomy 8,3b; Matthew 4,4b). In Deuteronomy 8,3a there is an obvious reference to the story of the manna, the heavenly bread, in Exodus 16. Matthew links up with Exodus via Deuteronomy that in its turn refers frequently to Exodus. Here in Deuteronomy 8,2 we clearly discover the reason for the testing, a reason that is in accordance with my explanation of Mark's story: "to humble you and test you, to know what was in your heart, whether you would keep His commandments or not". This text obviously formulates that the testing comes from God himself.

Matthew applies the same procedure for the first test and for the second one. In the discussion with the devil he puts the words of Deuteronomy 6,16a into Jesus' mouth: "You shall not put the LORD, your God, to the test" (Matthew 4,7).[a] Deuteronomy however continues with: "as you tested him at Massah" (Deuteronomy 6,16b). This addition refers to Israel's quarrel with Moses about the lack of water mentioned in Exodus 17,2 f. Now Matthew also links up with Exodus via Deuteronomy. For the third test Matthew proceeds in the same way. Here Jesus' answer to the devil is borrowed from Deuteronomy 6,13. The verses following immediately (Deuteronomy 6,14-15), remind us of the worship of the golden calf in Exodus 32. It was there and then that the wrath of God was kindled against the people and He threatened to destroy Israel from the face of the earth (Exodus 32,10), a threat that was subsequently averted by Moses.

Now it is conspicuous that the tests in Matthew are in the same order as in Exodus, and not in the order of Deuteronomy. This is once more a

---

[a]   I explained previously why I prefer to use here the verb "to test" (NEB) and not "to tempt" (NKJV).

sign that he had wanted to link up with Exodus seeing Deuteronomy only as an "intermediate stage". In table 5.1 I have summarized this in a diagram. I will round off this section with some exegetical annotations and point back to the previous section for those notions that already played a part in Mark.

Forty days and forty nights. Matthew doesn't copy Mark's expression "forty days" just like that. He adds "forty nights" and makes Jesus fast all that time. With the addition of "forty nights" he thoroughly underscores his identification of Jesus with Moses. For in Exodus it's said of Moses that he stayed on the mountain "forty days and forty nights" (Exodus 24,18). And when Moses visited the LORD on the mountain for the second time, that visit again lasted forty days and forty nights (Exodus 34,28). Evidently this central idea is so important that Deuteronomy repeats it four times (Deuteronomy 9,9, 11, 18; 10,10). Now, why the observation that Jesus had fasted all the time? Again the answer can be found in Exodus, for it is said about Moses' second visit to the Lord: "he neither ate bread nor drank water" (Exodus 34,28). The Oral Torah comments: "He didn't eat bread, only the bread of the Torah he ate, nor did he drink water, only the water of the Torah he drank".[152] This theme will be heard again in Jesus' answer to the devil's first test (Matthew 4,4).

The son of God. Many a person will read in the verses 3 and 6: "If you are *the* son of God"[153] associating this with the divinity of Jesus. To begin with, I would like to observe that this is an incorrect translation of the original text. In the Greek text the words "son" and "of God" aren't even one single expression. The text reads literally: "If (a) son you are of the God", whereas "son" and "of the God" are separated by the verb. How then could one take these words as a title, by writing them in capitals in the translation? Moreover, before the word "son" there is no definite article and so we should translate "a son". Before "God" however, the definite article is used, actually, as is almost always the case in New-Testament Greek. For this is about the one and only God of Israel. So a correct translation is: "If a son you are of the (only) God".

Table 5.1

*The linking-up of Matthew 4,1-11 with Exodus 16, 17 and 32
via Deuteronomy 6 and 8.*

EXODUS	DEUTERONOMIUM	MATTEÜS
Exodus 16,2 f. ⟶ Israel's grumbling because of lack of food, the bread from heaven	**Deuteronomy 8,3a** He allowed you to hunger and fed you with manna **Deuteronomy 8,3b** ⟶ That He might make you know that man shall not live by bread alone	**Matthew 4,4** Man shall not live by bread alone
Exodus 17,2 f. ⟶ The testing of the LORD at Massah and Meribah	**Deuteronomy 6,16a** ⟶ you shall not put the LORD, your God, to the test **Deuteronomy 6,16b** as you tested Him at Massah	**Matthew 4,7** You shall not test the LORD your God
Exodus 32,1 f. ⟶ The golden calf they worshiped That my wrath may burn hot against them and I may consume them[a]	**Deuteronomy 6,13** ⟶ You shall fear the LORD your God and serve him **Deuteronomy 6,14-15** You shall not go after other gods, lest the anger of the LORD be aroused against you and destroy you	**Matthew 4,10** You shall worship the LORD, your God, and him only you shall serve

---

[a] See also: Exodus 20,2-5.

It's not relevant now to think, in case of the expression "a son of God", of something that applies to Jesus only. This is clearly shown by other New Testamentary texts (e.g. Luke 3,38; John 1,12; Galatians 3,26). When the term "son of God" is applied to Jesus, it's also inappropriate to think of his supposed divinity. The dogma of the divine nature of Jesus is a doctrine developed in the Christian church only in later centuries. Such a doctrine about a human being is completely alien to Judaism and would certainly have been rejected by the Jewish Christians Matthew belonged to. The expression "son of God" had a entirely different meaning in the Judaism of those days. It alludes to a man who undertakes the task of manifesting the image and likeness of God on earth. In Tanakh this term is used for Israel (Exodus 4,22; Deuteronomy 14,1). However, if Israel isn't faithful to the LORD, they won't be his sons and daughters any longer (Deuteronomy 32,5, 18-20). The term "son" (of God) is used especially for the righteous king in Israel (Psalm 2,7). In the Apocrypha and in the Oral Torah the expression "son of God" means in general "a righteous one". He is someone doing the will of God, i.e. someone who lives in accordance with the Torah.[154] Jesus Ben Sirach says for example: "Be a father to orphans and like a husband to their mother, then *the Most High will call you his son* and his love for you will be greater than a mother's" (Ben Sirach 4,10).[155] The Oral Torah reads: "If the Israelites do the will of the Holy One, He will be praised, they will be called 'sons', but if they don't do his will, they will be called 'no-sons'".[156] A case in point is that Luke can use the word "righteous one" whereas Mark and Matthew use the expression "son of God" (compare Luke 23,47 with Mark 15,39 and Matthew 27,54). So in Matthew's story about the test in the desert we can also read: "If you are a righteous one, someone who does the will of God etc.". Indeed, this interpretation is entirely in accordance with the idea of the Oral Torah that only the righteous one is tested by order of God (see the previous section under "He was tested").

In addition to all this it's however possible that the term "son of God" evokes an additional association, viz. that of kingship as is the case in Psalm 2,7. In that case the use of the term "son of God" confronts the reader with some (further) questions: what direction will Matthew take with Jesus? Is Jesus only a righteous one or has he something to do with a possible kingship of Israel? And if so, what kind of kingship could Matthew have had in mind? But only the term "son of God" will not answer these questions. So for some answers we'll have to read on.

That these stones become bread. The character of this first test is: help yourself! Nobody will know your needs better than you do yourself. Follow your own feelings, your own experience, and, especially, save yourself! Use your abilities as a supposed "son of God" to intervene in the creation and to appease your hunger to your liking! Maybe you'd better translate the devil's words: "*If* you are a son of God" with: "*Because* you are a son of God",[157] meaning: "you *are* a son of God, so go ahead!" In the background-story in Exodus we can also find this theme of high-handed action. The people murmur against Moses and Aaron because in Egypt all things were better (Exodus 16,2-3). When God gives the manna with the explicit order not to leave anything of it until the next day (Exodus 16,4, 19), still there are some people trying to keep it (Exodus 16,20). When a double portion of manna is found on the sixth day with a view to the Shabbat, and one should gather a double portion because of the Shabbat-rest (Exodus 16,5, 22-23), yet there are some people going out on the seventh day to gather manna (Exodus 16:27). Already in Exodus 16,4b the meaning of this story is given: do the people live according to the LORD's Torah or not? Deuteronomy 8,3 comments: "but man lives by every *word* that proceeds from the mouth of the LORD". Man should unlearn being high-handed and self-willed. Jesus quotes this Deuteronomic comment on Exodus 16. Evidently Matthew wants to convince his readers that Jesus' actions were entirely based on the Torah, the central part of God's word. Just like Moses Jesus can alleviate his hunger with the bread of the Torah (see the above "Forty days and forty nights").

The pinnacle of the temple. The location of the second test is not the desert, but the temple in Jerusalem. Why now the temple exactly? Throwing oneself down is possible from any high place, isn't it? However, a tradition in the Oral Torah reads that if the messiah will reveal himself, he will come and stand on the roof of the temple. Then he will proclaim in Israel: "You, poor, the time of your salvation has come".[158] By taking Jesus to the roof of the temple the question arises if, possibly, we are dealing here with the messiah, the forthcoming king of Israel?

Throw yourself down. After the rejection of arrogance the question arises now whether it is allowed to test God or to force him to intervene in favour of his people. In the Exodus-background of this second test, viz. the story about the lack of water in Massah and Meribah, God is also challenged to act. At least that is the essence of the last sentence of the story (Exodus 17,7). The question of the people: "Is the LORD among us or not?" is a challenge directed to God to entice him to show that He is among them. In his answer to the devil Jesus quotes the commentary on this story as found in Deuteronomy 6,16 (Matthew 4,7). Now the question arises why Matthew chose this peculiar act of throwing oneself down for this second test. For although the devil motivates his advice to Jesus with a quotation from Psalm 91,11-12, even in this Psalm there is no immediate cause to speak about a self-performed fall into the depth. In Psalm 91,11 we only read about the protection by God's angels "in all your ways", but– as appears from verse 13 – these are the normal ways of life. An attempt at suicide, hoping to be rescued by God's angels, is outside the scope of this Psalm.

This second test however, has another background that explains this peculiar image of throwing oneself into the depth. We've seen already how the use of the term "a son of God" made the question arise of a possible kingship of Jesus in Israel. The roof of the temple as the scene of action aggravates the story to the issue of the messiah. Now, in those days, some people believed that the messiah would act in secret initially, but – at a certain moment – would reveal himself in the temple to the whole people by means of an amazing act. We find the echo of this belief in Luke 19,11 and John 7,4. However, another belief existed particularly among the supporters of the Zealotic freedom-fighters. They believed that, if the messiah would stand in danger of losing his life, God would send his host of angels down from heaven to assist his anointed one.[159] And it is especially this belief that makes the remarkable story of Matthew understandable. No doubt this belief was based on Psalm 91 and no doubt again, the Zealots would have associated this belief firmly with their armed struggle against the Romans. They often entered into combat with far too few people, but with an absolute trust in God (see also the verses 7-9 of Psalm 91). Matthew, for his second test, could have thought of this Zealotic belief, which is confirmed by his story about the arrest of Jesus in Gethsemane. There he makes Jesus say: "Or do you think that I cannot now pray to my Father, and He will provide me with more than twelve legions of angels?" But even then Jesus doesn't put God to the test. Armed combat is contrary to his idea of the Scriptures (Matthew 26,52-54). In this second test Matthew rejects, with an appeal to Exodus 17, the Zealotic belief that one can throw oneself into the fight for the sake of Israel's freedom because God will certainly send his angels to rescue his people in their moment of gravest danger. Surveying Matthew's gospel, he doesn't appear at all to be really interested in the political and military liberation of Jerusalem nor in the restoration of the temple. After all, he wrote his gospel not long after the destruction of the temple that happened in the year 70 CE.

With the rejection of the zealotic ideas and intentions which, undoubtedly, continued to have a grip on many Jews also after 70 CE, Matthew had to cope with a severe reproach from their side. Who didn't cooperate in the liberation from Roman hegemony, submitted himself in fact to Israel's oppressor and became a traitor and a collaborator, at least the Zealots thought so. In the third test Matthew will phrase an answer to that reproach.

All the kingdoms of the world and their glory. In the first century, there were of course independent kingdoms outside the Roman empire, but seen from within, it seemed to include all the kingdoms of the world. So Luke can safely write that a decree went out from Caesar Augustus to register *all the world* (in Greek the word *oekumene* is used; Luke 2,1). In the eyes of the first readers of Matthew's the devil showed Jesus the Roman empire especially. Now the third test comes down to this: because you are not willing to risk your life for the liberation of Jerusalem and the temple, you could just as well go and devote yourself to the Roman empire. Thus throw yourself down and worship. But

Matthew makes Jesus reject this idea with an appeal to Exodus 32, again via Deuteronomy. The middle course between armed combat that scorned life on the one hand and submission to Rome on the other, a middle course that didn't exist in the eyes of the Zealots, did exist in Matthew's eyes. This can be concluded from the location of this third testing.

An exceedingly high mountain. Now one could say: this test should take place on a very high mountain or else one shouldn't be able to see all the kingdoms of the world and their glory. But as will appear from the discussion of Luke's version of the testing in the desert, this will certainly be possible without mentioning a high mountain. Without doubt Matthew situated the third test, the very climax of his story, on a mountain, because of the important place a mountain occupies in his gospel. I have already discussed this in chapter 4. In Matthew the most important lecture of Jesus, the Sermon on the Mount, is, as its name says, given on a mountain. At the end of his gospel Matthew makes Jesus take leave of his disciples on a mountain too, viz. on the mountain of the Sermon on the Mount (see section 4.2). Situating the third test on a mountain Matthew points ahead to the mountain of this sermon. It is there that in his eyes, the middle way lies between Zealotism for one thing and the submission to Rome for another. His message: live in accordance with the Torah as interpreted by Jesus in the Sermon on the Mount! In that case the armed liberation of Jerusalem isn't necessary and you can also endure the Romans without submission. And if either the Romans or the Zealots make this impossible, you should accept martyrdom like Jesus did. The gist of it is: take upon yourself the kingdom of God!

Angels came and served him. It's conspicuous that, at the end of his story, Matthew did take over the serving angels from Mark, but not the wild beasts. Did he take the view that Isaiah's vision of the messianic kingdom of peace was not yet about to be realized? Or did the wild beasts remind him too much of Psalm 91 (especially verse 13), a psalm undoubtedly popular among the Zealots? (see above under "Throw yourself down"). Whatever the case may be, he could and did use the serving angels at the end of his story. The third test has, as we have seen (table 5.1), the golden calf in Exodus 32 as a Torah-background. Immediately after this event Moses too is sustained by an angel (Exodus 32,34; 33,2). So, in Matthew's case, the angels suit his identification of Jesus with Moses entirely.

5.4 Luke: the second rewriting (Luke 4,1-13)

In writing his gospel, Luke could make good use of the story about the test in de desert just before Jesus' appearance in public. This was undoubtedly caused by the function of the desert as a place of learning and a trial period. Also the idea that only the righteous will be tested, didn't stand in his way at all. Even Matthew's elaboration of Mark's story contained many elements that came in useful to Luke. The rejection of Zealotism as well as the rejection of submission to the Romans were also themes of importance to him. Yet there were all sorts of motives why he couldn't copy Matthew's story literally.

First of all Luke doesn't identify Jesus with Moses. He rather seems to avoid that identification. He doesn't take over the threesome we have read in Mark:[a]

- crossing the Red Sea // baptism in the river Jordan;
- journey through the desert // testing in the desert;
- entry into the land of Canaan // preaching in Galilee.

He interrupts the order of the baptism in the river Jordan followed by the testing in the desert by inserting an extended genealogical tree of Jesus (Luke 3, 23-38). It's true, he takes over Mark's forty days (Luke 4,2), probably because the number forty is frequently found in Tanakh, but he omits Matthew's expression "forty days and forty nights", because these words are associated too much with Moses. Luke also removes three other details because of their association with Moses and Exodus:

---

[a]   See the beginning of section 5.2.

- In Luke the second test, the worshipping of the devil (in Matthew the third test), doesn't occur on the mountain that is so characteristic for Moses. In some translations we read: "Then the devil taking him up into a *high mountain*" (Luke 4,5; NKJV), but in the original text not even a "high place" is found. The verb used in that place could best be translated with: "take up". Therefore one should translate: "And he (the devil) took him (Jesus) up and showed him all the kingdoms of the world". Obviously, Luke wanted to avoid any association with the mountain in Matthew, as appears from the rest of his gospel as well (see section 4.2).
- In the same test in Luke the words "throw down" (for the devil; cf. Luke 4,7 and Matthew 4,9) don't occur. A similar term does not occur either in the Deuteronomic background of this story (Deuteronomy 6,13-15), but it does in the Exodus-background of the story of Matthew (Exodus 32,8)[160]. In this way Luke breaks slightly away from the connection with Exodus.
- The end of Luke's story shows something similar. The angels who served Jesus, have disappeared from the final remark (Luke 4,13). Apparently, Luke can't use this parallelism with Moses in Exodus 32,34 and 33,2.

In comparison with Matthew, Luke slightly dissociates the tie of his story with Exodus yet in another sense. He changes the order of the second and the third test found in Matthew. Consequently, in his story, the tests are not in the same order as in their corresponding stories in Exodus. Now the quotations from Deuteronomy, on the other hand, are in the correct order: Deuteronomy 6,13 in Luke 4,8 and Deuteronomy 6,16 in Luke 4,12. Remarkably more parallelisms between Luke 4 and Deuteronomy 6 can be shown:

- The motive of food and eating (Deuteronomy 6,11; Luke 4,3-4);
- Serving only the LORD (Deuteronomy 6,13; Luke 4,8);
- Not putting God to the test (Deuteronomy 6,16; Luke 4,12);
- The motive of teaching (Deuteronomy 6,20; Luke 4,15);

- Liberation and redemption (Deuteronomy 6,21-23; Luke 4,18-19);
- The relation of Israel with the nations (Deuteronomy 7,1 f.; Luke 4,27-28).

It looks as if Luke abandons the parallelism with Deuteronomy at the moment the inhabitants of Nazareth don't want to take up Israel's duty to the other nations.[161] Here however, I'll restrict myself to the story of the testing in the desert.

Besides linking up with Deuteronomy instead of with Exodus, Luke had yet another reason to turn around the last two tests in Matthew. For his third test, the climax, plays in Jerusalem in the temple. This is completely in line with the plan of Luke's gospel and of the Acts of the Apostles, in which Jerusalem ever plays an important, central part.[162] Furthermore, I 'd like to observe that this reversal fits the argument Luke develops in both his books even better. I discussed this elsewhere and I will briefly summarize it here. Luke's work is, more than the other evangelists' work, an anti-Zealotic discourse. However, he doesn't reject the aims the Zealots pursued, but mainly their violent methods. The most important aim of the Zealots, viz. the liberation of Jerusalem from the Roman power, was also Luke's aim, this as opposed to Matthew! He shows however his fellow-Jews a different way to reach this aim, viz. the way of repentance of the gentiles and especially of the Romans to the God of Israel. If Judaism is able to reach that aim, then Jerusalem will be free. Therefore the question now is, why the order of Luke's second and third test fits better with this discourse than the order he found in Matthew.

Before Luke had written the story of the testing in the desert, he had already incorporated a story from which Zealotic readers could have concluded that he propagated submission to the Romans. For the census Joseph and Mary apparently submitted themselves willingly to, was a thorn in the flesh of the Zealots, and it had even been the direct cause of the origin of an organized Zealotic movement.[163] The argument of Luke 4,1-13 runs as follows. In the first test Luke makes it clear that Jesus based himself on the Torah and the Prophets. Then, in the second test, he immediately makes it clear to his readers that there is no question of submission to the Romans. Finally, in the third test, he shows that, in the end, his purpose is Jerusalem and the temple, but not in the way of the Zealots. In the following stories he indicates to his readers the course that should be taken to liberate Jerusalem. In my book *Luke the Jew* I discussed extensively how he handled this issue.[164]

5.5 Final remark

In the previous sections I showed how the evangelists as Jewish writers set about composing their stories. The example of the different versions of the story about the testing of Jesus in the desert is illustrative for the way they wrote all their stories as well. Undoubtedly it will be possible to formulate some objections against the given presentation. Maybe further research will oblige me to correct my argument on certain points. It is just a reconstruction after all. It will be clear however that the method I followed here, dulls the source-theories indeed. The Tanakh-backgrounds, the Oral Torah, the context of the historical situation the evangelists lived in, the literary analysis of the gospel-stories and especially the scrupulous comparison of parallel-stories in Mark, Matthew and Luke, all those are ingredients which could bring us closer to the evangelists, closer to Jesus and eventually to the Holy One, He will be praised.

6 And took his journey into a far country
The parting of the roads of Christianity and Judaism

6.1 The parting of the roads

The outline of the original movement of Jesus of Nazareth can be observed clearest in the gospels of Mark, Matthew and Luke. In the previous chapters I have shown that this movement was very closely connected with the rabbinical Judaism as we know it from the Oral Torah. The Jewish Christians saw Jesus first of all as a Torah-teacher (Matthew), or as an innovator of prophecy (Luke). One could come to see him as a messianic figure owing to his "doing and teaching" (Acts 1,1) concerning God's kingship in Israel – a kingship that could even be realized without political independence. He became an obvious counterpart of all those messianic expectations that were based on the ambition to overthrow the Roman regime violently as well. Jesus could be called "messiah" or "christos", i.e. "anointed one", because his life and teachings made every expectation of messianic figures that acted violently redundant. His Jewish followers still belonged entirely to Judaism and lived in accordance with the ancestral customs, despite the conflicts with some other Jewish groups they ended up in from time to time. Gentiles who felt attracted to the movement of Jesus, could join them as god-fearing gentiles and hardly differed from the many other god-fearing gentiles who had associated with Jewish communities elsewhere in the world.

This situation of the beginning "Christianity" as a part of Judaism, didn't last very long. Christianity grew into an independent religion that differed so much from Judaism that speaking about a Jewish-Christian tradition is wellnigh a contradictio in terminis. How could that be? The drifting apart of Christianity and Judaism was a complex historical process. Therefore I won't pretend to give a complete and an in every respect correct description. Nevertheless, as I see it, some outlines of this process can be observed clearly enough. Nowadays it's called the "parting of the roads".[165] Yet, no indications for this parting of the roads are found in Matthew and Luke. At the most we find a severe polemic with other Jewish groups in their gospels, but no rejection of Judaism whatsoever. On the other hand, however, the letters of Paul do show clearly the main features of this process of alienation. In fact, his letters are the first phase of the parting of the roads.

A consequence of Paul's actions was that independent Christian communities of gentiles came into being detached from the synagogue. When after Paul such communities developed in great numbers, new Christian ideas were formed, partly influenced by gentile ideas, that drifted further and further apart from their Jewish origin. That was the second phase of the parting of the roads. And then, halfway through the second century, the third phase started. The till then formed Christian faith was subjected to a reflection with the help of defining problems and concepts from the Greek-Roman philosophy, after which the Christian doctrine reached its final form and meaning. At the beginning of the third century this process was essentially completed: from now on Christianity was founded strongly and dogmatically in itself, only to be refined and completed in later centuries. The question is, however, whether this foundation was in agreement with the original intentions of Jesus and the evangelists. The Christian dogmas, as developed in the first centuries, are like "mountains hanging on a hair": their implications are many, but their evidence from the Scriptures is small. In the next sections I will describe the three phases of the parting of the roads in the light of their most important aspects.

6.2 The first phase: Paul

Jesus' first followers made up a typically Jewish movement. As far as gentiles were involved they didn't differ initially from the God-fearing who could be met in the synagogues everywhere in the Diaspora. At first this situation changed only gradually but later, when Paul of Tarsus became a member of the movement, it speeded up considerably. Now it's likely that we have got an incomplete image of Paul from his letters, and it's equally likely that he wouldn't have written down the majority of his ideas, but handed them down orally to his disciples. Not even all his letters are preserved (see e.g. 1 Corinthians 5,9; 2 Corinthians 2,4; 7,8).[166] Therefore, it is quite possible that the present collection of Paul's letters is a selection made by later generations. Nevertheless we can establish with certainty that Paul's letters represent an entirely different atmosphere and completely different ideas than those found in the gospels and in the Acts of the Apostles. Paul's line of argument doesn't involve concrete stories, but abstract arguments. His letters are more like the explanations of a philosopher than those of a rabbi.

Contrary to the evangelists Paul is hardly interested in the life of Jesus of Nazareth. He even acknowledges as much (2 Corinthians 5,16). So we'll find little information about Jesus' life and teachings in Paul's letters. We are told about Jesus that he was "born of the seed of David according to the flesh" (Romans 1,3), "born of a woman and born under the law" (Galatians 4,4). Of Jesus' actions only the last supper with his disciples is mentioned (1 Corinthians 11,23-25). Paul's interest in Jesus confines itself chiefly to his sufferings (2 Corinthians 1,5; Philippians 3,10), his death[a], his burial (1 Corinthians 15,4) and his resurrection[b]. No doubt the reason for this lack of interest in the "earthly Jesus" lies in Paul's idea that the earthly form of the Christ ought to be considered a humiliation of his heavenly origin (cf. 2 Corinthians 8,9; Philippians 2,8). In Paul's view Jesus is just the incarnation of the Christ who exists, form the beginning, with God in heaven (cf. Colossians 1,15-23).[c, 167] As such

---

[a] Romans 3,25; 5,6; 6,3, 5, 8, 10; 14,9; 1 Corinthians 1,17, 23; 2,2, 8; 5,7; 8,11; 11,26; 15,3; 2 Corinthians 4,10; 5,15; 13,4; Galatians 2,20; 3,1, 13; 6,14; Philippians 2,8; 3,10.

[b] Romans 1,4; 4,24; 6,4, 5, 9; 7,4; 8,11; 10,9; 14,9, 15; 1 Corinthians 6,14; 15,4, 12, 20; 2 Corinthians 4,14; Galatians 1,2; Philippians 3,10.

[c] Although today the letter to the Colossians is no longer seen as an original letter of Paul's, but rather as a letter written by one of his disciples (see the endnote), Paul's ideas with respect to this issue are probably represented correctly in this texts.

the Christ is an instrument in God's hand to restore the breach between God and humanity.[a]

Paul's theology and ethics aren't based peculiarly enough on the words and deeds of Jesus except for his way to the cross. In two cases only he says he'd received an order of the Lord (1 Corinthians 7,10; 9,14). In both cases however he appeals to the Torah, so that the word "Lord" had better be interpreted as the Jewish substitute for the name of God and not as a description of Jesus (in both cases in Greek the word *kurios* can be used). It seems that Paul didn't know the Torah-teacher Jesus at all. In Paul's view, the Torah is linked up rather with sin and death (see e.g. 1 Corinthians 15,56) than with life and redemption. In his wake his disciples can even claim that Jesus had abolished the Torah (Ephesians 2,15).[b] At this point, the contrast between Paul's way of thinking and that of Matthew and Luke couldn't be larger. Nevertheless it's remarkable that Paul based his theology and ethics repeatedly and directly on Tanakh. He frequently quotes the Torah (the Law), the Prophets and the Psalms.[c] Especially with respect to the Torah this is remarkable at the very least, because, as "the law", it is frequently judged very negatively (Romans 3,20, 28; 4,13-15; 5,20a; 6,15; 7,5-6, 8-11; 8,3; 9,31-32; 2 Corinthians 3,7; Galatians 2,15-21; 3,2, 10-13; 4,24; Philippians 3,8; etc.).

In addition to all this we have to consider that for some time Paul probably lived in the environment of the strict Pharisees (Philippians 3,5), a Pharisaic wing closely related to the Zealots (see e.g. Romans 10,2). These Zealots took the view that their violent actions could precipitate the coming of the messiah (Greek: *christos*) (cf. Romans 10,6-7). They didn't want to have any dealings with gentiles (this explains the word "jealousy" or "zeal" in Romans 11,11; see also Galatians 4,17). Paul

---

[a] See e.g. Romans 6,4; 7,25; 8,32, 39; 1 Corinthians 1,9, 30; 3,11, 23; 6,14; 8,6.

[b] What holds for the letter to the Colossians (see the last but one note), holds also for the letter to the Ephesians.

[c] E.g. in Romans 4,1-3, 7-8; 7,2-3; 9,15, 25-29, 33; 10,15-16; 12,19-20; 13,9-10; 1 Corinthians 1,19, 31; 2,9; 3,19-20; 5,1 e.v.; 9,9, 13; 10,1-11; 14,21; 15,55; 2 Corinthians 6,2, 16-18; 8,15; 9,9; 13,1; Galatians 3,6, 8, 10.

himself clearly indicated his affiliation to these Zealots (Galatians 1,14). His violent persecution of Jesus' followers before his conversion has all the traits of a Zealotic action (1 Corinthians 15,9; Galatians 1,13, 23). In this context he himself uses the word "zeal" (Greek: *zèlos* in Philippians 3,6). In those Zealotic circles the observance of the Law didn't exactly go hand in hand with mercy. Additionally, after his conversion, Paul wrote for gentiles (Romans 1,6, 13; 11,13; Galatians 4,8). He wanted to protect them against his former, strict Pharisaic and Zealotic idea of the law. The consequence was that he wrote about the Torah (the law) in a way that ultimately had to end in the dissolution of the Torah. In Paul's thought the Torah is pushed aside by Christ from the centre of the revelation.[a] And just there lies the beginning of the parting of the roads between Christianity and Judaism. But it could have been done differently.

The joyless idea of the law we find in Paul's letters, isn't in any sense characteristic for the Judaism of those days. In the enlightened Pharisaic School of Hillel, the founder of today's Judaism, we come across an idea of the Torah that is a lot more joyful and merciful. Matthew's and Luke's ideas of the Torah are closely related to the ones we meet in the School of Hillel. This school considers the Torah the very instrument that God gave to Israel to restore the breach between Him and the world. People like Moses, Joshua, the prophets en later the rabbis – however great – always remain subservient to the Torah. In Matthew and Luke we find this idea also with regard to Jesus. As long as Jesus' followers were chiefly Jews this was understood. However, when in Paul's wake more and more Christian communities from the gentiles came into being, communities which very soon lost any contact with Judaism, the way was cleared for a Christian church that estranged itself from its origin more and more.

---

[a]   Romans 2,14-16; 3,21-22; 8,3-4; 10,4; 1 Corinthians 1,24; 5,7; 9,20-21; 10,4; 15,56-57; 2 Corinthians 3,7-8, 12-15; 5,16-21; Galatians 2,16, 19-21; 3,2, 5, 13, 19-25; 4,4-5, 21-31; 5,4, 18; Philippians 3,9.

6.3 The second phase: the intrusion of gentile ideas

In the letters of Paul the influence of Greek-Hellenistic thought is already clearly noticeable. The notions of "body" or "flesh" on the one hand and of "spirit" on the other – for the rabbis still two aspects of one and the same earthly reality that complete and influence each other – are, in Paul's thinking, a contradiction rather than a twofold unity, moreover a contradiction that tends towards two independent realities.[a] Every now and then earthly matters are entirely spiritualised by Paul, for example death (Romans 6,6), the Torah (the law) (Romans 7,14) and the resurrection of the dead (1 Corinthians 15,44). After Paul, there is a growing influence of ideas and conceptions from the gentile cultures and religions on the Christian communities from the gentiles. This leads to a re-interpretation of many originally Jewish words and stories resulting in a complete alienation of Christianity from Judaism. I will confine myself to some examples of this re-interpretation.

In the gospels Jesus is sometimes described by the words "son of God" (e.g. Matthew 4,3, 6; 27,54). We have already seen that in Judaism this expression "son of God" doesn't refer to the divinity of a person at all, but only to the extent in which someone – through his way of life – makes God's image and likeness visible in the world. In fact, this should be everyone's task (see section 5.3). The gentile world however didn't have the slightest idea of this human notion of the term "son of god". He who was the son of a god, was divine himself. After all the gentile world was full of gods in human form (c.f. Acts 14,11-12), demigods and rulers who descended from gods. At an early stage already the idea of the divine nature of Jesus entered the Christian church. Ignatius of Antioch (about 110 CE) wrote for example about "Our God, Jesus Christ".[168] For him God and Christ were inseparably joined to each other, for Christ is God.[169] Some decades later the apologist Justin quite frankly explains to his readers the divinity of Jesus with the aid of the Greek demigods, the

---

[a]   Romans 1,4; 2,28-29; 7,14-15, 26; 8,1-16; 1 Corinthians 2,10-16; 3,1; 5,3; 9,11; 15,45; Galatians 5,16-17; 6,8; etc.

sons of the supreme god Zeus. He adds that the Christian story resembles those stories indeed, but is nevertheless superior.[170] In this way the Christian doctrine became a bettered version of the gentile mythology.

The same phenomenon occurs with respect to the so-called virgin birth of Jesus. In Matthew's and Luke's birth-stories about Jesus, Joseph doesn't seem to play a part as the natural father of the child (Matthew 1,18 f.; Luke 1,26 f.). According to both evangelists Mary's pregnancy is caused by an interaction of God himself (Matthew 1,18; Luke 1,35). However, divinely inspired births happen in the Oral Torah as well. Examples are the births of Isaac of Sarah, of Esau and Jacob of Rebecca, and of Obed of Ruth.[171] In no way whatsoever an argument could be derived from suchlike stories with regard to a possibly divine nature of the newborn child. This changed however, as soon as the birth-stories of Jesus ended up in an originally gentile environment no longer familiar with the Oral Torah. Stories about divine births are found in the entire gentile-world and strongly support claims on divinity there. For example, Alexander the Great's mother Olympias (356-323 BCE) was said to be a virgin at his birth. This was considered to be proof of his divine nature.[172] Remus and Romulus, the founders of the city of Rome, were also said to descend from the war-god Mars and the Vestal virgin Rhea Silvia.[173] The Roman empire was thus founded by the sons of a god. Early on in Christianity, one started to consider a poem, written by the Roman poet Virgil about 40 BCE, as a prediction of the birth of Christ. This poem is about a boy born of the "divine virgin". The child is described with words like "child and darling of the gods" and "glorious offspring of Jove".[174] The idea that important people, because of their close relation with the divine world, might have a divine nature themselves, was already present as a matter of course in the pagan world of those days. This explains why the belief in Jesus' divinity already occurred so early in the circles of Christians from the gentiles. This idea however, is entirely inconsistent with the Jewish origin of the gospels.

Indeed, the ideas of the Christian church were strongly influenced by the gentile realm of thought and mythology, not only with respect to the divine nature of Jesus, but also with regard to many other issues.[175] The influence of the non-Jewish world on Christian thought however, was to become very powerful from the middle of the second century CE. From that time onwards, the Greek and Roman philosophy in particular was going to leave its mark upon the development of the doctrine of the church.

6.4 The third phase: the influence of the Greco-Roman philosophy

From the middle of the second century CE an ever increasing number of intellectuals became members of the Christian church. Without any exception they were educated in the schools of gentile philosophers and lawyers.[176] The apologist Justin (c. 100 – c. 165 CE) for example was studying Stoic and Platonic philosophy at his conversion to Christianity.[177] The Latin church-father Tertullian (c. 157 – after 220 CE) was educated in Rome, where he worked as a lawyer afterwards.[178] The Greek church-father Origen, born from Christian parents around 185 CE, was very well schooled in Greek philosophy.[179] From their philosophical background many of them were seeking for certainty when they came into contact with Christianity as was the case for example with Clement of Alexandria (c. 180 CE).[180] Therefore it's not surprising that most Christian authors of those days didn't look upon their conversion to Christianity as a breach with the past. And even with respect to those authors who did experience their conversion as a breach, it must be observed that, after all, this wasn't a real breach.[181] The ideas of the Stoic and Platonic philosophy brought along by all these apologists and church-fathers from before their conversion, would give the Christian theology its definite form and meaning.

For some obvious reasons some philosophically schooled intellectuals of those days could be attracted to Christianity. Already the Greek philosophy had clearly shown a certain development into the direction of monotheism.[182] The Stoics for example considered the world-history as embodied in a supreme being they addressed as "father".[183] They fought the polytheism of their days with philosophical arguments.[184] This tendency towards monotheism could even be perceived in certain cultic movements like the Isis-cult.[185] The belief in one god who maintained a relation with man, was widespread in those days. But the all important question was, what then the character of this relation would be.[186] Especially the close tie between God and man that Christianity had inherited from Judaism, offered many people who couldn't manage the answers of philosophy, a hold in a confused world.[187]

Philosophy paved the way for Christianity not only with regard to the idea of God but also in the area of ethics. The Christian faith owed its highly ethical standards to its Jewish origin. This made the joining of Christianity with the ethical movements within the Greek philosophy very easy indeed.[188] At the same time, the Roman part of the civilization of those days was attracted to issues of practical morality as well.[189] In the ethical sphere, especially Stoicism laid the foundations for Christianity. It preached a strict , ascetical morality, disregard of outward appearances and a general love of mankind that broke through all borders, nations and classes .[190] Thus we can see that, at the end of the second century, the Christian writers adopt the ethical principles of the Stoic writers almost without any change.[191]

There are several reasons why the apologists and church-fathers reflected upon the Christian faith with the aid of Greek philosophical ideas. Besides the fact that they were very conversant with all these ideas and hadn't much awareness of the Jewish background of the gospels as well, it was also necessary for the public they wrote for, to avail themselves of the language and the notions of the philosophical movements of their days. It's true, they wrote to obtain more followers[192] and to introduce their faith into the educated circles of their days.[193] After all, philosophy was very appropriate for the fight against all kinds of heresies and for the defense against imputations of non-Christians, because it constituted a common language in the broadest sense of the word, that was understood by their opponents. In that situation it was unavoidable however, that the ideas of the opponents influenced

Christian thought.[194] Especially when people from the higher classes of the society began to join Christianity, Christian authors sought more and more alliances with Greek and Roman traditions.[195] Eventually Stoicism and Platonism became the philosophical basis of the Christian theology.[196]

As observed before, most apologists and church-fathers didn't experience their change to Christianity as a breach with their philosophical past. Justin, Clement of Alexandria, Origen and Tertullian saw a positive connection between the Greek philosophy and the Biblical writings.[197] Aristides (midst 2nd century), Justin and Athanagoras (c. 177 CE) were diligently searching in the Greek philosophy for all valuable issues that could be adopted by Christianity.[198] According to Justin the Greek philosophy was, just like the Christian philosophy, a revelation of the divine Word, of which a seed would be planted at birth into every man's reason.[199] He relies especially on Platonism and adopts its theory that the divine revelation had already occurred in olden times. So with regard to the original philosophical tradition Christianity is not something new, but the gentile philosophies of its days had deviated from the ancient divine revelation.[200] In Justin's eyes Christianity was therefore the final stage in the development of philosophy.[201] He argues that Plato had known the entire Old Testament, and takes the view that philosophers like Heraclitus, Socrates and Plato should be called Christians before Christ.[202] According to Justin Christianity is the only true successor of the ancient Platonism.

According to Athanagoras, too, the gentile philosophers could already have enjoyed an affinity with the inspirations of God.[203] Clement of Alexandria considers philosophy an appropriate training of thought. The positive value of philosophy is that it constitutes a preliminary instruction to find the truth. In his opinion some philosophers had a presumption of the truth, and that's why philosophy could be seen to a certain extent as the work of Providence.[204] Moreover, he is of the opinion that Greek philosophy had, by God's decree, prepared the gentiles for Christ, like the Torah had done for the Jews.[205] Minucius Felix (c. 200 CE) was convinced that certain Christian ideas were already present among the poets and thinkers of antiquity. For him, Christianity was the highest fulfillment of the ideals of the gentile philosophy.[206] At last, the church-father Origen answered all kinds of questions usually from Greek philosophy only.[207]

However, not all Christian writers were that positive about Greco-Roman philosophy. Irenaeus (c. 140 – c. 202 CE) spoke negatively about the Greek philosophy that was, in his eyes, the cause of heresies. Nevertheless it is obvious that he was not ill disposed toward all philosophy.[208] In his opinion the gentiles had, through providence, already been acquainted – to a certain extent – with God's revelation. This was especially the case with Plato.[209] More or less the same attitude towards philosophy we see with Tertullian. Notwithstanding the fact that he ran down Greek philosophy – especially Platonism had to bear the brunt[210] –, he yet used the philosophy of Stoics like Seneca and Musonius Rufus for the construction of his own philosophical theories.[211] He approvingly underscored the presumed affinity to Christianity of philosophers like Seneca.[212] He started from a collection of "tools for common use" (*utensilium communionem*) of Christianity and philosophy. The Christians moreover would have the privilege of the correct use.[213] Later Lactantius (c. 250 – c. 325 CE) shows a similar attitude to philosophy as well. For him philosophy had no value whatsoever, but nevertheless he tried to systematize the Christian doctrine with the aid of philosophy.[214] From this all it is clear that even those Christian authors who openly rejected philosophy, couldn't in practice withdraw from its influence. So it's not surprising that many Christian publications since the second century try to compete with the philosophical ideas of the Greek-Roman world.[215]

It's not my intention to deal comprehensively with the consequences of the influence of Greco-Roman philosophy on the Christian doctrine. That's beyond the scope of this book. Therefore, in the following paragraphs, I will only indicate some issues that, in my eyes, are important for the parting of the roads of Christianity and Judaism. First there is the way the concept of God developed in Christianity under the influence of philosophical thinking about divinity. To fight polytheism the Greek-Christian apologists copied the arguments of the gentile philosophy.[216]

They used the weapons of the Greek philosophy to attack the Greek gods.[217] The Latin-Christian authors Tertullian, Minucius Felix, Arnobius (c. 300 CE) and Lactantius derived their arguments from Cicero's *De Natura Deorum*.[218] In this way a Christian concept of God was created that borrowed its essential features from gentile philosophy, but that was also far removed from the Biblical-Jewish concept of God the evangelists lived with. Aristides (c. 140 CE) defended his Christian concept of God in Platonic terms against the Greek, the Barbarian and even against the Jewish concept of God.[219] Justinus (c. 150 CE) as well described God in Platonic terms as the father of everything.[220] In his eyes the highest aspiration of Christianity and of Platonic philosophy as well is a transcendent and unchanging God.[221] It is especially this concept of an unchanging God, borrowed from Platonism, which was going to influence Christian theology deeply and fundamentally. In the central issues of his theology Irenaeus for example shows to be convinced of these Platonic ideas.[222] The terms in which he speaks about God, are indeed very far removed from Tanakh and from the gospels. God created the world by his own free will, free from any pattern of creation outside himself. God's freedom is unlimited and so is his power. God's will coincides with his power, his wisdom and his goodness. God is unlimited, all-containing and knows no border. He doesn't need any glorification by man, for he is perfect in himself. It's only by his grace that he will accept glorification.[223]

The unbridgeable gap between God and man, so characteristic for Greek philosophy, but entirely contrary to Tanakh and the gospels, should be closed in Christian theology as well as in Greek philosophy by mediating notions. In philosophy the "Logos" acts as such, i.e. the Reason which rules the world. Plato has the divine Ideas that mediate between God and creation. In Christian theology the part of the Logos will be taken up by Christ. Already Justin clearly identifies Christ with the Logos: "His [God's] son however, the only one who is his son in the proper sense, the Logos, who was in him [God] and was begotten before the creation, he is called the Christ because he was anointed and God ordered all things by him."[224, a, 225] In this view the Logos is at the same time the creating, revealing and redeeming Word of God.[226] Christ, the Logos, is God's first creation that already existed before the creation of the world. Irenaeus concludes from the pre-existence of Christ, that he had always revealed the Father also before his incarnation. In this way the newness of Christianity that was difficult to bring in line with the idea of an unchanging God, was put into perspective and restricted to its minimum.[227] It's also obvious that these ideas have largely influenced the way in which one was going to read the so-called Old Testament.

If Christ already existed before the creation of the world, it had to be possible to discover his presence in the "Old Testament". Justin is of the opinion that Christ is hidden behind all kinds of Old Testament-expressions.[228] Irenaeus explains extensively that the prophets, as limbs of the body of Christ, had foretold all aspects of Christ's life.[229] Justin, Irenaeus, Clement of Alexandria and Origen develop, all in their own way, the doctrine that Christ had come to fulfill the prophecies. In this way the "Old Testament" has been devaluated into a rough draft, a preparation or a foreshadowing of the New Testament.[230] Irenaeus for example is of the opinion that the exodus from Egypt was a foreshadowing of the Christians who broke with the gentile world.[231]

The same devaluation that the "Old Testament" endured, was shared by its Hebrew text as well. The church-fathers considered this text as less inspired than the Septuagint, the Greek translation of Tanakh.[232] Many incorrect opinions about the "Old Testament" are found in the writings of many Christian authors. Clement of Alexandria for example is of the opinion that fear is characteristic for the "Old Testament", whereas love was added to it by Christianity.[233] In that way everything Tanakh has to

---

a   As I see it, this interpretation doesn't hold good for the "logos" in John 1, like a Jewish exegesis of the prologue of the gospel of John has shown (see the second endnote). However, this will not mean that Justin and those who came after him, couldn't have interpreted it in such a way. The problem is here that the words "the word became flesh" (John 1,14) are connected too one-sidedly with Jesus, an interpretation to which the text itself doesn't force at all.

say about love and mercy, is simply overlooked! According to Justin the law of Moses had only a temporary value and was replaced by the law of Christ that addresses mankind as a whole.[234] In that way the universalistic tendency of the Torah is completely disregarded. The covenant of God and Noah for example is a covenant with all generations of the earth (Genesis 9,8 f.). This indicates that the Torah, at least partially, is meant for all mankind. Finally, Irenaeus is of the opinion that the relation between God and man in the "Old Testament" is characterized by the obedience of a slave to his lord.[235] But Tanakh describes that relation rather as one of a father and his children.

With all this, we are far removed from the Oral Torah and from the gospels. Even the methods of interpreting the Scriptures that began to take root in the church, had few in common with the midrash-approach of the evangelists. From the second century until the middle ages especially the allegorical method of Bible-interpretation dominated in the church. The allegoresis is a method of interpretation that tries to discover the supposedly hidden or symbolic meaning behind the Bible-story. This method was developed by the Greek philosophers trying to overcome the problems that arose from a literal interpretation of the old Greek myths.[236] The Jewish-Hellenistic philosopher Philo of Alexandria, a contemporary of Jesus', had already applied this allegorical method to the Septuagint. In this way he tried to harmonize the law of Moses with the Greek philosophy. From Alexandria in Egypt the allegoresis was spread throughout Christianity, although other methods of Bible-interpretation also were maintained.[237]

Actually, the first Christian allegory is already found in the New Testament, especially in Paul's letter to the Galatians. The words in this letter, characteristic for the allegoresis run as follows: "This is something being allegorized" (Galatians 4,24).[238] Then, in the story of Sarah and Hagar (Genesis 16,1 f.), Hagar is interpreted as "the present-day Jerusalem" (Galatians 4,25), i.e. "Mount Sinai which generates slaves" (verse 24). Contrary to this is the interpretation of Sarah as "the heavenly Jerusalem" that is free (verse 26). In this way Ishmael is identified with the Torah-abiding Jews who are faithful to the Torah, whereas Isaac represents "you, brothers, children of the promise" (verse 28).

In this first Christian allegory we could observe a conspicuous feature of the allegoresis. Ignoring the original meaning of the story, this method manages to change its meaning into its opposite to encourage the own belief of the interpreter. The interpretation of the words, names and images is not defined by knowledge of the time the story was written in. Paul completely ignores the fact that the writers of Genesis had in mind that Isaac represented a stage in the genesis of Israel's loyalty to the Torah. Moreover, the allegorical interpretation doesn't fit in with a tradition of interpreting the Scriptures that is directly connected with the Jewish-religious environment from which the books of the Bible originate. In this case that tradition is found in the Oral Torah which should be seen as a link between Tanakh and the Judaism of the first century. In the allegoresis the "deeper sense" of the story is defined by the own situation and the pre-existing opinions of the interpreter, i.e. Paul in this case. In this way one is able to insert all kinds of meaning into the texts that were never intended by the authors. Indeed, there are hardly any criteria in the allegoresis the interpretation of the text should correspond to. Perhaps the only condition is the inner consistency of the interpretation, i.e. the meaning of the images must be the same throughout the whole story. A skilled allegorical exegete however will make this happen, because his interpretation could easily be disputed. If, in Paul's interpretation, Hagar, the bondswoman, is the symbol of Mount Sinai, i.e. the Torah, Ishmael must be Judaism. If Sarah, the free woman, is the symbol of the promise, Isaac must be Christianity. That's consistent. But in that case Paul is really very far removed from the original meaning of this story in the book of Genesis. The allegoresis therefore opens the door to all kinds of uncontrolled speculation.[239]

In the scope of this book it's important to compare the allegorical method with the midrash-method as discussed in chapter 4. Even in the midrash the images used, often have an underlying or "deeper" meaning. The interpretation of the midrash however is monitored by a number of checks. Earlier written Bible-books don't refer to later historical situations, but, the other way round, later written Bible-books make use of themes and stories from earlier Bible-books to investigate their own situation. The writer of a midrash-story doesn't impose his already formed opinion on the story in Tanakh, but he studies Tanakh to form an opinion about his own situation. The gospels aren't written to show that Tanakh refers to Jesus, but to show that Jesus came up to the intentions of Tanakh. Instead of dissolving Tanakh as the valid Scripture, this means that Tanakh stays the guide for life, also for Jesus.

Moreover, a complex of more or less fixed meanings of the images used, is found in Tanakh and in the Oral Torah. The evangelists frequently use all these images. That is why it is impossible to interpret the gospels without using Tanakh and the Oral Torah. The vineyard for example is an image of Israel.[240] Sometimes the dove is an image of the spirit of God, sometimes of Israel.[241] Pigs symbolize Romans as does Esau, or Edom or Edomites.[242] Horses and chariots indicate violence of war.[243] By contrast the fig tree is an image of the messianic age when the world will be a place full of peace.[244] I could go on and on in this way. These patterns of the various meanings of the images now create the best guarantee that the stories can't be used contrary to their meanings and at cross-purposes as a result of a headstrong exegesis. Unfortunately, in Christianity the methods of the midrash were only followed by the Jewish Christians, like the evangelists, in the first century and in the beginning of the second one. Today they are rediscovered at the expense of a lot of trouble.

After all this, only one conclusion could be drawn: at the end of the second century the Christian church had already completely alienated itself from its Jewish origin. Under the influence of Greek-Roman thought the Christian faith of those days had developed into a direction diametrically opposite to the evangelists' idea of their mission. The parting of the roads of Christianity and Judaism was definite from the midst of the second century onwards.

6.5 From anti-Judaism to the Holocaust

The strong influence the Greek-Roman world had on the Christian thought, was responsible for the unlimited anti-Judaism that has developed in the church from the middle of the second century onwards. Also with respect to this anti-Judaism there is a continuous line from the Greek-Roman paganism to Christianity. Many anti-Jewish opinions could be found with the pagan authors of antiquity. This pagan anti-Judaism is almost always caused by the strangeness of the Jews as a religious group in the ancient society.[245] One took offence at the Jewish way of life and at their customs, which always forced the Jews into a certain form of separation. Their refusal to participate in the worship of the pagan gods, to eat from the pagan tables, to participate in libations, prayers and sacrifices, was for many gentiles an incomprehensible form of superstition or godlessness. The loyalty to the only God and the stubborn perseverance to live in accordance with his law, the Torah, were completely contrary to the syncretistic attitude of the Greek-Roman civilization, which was so "tolerant" to think that all gods ought to be honored.

Besides this anti-Jewish movement there was a movement towards Judaism as well. Many gentiles joined Judaism as those who feared the God of Israel or as proselytes. Early Christianity among the gentiles originated from this movement. However, when those gentile Christians began to form autonomous communities, giving up their orientation on Judaism and coming more and more under the influence of pagan-religious and philosophical ideas, their pro-Jewish attitude made way for an anti-Jewish attitude that already existed in paganism.

Here I will not deal with the development of anti-Judaism in the church extensively. Other scholars did so comprehensively and expertly for the last few decades.[246] Therefore I will confine myself to a brief sketch and some examples. As early as circa 135 CE a Christian writing was published, the so-called Letter of Barnabas, which had a fierce anti-Jewish content. In this letter the vehement attacks against the Jews are especially aimed at depriving them of the "Old Testament". According

159

to the writer it had already been a Christian book from its very first word.[247] The Jewish interpretation of the "Old Testament" is violently attacked indeed and the Jews are depicted as the victims of a bad angel.[248] The Letter of Barnabas differentiates within the Old Testament in a very special way between the words God speaks to his people: when favorable they are meant for the Christians, when unfavourable they are meant for the Jews.[249] Justin will continue along this line some decennia later. He also remarks that the Scriptures don't belong to the Jews anymore, but to the Christians. He calls them "ruthless", "stupid", "blind" and "sly", whereas he dwells on their supposedly excessive sense of lust. Exactly the same reproaches the Jews were burdened with earlier by the pagan anti-Semites.

From now on this tenor will determine Christian thinking, speaking and writing about the Jews until today. What's worse, over the centuries a process of demonizing the Jews started in Christianity with, as its climax, the annihilation of the six million Jews in the German extermination camps: the Holocaust. Over the centuries, ninety-six church-councils and hundred and fourteen popes promulgated all different kinds of laws and regulations against the Jews that made them the pariahs of the Christian society. Once in power, Hitler could draw from rich Christian sources for the murder of the six million as well as for its motivation: he could already find the ideas of the Endlösung, the total annihilation of the Jews, in the writings of the church-fathers.[250] And in this respect the Reformation didn't improve matters either. Luther already wrote the scenario of the Holocaust for the greater part:[251]

"What then should we, Christians, do with this damned and rejected race of the Jews? For they live among us and we know that they tell lies, they slander and swear. We cannot tolerate them, if we don't want to participate in their lies, their curses and their slander. Full of prayer and solemn piety we ought to practise a merciful rigour. Let me give you my honest advice.

Firstly, their synagogues should be set on fire and what will not burn, should be covered with mud. This should be done for the honour of God and Christianity, in order that God might see that we are Christians having no patience nor approving that his son and his Christians are submitted in public to lying, cursing and slandering.

Secondly, their houses should be broken down and destroyed. They should be sheltered in stables like gypsies, in order that they will realize not being masters in our country, as they proudly tell, but unhappy prisoners, as they continuously complain to God.

Thirdly, their books should be taken away from them.

Fourthly, their rabbis should be forbidden, by death penalty, to teach any longer.

Fifthly, they will not be allowed to move freely. Let them stay at home.

Sixthly, they will be forbidden to take interest. The money one shall take away from them, should be spent to help a Jew who wants to be baptized.

Seventhly, they should be put to hard labour.

Dear princes and nobles who have Jews living in your country: if this advice will not suit you, find something better, so that you and we all will be releaved of this unbearable, diabolic burden, the Jews."

Add to this the gas-chambers and one will get the Holocaust. How could Christians live with such a history?

7 When he came to himself
A new Christian orientation on Judaism

Entirely against the tendency of nineteen centuries of church-history, a change can be observed in the attitude of Western Christianity towards Judaism after the Second World War. After nineteen centuries of estrangement and enmity a conciliation between Christians and Jews is happening today, history never showed before.[a] This is the subject of the last chapter of this book.

7.1 A new Christian interest in Judaism

The change in attitude of Western Christianity towards Judaism, after the Second World War, was caused by four factors mainly: how to deal with the Holocaust; the foundation of the State of Israel; the rediscovering of the Hebrew Bible; and the discovering of the Jewish character of the New Testament. These factors cannot be detached from one another because of their interactions. In order to characterize these developments in brief, I'll make some remarks on each of them without paying much attention to their complex interactions. I will confine myself to the Dutch situation mainly, although, without any doubt, this situation hasn't been representative in every respect of Western Europe and America as a whole.

a. How to deal with the Holocaust
Immediately after the Second World War a growing number of church-leaders began to realize that the Holocaust was a direct effect of the viru-

---

[a] Unfortunately, the Eastern Christianity shows less of this change. In my eyes, this is mainly caused by the strong Platonic character of the Eastern Orthodoxy, and recently strengthened by the Israeli-Arabic conflict in which Eastern Christians identify themselves more with the Arabs than with the Israeli.

lent anti-Semitism that had kept Europe in its grip for centuries. Starting from the idea to prevent such things like that ever to happen again, international conferences were organized, inter-religious consultations were started, ecclesiastical study-centres were founded and national councils for Christians and Jews were erected in several countries in Europe from 1946 onwards. In Great-Britain such a national council was already erected in 1942.[252] And in 1974 the International Council of Christians and Jews was founded in Basel in Switzerland.[253]

In the Netherlands the Inter-denominational Contact Israel (ICI) was founded in 1946 with eight participating protestant churches and from 1974 the Roman Catholic church joined it. Fighting anti-Semitism was its main issue. But , initially the "disclosing of the gospel to the Jews" also continued to play a large part in the thoughts of many church-leaders concerned.[254] In the fifties and sixties, however, there weren't many direct contacts with the Jewish Congregations after all.[255] This only changed in the seventies under the influence of international developments. In 1981 the Dutch Council of Jews and Christians (OJEC) was founded,[256] which made itself heard, especially in the eighties and nineties. In combined press-declarations and other publications one tried to denounce anti-Semitic statements and to enlighten many subjects from both sides in order to create a better understanding for each other's opinions and thus to fight prejudices.[257]

One of the results of the process of dealing with the Holocaust and fighting anti-Semitism was that one became more and more aware of the age-long Christian founded anti-Semitism.[258] Numerous studies showed that anti-Semitism had been an inseparable element of almost nineteen centuries of Christian theology and church-history.[259] In thousands of sermons, prayers, encyclical letters, regulations, epistles, articles and books, large numbers of Christian theologians and church-leaders abused the Jews for centuries, creating the climate in which the Nazi's could execute their brutal plans. In section 6.5 I already showed that even Martin Luther, one of the most famous founders of the Reformation, was every bit as bad as his Catholic predecessors with regard to Christian anti-Semitism.

Dealing with the Holocaust and the ecclesiastical and theological anti-Semitism, however, seems to have been the problem of one generation mainly.[260] The Church-and-Israel activities and the co-operation of Christian and Jewish communities flourished in the eighties and nineties of the last century. However, now that the generation that consciously experienced the Second World War, passes away, and those who grew-up with the stories, retire, the spirit to fight anti-Semitism is dying also in the Dutch churches. Even the consultative bodies of Jews and Christians are leading an ever more marginal existence. Until today, many churches and theologians find it hard to deal honestly with the anti-Semitic past of Christianity, let alone to reject it radically. Therefore the question remains whether dealing with the Holocaust could have been the most important factor that caused a new Christian approach to Judaism.

b. The foundation of the State of Israel

More important than the Holocaust was perhaps the foundation of the State of Israel in 1948, that took place three years after the end of the Second World War. Now, for the first time since the beginning of their religion, Christians were forced to recognize the Jews as a nation with a free and independent existence.[261] The stereotypical image Christians had about Jews for centuries, viz. they were a stubborn people rejecting the salvation of God in Jesus Christ and, therefore, constantly suppressed, persecuted and hunted – the Holocaust could in fact be considered as the ultimate confirmation of this theology! –, that stereotypical image crumbled. Apparently the national independence of the Jewish people could originate from the largest mass-murder in the history of men. One even needn't believe in an Almighty God or in Providence to consider this a first-rate religious-historical phenomenon. The traditional Christian view on Judaism no longer tallied! Therefore, I'm afraid that, without the foundation of the State of Israel, the Holocaust wouldn't have influenced Christianity that much.

In an early stage already, many churches experienced the foundation of the State of Israel as a theological problem. How could this foundation be explained against the background of the traditional substitution-theology that assumed that the church had taken over Israel's place in God's plans with the world. Study groups were put to work and church meetings began to deliver statements about the relation of the church and the Jewish people. Many churches set up centres to study this new relation. Many Christians supported the State of Israel as a form of paying back the Christian guilt of anti-Semitism.[262]

A positive effect of all this reflection on Israel has been that the substitution-theology and the mission among the Jews were dropped rather quietly. Instead, a so-called theology of two-ways arose in which Christianity as well as Judaism were seen as legitimate continuations of the Biblical tradition: two ways leading to the same God.[263] In many churches the opinion is entertained that God "yet has a plan with Israel" and that ultimately, with the Second Coming of Christ, the Jews would recognize Christ as their messiah.[264] The Christian mission among the Jews has become an almost historical phenomenon now.

In the seventies, eighties and nineties the Church-and-Israel departments of the various churches and sympathizing publishers, published a large amount of study material on all kinds of aspects of the relation of Judaism and Christianity.[265] Unfortunately, in many Christian views about Israel not Judaism but the State of Israel appeared to be the dominant issue. During the first three decades after 1948 this led to much sympathy because the State of Israel was mainly erected by social democratic, European Jews and had to hold out against an extensive, hostile, Arabic neighbourhood. However, after the conquest of the occupied territories in the Six Day War in 1967 and the victory of Israel in the Yom-Kippur War in 1973 the image changed from a nation threatened by the Arabs into the image of a military superpower. Moreover, with the arrival of many Jews from Arabic countries, Ethiopia and Russia, Israeli policy became ever more right-wing. The hard line of the occupation of the conquered areas, the policy with regard to the settlements and the Palestinian revolts in 1987 and 2000, all this continued to change the image of Israel from a threatened nation into the image of a suppressor of a neighbouring people.

This is not the place to go into the political aspects of this problem. It's a fact that this negative representation of the State of Israel permeated the churches as well.[266] Since the seventies discord grew between the supporters of Israel on the one hand and the advocates for the Palestinian issue on the other. The Israel-departments of the churches often were diametrically opposed to the supporters of the world-diaconal departments that saw Israel as a nation like all other nations.[267] The State of Israel, involved in a long-lasting state of war, couldn't simply fulfil the high moral standards many Christians projected on it from a peaceful Europe, standards, however, they seldom apply to Israel's enemies. After all, in the Marxist-inspired "theology of the poor" the material circumstances of men weigh heavier than their cultural, social, moral of religious choices. This causes many left-wing Christians to adopt an over-critical attitude with regard to the "rich" Israel and an often less critical sympathy for the "poor" Palestinians and their rich Arabic allies.[a]

As a result of this development of the public opinion with regard to the State of Israel, the interest in Judaism became under heavy pressure within the churches as well. This too, had repercussions on the Church-and-Israel departments. They flourished in the eighties and nineties. Today in 2010 they only play a marginal part because many Christians no longer wish to see the existence of the State of Israel as a phenomenon of religious significance. Yet it can be established that the foundation of the State of Israel made a lasting contribution towards the disappearance of the substitution-theology and the mission among the Jews, and as a result caused Christian anti-Semitism to diminish considerably.

---

[a] The part the media played and are still playing in this conflict should not be underestimated. The Israeli society is an open Western society including freedom of press, in which – in principle – everything happens in public. The Palestinian and Arabic societies on the contrary are closed societies without freedom of press, in which many things happen behind closed doors and in which the public stories are often much more beautiful than reality. Western journalists and media often match Israeli reality with public stories from Palestinian and Arabic side. Thus a tremendous black and white distortion occurs.

c. The rediscovery of the Hebrew Bible

More or less parallel to the previously discussed changes in the relation of Christianity and Judaism a third development took place that I'd like to call the "rediscovery of the Hebrew Bible". Of course, Christianity already had the disposal of the Old Testament from the beginning of its existence, but for centuries it had been read in the Greek and Latin translations of the Septuagint and the Vulgate. It's true, the Renaissance and the Reformation rehabilitated the Hebrew text of the Old Testament within the churches, and its translation was coupled with great interest in the Rabbinical literature,[268] but the book remained the "Old Testament", i.e. predominantly of interest as a preparation to the New Testament. Already before the Second World War, however, some Christian theologians, following liberal-Jewish scholars like Martin Buber and Franz Rosenzweig, began to read the Old Testament as the "Hebrew Bible" with its own revelation independent of the New Testament.[269] This "rediscovery of the Hebrew Bible" was attended by a changing view on the Hebrew language which was no longer interpreted from Greek-Latin and Christian sources and ideas, but which was from now on seen as an expression of Hebrew-Semitic thought preserved in Judaism.

After the Second World War this approach gained acceptance increasingly in certain theological circles and university studies in the Netherlands.[270] Following this approach, the interest in the rabbinical literature began to grow.[271] In many places in the Netherlands discussion groups and "study-houses" came into being in which not only the Jewish interpretation of the Hebrew Bible was studied but often all kinds of modern developments in theology as well. In the beginning of the nineties the number of study-houses was estimated at more than a hundred.[272] Moreover, the number of Christians in the Netherlands that began to study Hebrew grew considerably in the last decades of the twentieth century. Many of them wished to obtain a better understanding of the Hebrew Bible and of Judaism.[273]

Unfortunately, the Christian affinity for Judaism didn't – for the greater part – go beyond liberal Judaism, and the interest in the Hebrew

Bible had a more literary-functional than a halakhic (Jewish legal) character. Discussions about the practical consequences of the Hebrew Bible as an independent source of revelation were generally restricted to political and social problems which often were approached from a left-wing political orientation. For some the study of Hebrew and Marxist-inspired social criticism appeared effortlessly consistent.[274] This development had, however, only little influence on the daily life of most Christians or on the ecclesiastical practice of worship and diaconal work. The worship of most churches remained founded on the liturgical structures of the classical Christian doctrines.[275] Likewise the national and international diaconal departments were more inspired by pastoral theology, social and psychological sciences and social-criticism than by a thorough study of the Jewish character of the Hebrew Bible.

Nevertheless, the biggest profit of this "rediscovery of the Hebrew Bible" has been that, in many churches, the "Old Testament" is no longer seen as a simple foreshadowing of the New Testament, but can be read as an independent source of religious inspiration. The second point is that many Christians experience studying the rabbinical literature like the Talmud and the Midrash as an enrichment of their lives.

d. The discovery of the Jewish character of the New Testament
After the rediscovery of the Hebrew Bible the discovery of the Jewish character of the New Testament was bound to come. In the years after the Second World War more and more Christians came to the conclusion that the New Testament could no longer be read without a thorough knowledge of the Judaism of the first centuries.[276] In addition to the Christian anti-Semitism, the significance of the State of Israel and of the Hebrew Bible, the Jewish origin of Christianity became a subject of study as well.

This new orientation on the Jewish character of the New Testament and of the early Christianity offered many people an alternative for the erosion the classical Christian theology had undergone by the technical-scientific and social progress of the Western-European culture in the course of the twentieth century. This development led to a strong secularisation and to disorientation in the theological area. Old doctrines no longer appeared to be able to withstand scientific criticism. Traditional Christian opinions no longer appeared to be able to give answers to contemporary questions and problems. The Greek-Roman foundation the Christian doctrine had been built on for centuries, no longer appeared to be able to resist the changes in Western thought. Consequently Christian theology ended up slowly but surely into a crisis of certainties.

Many people found a way-out out of this crisis by linking their theology to present-day social and philosophical movements like Marxism, Existentialism or Feminism. Others even tried to re-interpret the Christian faith with the help of social sciences like sociology, psychology and even psychiatry. Another way to react to this crisis is, however, to reflect again on the Jewish origin of the Christian faith and to redefine it next, starting from its sources. Consequently, Christians of all centuries have necessarily met Judaism, and this – as I have shown in this book – will have far-reaching consequences for the exegesis of the New Testament. However, the revision of the Christian faith from her Jewish sources[277] has appeared to be a slowly advancing process of which many Christians who reap its fruits, are entirely unaware.

As in the domain of science and society, the influence of Judaism in the domain of the Christian faith is often a little visible, subcutaneous process. Only a few Westerners would endorse that we are largely indebted to the Jewish influence on the Western culture for our present democratic society with its strong pressure on individual freedom, social equality and justice, and scientific progress. Only a few will recognize that the modern Western concept of man has developed from the Jewish concept of man.[278] Does one feel embarrassed about it? The Jewish influence on Western culture is only marginally a subject of scientific study as is the Jewish influence on the development of Christianity. There is hardly any systematic research into the phenomenon that all important "heretical" movements in Christianity originated in areas with a large and influential Jewish population. Consciously studying the Jewish character of the New Testament and of early Christianity, and having the courage to draw the obvious conclusions for faith and life is still experienced by many Christians as a threatening activity which had better occur in or outside the margins of the church. However, the influence of it on Christianity as a whole is unavoidable. Who feels inspired by Jesus of Nazareth and will live from the New Testament, won't be able to get around Judaism. In the next section I'll show that when studying the Jewish character of the New Testament, we'll get help from Judaism itself.

7.2 The Jewish interest in the gospels

It is conspicuous now that a more or less comparable development took place among the Jews. For centuries they had no or only little interest in the New Testamentary writings. After all, these were the holy books of their suppressors. This situation began to change at the beginning of the twentieth century when large groups of Jews settled in the land of Israel. Once back in their own land they could no longer ignore these writings from the first centuries of the Common Era. So one began to read the New Testament, although in the same way as one was going to read the Qumran-scrolls some decades later. Since those days it is read as a collection of Jewish writings, i.e. writings of a religious movement in the Judaism of the first century.[279]

This new interest of Jewish scholars in the New Testament had already begun before the Second World War. One of the first Jewish scholars who took the study of the New Testament in hand, was the linguist, historian and Zionist Joseph Gedaliah Klausner (1874-1958).[280] Coming from Russia he had settled in Jerusalem in 1919. There, in 1922 he published his book "Jesus of Nazareth" in Hebrew. Later, this book was to be translated into many European languages. Contrary to the Jewish writers before him, Klausner emphasized the fact that Jesus was a Jew. He argued that Jesus had been a self-conscious Jew who had never rejected Judaism and who had seen himself as a Jewish messiah. In 1939 his book "From Jesus to Paul" was published in which he mainly discussed Paul against his Jewish and Hellenistic background. In that book he argued among other things that without Paul Christianity would never have developed into a world religion.[281]

After Klausner many Jewish scholars can be mentioned who were engaged in studying the New Testament.[a] Their publications contributed a lot to a better understanding of the Jewish character of the New Testament writings. As an example I will confine myself to the Jewish scholars David Flusser and Pinchas Lapide who, in the eighties, gave a tremendous stimulus to the Christian orientation on Judaism through their many publications. With his book "Jesus" Flusser wanted to show that it is possible to write a biography of Jesus.[282] To reach this aim he especially used the three synoptic gospels (Matthew, Mark and Luke). They rather faithfully paint Jesus as a Jew of his days. According to Flusser these gospels show us Jesus not as a redeemer of mankind, but as a Jewish miracle worker and preacher.[283] Flusser's method aims to release, within the three synoptic gospels, the old traditional tidings about Jesus from the editorial work of the evangelists.[284] Then, to understand Jesus, knowledge about Judaism of his days is vital.

In his book "He taught in their synagogues" Lapide likewise is in search of the historical Jesus.[285] In this context he speaks about the "fifth Jesus" to distinguish the real Jesus from the ones of the four evangelists.[286] An important element in the methods of both is "retranslating" the Greek of the evangelists into Aramaic and Hebrew which were, in their eyes, the languages of the original traditions.[287] The large merit of Flusser and Lapide is that, in this way, they have shown that Jesus never dissociated himself from the Judaism of his days neither transgressed or untied essential rules of the Jewish practice of life.[288] Through many other publications they provided valuable contributions to the study of the New Testament as well.

---

[a]   In the first Dutch edition of this book in 1986 I wrote in a footnote: "It would be recommendable to publish an overview-study on all these scholars and their work shortly". Today, 25 years later, as far as I know, scientific theology hasn't yet produced such a study, certainly not in the Netherlands.

However, without altering the large merit of Flusser and Lapide, I think that their approach to the gospels falls short with regard to an essential point. Their perspective is mainly linguistic and historical. Both of them are in search of the historical Jesus and they try – and justly so – to show that he was a Jew true to the Torah. But the point is that this search for the historical Jesus goes hand in hand with an opinion about the evangelists which is, in my eyes, not correct.

The supposition Flusser and Lapide base their work on, is that the gospels rest on historically reliable tidings about Jesus formulated in Hebrew and Aramaic. These original tidings would have reflected the words of Jesus more or less correctly.[289] An opinion frequently found in their publications is that the so-called Greek evangelists were no longer acquainted with the Jewish customs and ideas, and certainly not with the Hebrew and Aramaic languages. These "Greek" evangelists often mistranslated the original Aramaic and Hebrew tidings out of ignorance. They made reading and writing errors. They stylistically shaped these original tidings to embellish their own writings and wrote a new message across the original one.[290]

The effect of this approach was that Flusser and Lapide weren't very much interested in the so-called theology of the evangelists. Flusser wrote for example: "In general it remains to be seen whether the synoptics (Mark, Matthew and Luke) – Luke maybe being an exception – show a personal theological tendency in their work. Clearly the synoptics don't propagandize their own personal theological creed, but wanted to write down ancient traditions of Jesus' words and deeds in the first place".[291] Elsewhere, Flusser touches the sore spot: "If the synoptics were the final results of the creative activity of the early Christian communities and of the originally theological ideas of each of the evangelists, one should begin with the theological analysis of the gospels and one shouldn't be able to penetrate, by means of a philological approach, the older layers of the tradition, and consequently the words of Jesus himself".[292] It will be clear that I have a lot of difficulty with this opinion. Their approach reduces the evangelists to rather unreliable historians. They collected original tidings written in a language they didn't master, mistranslated them frequently, added and omitted material, doing so without a certain vision. Flusser even contends, that Luke's ignorance in a specific case could guarantee the historical reliability of his tiding.[293]

In this book and in my book *Luke the Jew* I have tried to show that at least Matthew and Luke wrote their books as a product of their own "theological ideas" indeed. The weakness of Flusser's and Lapide's method is that a purely linguistic-historical approach won't be able to reveal this. So in my view, a linguistic analysis should be preceded by a theological-literary analysis which ought to depart from the idea that the gospels are the personal midrash-stories of the evangelists. It's true, such an approach will not bring us nearer to the historical Jesus but will do so to the evangelists. And only through them Jesus would come to us. Therefore I plead that in the Jewish approach of the gospels a shift will occur towards the evangelists who will then be seen as narrators of midrashim. Only then Christianity will very much appear to be permanently dependent on Judaism, if it wants to survive anyway.

7.3 Anti-Judaism in the gospels?

Reading the gospels as the midrashim of the evangelists and no longer as a random collection of later touched-up, historical traditions, we can answer all kinds of questions in the domain of the New Testament in a way that differs rather a lot from what is usually done. In this section I'll demonstrate this by means of the question after the so-called anti-Judaism in the New Testament.

The age-long theological and ecclesiastical anti-Judaism that became so sharply visible to our generation, also actualized the question after the anti-Judaism in the New Testament and especially in the gospels. In my view some people too easily answered this question positively. Merely the fact that all New Testament authors, including Luke, were Jews,[294] should make exegetes cautious to use the word "anti-Judaism" in the context of the New Testament. It's impossible to bring out this issue completely here and therefore in the next paragraphs I'll confine myself to a single example.

Usually, theories about anti-Judaism in the gospels aren't isolated cases. In general they are accompanied by suppositions with regard to the age, the origin and the interdependency of the gospels. Some scholars for example are of the opinion that Mark was written first, next came Luke and at last Matthew. They subsequently perceive a growing anti-Judaism as well, when they are going to read these three gospels in their presupposed order.[295] The idea behind this conclusion is that already in the first Greek-speaking Christian communities in which the gospels developed, there was a progressive estrangement from Judaism. No notice is taken of the possibility that the gospels could very well have been developed in Greek speaking communities of Jewish adherents of Jesus. Many considerations on this subject interpret the conflicts in the gospels too easily as the forerunners of the great conflict between Christianity and Judaism in later centuries. In that case not only the multiplicity of the movement around Jesus of Nazareth is overlooked, but one also ignores the fact that the Judaism of those days was much more diversely made up than today's Judaism. The Judaism at the beginning of the first century CE differed considerably from the Judaism at the end of the same century. What was left of Jewish groups like the Sadducees, the Herodians, the Essenes, the Zealots, the adherents of John the Baptist and other charismatic leaders? What was left of the different kinds of Pharisees of Jesus' days? Moreover, all these Jewish groups had their own multiplicity in the days of Jesus. And the large majority of the Jewish people, which group did they belong to?

The Judaism of today is to a considerable extent the continuation of the Jewish people guided by the School of Hillel, a small group of Pharisees which was not too influential in the days of Jesus. The later rabbis of this Pharisaic school don't even call themselves "Pharisees" and in their writings the word "Pharisee" has often got the same negative sound as it has in the gospels.[296] Therefore, the analysis of the gospels should answer two questions before one could ask after the anti-Judaism of the gospels:

1. Are there really any references in the gospels to enmity between Jesus and the School of Hillel or their ideas?
2. And are there really any references to a hostile attitude of the evangelists with regard to the School of Hillel and their ideas?

It's only after these questions will be answered positively, that there could be some reasons , in my view, to speak about anti-Judaism in the gospels and the Acts of the Apostles. In "Luke the Jew" I have shown that, at least for Luke, this isn't the case at all. On the contrary, Luke assumes a more or less natural alliance between the representatives of the School of Hillel and the adherents of Jesus (e.g. in Acts 5,34-40).[297]

Much "proof" of anti-Judaism loses its validity as soon as the gospels are read as midrashim and no longer as touched-up history. Luke's version of Mark's Nazareth-story for example is put forward as proof of Luke's larger enmity against the Jews.[298] The scene in Mark is still limited to opposition against Jesus (Mark 6,1-6), whereas Luke's version finishes with an attempt to execute Jesus (Luke 4,14-30). However, if one is going to read Luke's story as part of the total composition of his gospel, assuming it to be a midrash directed against the Zealotic and Sadducee mentality to press home their religious issues with violence,[299] it'll be difficult to maintain that anti-Judaism is the issue at stake here. So I take the view that one is only allowed to speak about anti-Judaism with the New Testament authors if it appears clearly from the set-up of their writings that they openly and repeatedly tried to discredit Judaism with the Christians from the gentiles. It's my firm conviction that this certainly is not the case with Mark, Matthew and Luke, and not even with John.[300]

In the next section I'll present a midrash-exegesis of Luke's story of the lost son, a story that could get a new and actual meaning for Christians of the twenty-first century who are trying to define a new position of Christianity and church in relation to Judaism.

7.4 The return of lost son (Luke 15,11-32)

At first sight the parable of the lost son (Luke 15,11-32) is a simple tale of a conversion. However, there is always more behind a Jewish story from those days than meets the eye at first reading. If it's just a tale of conversion, what value should be attached to the curious part of the elder son? Why is this such a long-drawn-out story and why does it contain so many details? And why does it stop so suddenly and at such a strange moment, with an open end? I'll make some exegetical remarks on this story with the intention of showing its outlines. Then it will appear that we are having to do with more than only a moving story about an unfaithful son who starts to see the error of his ways and repents. The story appears to hide a message which is topical for Christianity, even today.

Then Jesus said: A certain man had two sons (verse 11).

Two sons. Why two? Why not one? Why not more than two? The theme of a father and two sons is found several times in Tanakh, for example:

- Adam with Cain and Abel (later Abel's place is taken by Seth),
- Abraham with Ishmael and Isaac,
- Isaac with Esau and Jacob,
- David with Absalom and Salomon.

The meaning of the theme of these two sons always transcends their individual existence by far. Cain represents the dead end of murder and vendetta (Genesis 4, 17-24). Abel symbolizes the vulnerability of human life, and Seth the ongoing way of the revelation. Also in the pairs of Isaac-Ishmael and Jacob-Esau tradition opposes non-tradition. In the pair of Salomon and Absalom the right continuation of the Davidic monarchy opposes the wrong one. Remarkable for this pair is the affinity between both names: the name *Salomon* is derived from *shalom*, "peace" – indeed Salomon is the prince of peace par excellence –, whereas the name *Absalom* means "(my) father is peace". In the last name one senses the criticism of the story-teller: Absalom himself is not exactly peaceful, his father David on the contrary is all peace in the story of Absalom (2 Samuel 15-18). That's why, from the beginning of our parable, we'll have to take into consideration that both sons represent two quite different issues in a discussion which transcends the specific images used in the story.

And the younger of them said to his father: Father, give me the portion of goods that falls to me. So he [the father] divided to them his livelihood (verse 12).

The younger. Who is this father and who are these sons? In the above-mentioned stories in Tanakh about fathers with two sons, it was always the younger one who continued the tradition. This ever returning theme in Tanakh has a clear meaning. God's involvement with man continually turns the existing relations and patterns of expectation upside down. The tradition of the revelation, God's influence in the world, doesn't run automatically via the older and stronger one, the one who has first claim. At the same time, Israel is implicitly told that it is a late arrival among the nations. In Genesis the theme of the younger son who pursues the tradition, is closely connected with Israel's election for the benefit of the other nations. Why does Luke ignore this theme in his parable of the lost son and why does he make the younger son abandon the tradition?

Supposing that both sons in this parable represent nations, religions or cultures, in Luke's days, the elder son could only be Israel and the younger one the representative of the nations. Tanakh does indeed support this interpretation. In Exodus 4,22 the LORD calls Israel "my first-born son". No Jew in Luke's days would have taken this parable seriously if Luke had represented Israel as the younger son. Ever since the exodus from Egypt Israel is God's first-born son and the nations have to make do with the position of a "younger son".

Father. Against the above-mentioned background it's not necessary to interpret the father in this story as God himself (see also the verses 18 and 21, that make a difference between the father and heaven). The father-figure in the above-mentioned Tanakh-stories is always the personification of the tradition the sons can separate themselves from but can also accept. In the vision of the book of Genesis all nations are ultimately secessions from the one line of tradition that began with Adam and that arrived at Israel via Noah, Abraham, Isaac and Jacob. As such, the father in all these stories is the one who represents the covenant with the only God. Who estranges himself from the father, alienates himself from God as well.

Give me. The request of the younger son is not motivated. The scene mirrors the actual situation: the nations have moved away from God from the outset to go their own ways. Here, Luke presents a very short summary of the first chapters of Genesis.

The goods. Here Luke uses the Greek word *ousia*, that signifies much more than material goods only. It's about the essence of someone's existence, not only his real property and possessions, but also his character, his personality, all one really is. In the Torah Israel is told that they are God's "goods" or "property" if they would listen attentively to him and would keep his covenant (Exodus 19,5; see also Deuteronomy 7,6 and 14,2). In these verses the Septuagint uses the word *peri-ousios*. One recognizes the word *ousia* in it. So in our parable the son demands a part of his father's right to exist. Or, as Genesis 3,5 words it: the nations wish to be like God. They think they are entitled to the divine revelation and are allowed to use it to their own ends.

So he divided to them. It is conspicuous that the demand of the younger son appears to be granted immediately. However, in one respect this is not strange at all. Who has been educated in the tradition of the father and nevertheless makes such a request, has evidently made up his mind. In Genesis 4 too, not the slightest obstacle is put in the way of Cain's offspring. Who lives that close to paradise, has obviously made his decision: he doesn't want anything more to do with it. God doesn't hold back man when he, by any means, wants to go his own way, not even when this way perishes in the great flood.

His livelihood. Here, Luke doesn't use the word "goods" (*ousia*), but the word "livelihood" (*bios*). When he uses this word again in verse 30, in Greek it is about "eating". So a possible explanation could be that the father doesn't really grant his son's request. He only divides the least important, immediately available means of support among his sons. So metaphorically speaking: the nations don't receive the revelation (*ousia*), but only the creation, the living nature (*bios*), the world.

And not many days after, the younger son gathered all together, journeyed to a far country, and there wasted his possessions with prodigal living (verse 13).

Possessions. Here Luke uses the word *ousia* again. What is still livelihood (*bios*) in the house of the father, becomes his "capital" or his "fortune" (*ousia*) when the son goes his own way. For the gentile religions the creation, the earth and the living nature *are* the revelation of the divine world. Son, moon, stars, lightning, thunderstorms, rain, rivers, oceans, fertility, the changing seasons, trees, animals, they all are gods or aspects of gods one is favoured or threatened by according to one's ability to win their sympathy. What is "livelihood" (*bios*) in Israel, is "possession" (*ousia*) in the gentile world.

But when he had spent all, there arose a severe famine in that land, and he began to be in want (verse 14).

Had spent all. In Luke's days, at the end of the first century, there was a clear tendency among the gentiles to lose the faith in the traditional nature gods.[301] Especially in the higher classes the traditional religion was more and more superseded by a completely different approach of reality, viz. that of philosophy. But even this approach didn't bring the expected certainty and unanimity. In addition to this, many new ideas in the field of religion invaded the Greek-Roman world from the East as well. Religiously and philosophically the gentile world of Luke's days was, to a great extent, characterized by a major instability which had given many people the feeling **to be in want**.[a] There was only one factor in this confusing totality which provided a certain stability: Rome's authority based on military power and furnished with the clearly religious legitimation of the emperor-cult.

> *Then he went and joined himself to a citizen of that country, and he sent him into his fields to feed swine. And he would gladly have filled his stomach with the pods that the swine ate, and no one gave him anything (verses 15-16).*

Joined himself to. The Greek text reads literally: he stuck to a citizen of that country. Clearly, the younger son isn't his own master in his new dwelling-place. It may appear like this for a while, but in times of need he is subjected to and dependent on a ruling nation. This is exactly the situation of almost all nations in Luke's days. The Romans ruled the greater part of the known world of those days. They allowed the conquered people a certain degree of autonomy. However, when the interests of the Roman empire were at stake, they didn't hesitate to strike hard. The nations would be well-advised, especially in case of need, to "stick" to the Romans. This was the only way to survive.

A citizen. The word "citizen" in Greek (*polites*) is, just like in English, derived from the word "city" (*polis*). Thus, the literal meaning is "city-dweller". The Roman society of the centuries before and after the beginning of the common era was a society of large landowners. They lived in the cities, but owned large estates that were made productive by large numbers of slaves. For the impoverished citizens the Roman cities initially knew a system of sustenance based on tradition. The poor had to secure a protector or *patronus* among the rich citizens. Then, as a *patronus*, this one was responsible for the welfare of his faithful

---

[a]   See also section 6.4.

followers.[302] It seems that Luke has incorporated such a background in his story.[a]

Into his fields. The institution of the *patronus* was mainly an institute of Romans amongst themselves. As a stranger the younger son had to work for his "*patronus*" on one of the fields of his estate. A direct lessening of his needs wasn't in for him. His position resembled that of a slave.

Swine. Pigs are unclean animals for the Jews, their meat is not to be eaten. Therefore, to keep pigs is a business of non-Jews. This is, however, not the only reason why Luke introduces these animals into his story in this place. In his days Jews often compared Romans with swine. The main reason for this was that the Roman legion that occupied the land of Israel, had a wild boar in its standard.[303] Therefore, Jewish listeners of those days associated the story even more strongly with the Roman empire: the nations in their need who made themselves subservient to the Roman boar. This appeared to be the only way to survive for all nations.

To feed. This word reveals exactly the central point in this phase of the story. The Roman citizen was less interested in the hunger of the younger son than he was in the feeding of his pigs. For the Romans the starvation of the nations was of lesser interest than the consolidation of their own economic, military and religious power.

And no one gave him anything. It's hardly possible to find a more violent contrast to the care the Torah prescribes on behalf of the poor, the hungry and the stranger. A critical note of Luke's with respect to the social conditions in the Roman empire.

But when he came to himself, he said, 'How many of my father's hired servants have bread enough and to spare, and I perish with hunger! I

---

[a] In such a situation a penniless non-Roman stranger usually sold himself to a rich citizen. Luke however couldn't use that variant because of story-technical reasons. After all, later in the story, the younger son should be able to return to the father without a rebellious escape from slavery.

will arise and go to my father, and will say to him, "Father, I have sinned against heaven and before you, and I am no longer worthy to be called your son. Make me like one of your hired servants."' And he arose and came to his father (verses 17-20a).

Hired servants. A hired servant in Israel is a free man and a full member of the Jewish community. The hired servant is more characteristic for the Jewish economy than the slave. Slavery did exist, but was governed by many restrictions. The Torah prescribes, for example, that the work of a slave may not be heavier than the labour of a hired servant (Leviticus 25,39-40a). Slaves must be set free at the beginning of the jubilee (Leviticus 25,40b-41). Another regulation even says that an Israelite should be released after six years of slavery (Deuteronomy 15,12). In the Torah the esteem of man's freedom is so comprehensive that a slave who refuses to be released because he feels at home with his lord, should be punished with an awl through his ear (Deuteronomy 15,16-17). This restrictive attitude with regard to slavery stems from the fundamental idea of the Torah that all the members of God's covenant are equal. Numerous are the rules that refer to the mutual care of Israelites. Consequently, in Luke's days, only a relatively small number of Jews was in non-Jewish slavery. On the one hand a Jewish slave was less attractive for a non-Jewish owner because he didn't work on the Sabbath, and on the other hand many Jewish slaves bought their freedom or were bought off by their co-religionists.[304] The Jewish idea of man as a free and equal member of the community was very attractive to many non-Jews who lived in a Roman society based on slavery. The younger son, who was more or less in the position of a slave, now craves for the position of a free hired servant of his father's.

Bread enough and to spare. In the Oral Torah eating bread is very often used for "living in accordance with the tradition". The Hebrew words for bread (*lechem*) and for life (*lechajim*) differ one consonant only. The connection between bread, life and the Torah is already made in the Torah itself, viz. in Deuteronomy 8,3. There it says that the manna, the bread of the desert, is nothing else than a sign of God's word. Who lives in accordance with the Torah, lives on bread that will always be there.[a] In their spiritual hunger many non-Jews of the first century turned their eyes towards the Jewish religion that was based on the high ethical standard of the Torah. That's bread galore, "bread enough and to spare".

Arise and go to my father. Many non-Jews visited the synagogues of the diaspora as God fearing people. There, they were taught the Torah and its explanations. There also, they unlearned their paganism and learned to listen with "Jewish" ears. In the Acts of the Apostles Luke tells occasionally about these God-fearing non-Jews and their longing to hear the word of God. Once they had taken the path towards the synagogue, many of them went one step further. They didn't confine themselves to fearing God, but converted to Judaism and became proselytes. There must have been a large-scale proselytism already from the days of the Babylonian exile. The enormous extend of Jewry in the first century – according to some estimates the Jews constituted 10% of the population of the Roman empire – can't be explained from the natural growth of a small nation. Here, only the conversion of many gentiles to the Judaism in the diaspora offers an explanation. Luke describes this influx of gentiles as the return of the younger son to the house of the father. This representation is consistent with the representation of Genesis in which all people descend from this one line of tradition.

> But when he was still a great way off, his father saw him and had compassion, and ran and fell on his neck and kissed him. And the son said to him, 'Father, I have sinned against heaven and in your sight, and am no longer worthy to be called your son.' But the father said to his servants, 'Bring out the best robe and put it on him, and put a ring on his hand and sandals on his feet. And bring the fatted calf here and kill it, and let

---

[a] See also section 5.3 "That these stones become bread".

us eat and be merry; for this my son was dead and is alive again; he was
lost and is found.' And they began to be merry (verses 20b-24).[a]

Began to be merry. One of the many background-stories to this story
that can be found in Tanakh, is the story of Isaiah's vision of the
messianic meal (Isaiah 25,6 f.). It's a meal of "fat things full of marrow, of
well-refined wines on the lees", laid on by the LORD for all nations. Luke
experienced the flow of gentiles to the synagogue as the fulfillment of
Isaiah's prophecy. The younger son is received with a feast: the nations
are coming back to God's table!

Now his older son was in the field. And as he came and drew near to the
house, he heard music and dancing. So he called one of the servants and
asked what these things meant. And he said to him, 'Your brother has
come, and because he has received him safe and sound, your father has
killed the fatted calf.' But he was angry and would not go in (verses 25-
28a).

He was angry. In Luke's days a large part of the Jews were not so keen
on admitting interested gentiles to their communities. Especially those
groups which wanted to adhere strictly to all the prescriptions of the
Torah, were plainly opposed to those non-Jews joining them too easily.
For instance, the strict Pharisaic School of Shammai was known to be
unfavourably disposed towards any contacts with the gentiles.[305] The
religiously inspired freedom-fighters of the Zealots didn't want anything
to do with gentiles as well unless they joined Judaism through circumcision.[306] Undoubtedly, this attitude was caused by the sincere fear that
Judaism would become watered down, if contact with gentiles and their
entry into Judaism shouldn't be subjected to very strict rules. Especially

---

[a]   In stories like this one the Greek word *doulos* needn't necessarily be translated
with *slave*. The Septuaginta often translates the Hebrew word *èvèd* ("servant")
with *doulos*, for example in Jeremiah 7,25 where it is used for the prophets, the
'servants of the LORD'.

many Jews living in the land of Israel – the oldest son par excellence –
looked Argus-eyed at the developments in the Diaspora.

> *Therefore his father came out and pleaded with him. So he answered and*
> *said to his father, 'Lo, these many years I have been serving you; I never*
> *transgressed your commandment at any time; and yet you never gave me*
> *a young goat, that I might make merry with my friends. But as soon as*
> *this son of yours came, who has devoured your livelihood with harlots,*
> *you killed the fatted calf for him.' And he said to him, 'Son, you are*
> *always with me, and all that I have is yours. It was right that we should*
> *make merry and be glad, for your brother was dead and is alive again,*
> *and was lost and is found' (verses 28b-32).*

Here the story comes – rather unexpectedly - to its end just like the story
of Jonah: Jonah resists God, God admonishes him and that's it! The elder
son resists the father, the father admonishes him and that's it! The meaning of such an open end is clear: here we meet the people whom the
story is meant for and who are invited to stop their resistance. The
parable of the lost son is an appeal to the very strict, Torah-abiding
groups in Judaism, to abandon their negative attitude against those who
fear God and against proselytes. In the flow of gentiles towards the
synagogues in the diaspora of his days, Luke saw the fulfillment of the
prophecies regarding the last days. This parable reveals the great care he
took to stay on speaking terms with his opponents within Judaism. On
the basis of Tanakh he indirectly presented them with his views by
means of a parable. How would they react? This story is addressed to a
Jewish public. It is about a discussion of Jews among themselves.[307]

All this raises two considerations. Firstly, I find that nowhere in this
parable a mediator acts with regard to the return (the conversion) of the
younger son (the nations) into his father's house. Christian theology,
entirely based on the remission of sins through the sacrificial death of
Jesus, has insuperable difficulties with this story indeed.[308] A suchlike
theology however is chiefly based on the letters of Paul. Luke on the other hand doesn't connect Jesus' death anywhere with remission of sins

and reconciliation.[309] In the Acts he paints Paul in a way that differs totally with the Paul the Paul we know from his letters. For Luke Jesus was a Jew among the Jews with whom a non-Jew could only come into contact by joining Judaism.[310] Nowhere Luke intends to establish a Christian church separated from Judaism. Nowhere in the Acts Christian communities are founded. Wherever Paul arrives, he approaches the Jews first. He often meets brothers who are already there, as in Rome (Acts 28,15). In Luke's eyes the conversion of the gentiles was a conversion to Judaism and not to a new and independent Christian religion.

In the second place, unfortunately, I am obliged to say that Luke's program failed. The Christian communities soon cut their ties with Judaism. As I have shown in chapter 6 Christianity became an independent religion with, ultimately, a strong anti-Jewish character. The younger son wreaked havoc in the house of the father and began to persecute his older brother bloodily. That was the sad sequel to the parable of the lost son, a sequel, finally, many Christians only dared to consider some decades after Auschwitz. Yet, after nineteen centuries, this parable of Luke's can help us to reach a new orientation with regard to Christianity and the church. Like the younger son, we will have to stand up and return to the father-house of the Jewish tradition. However difficult that may be. Before I will continue to examine this matter in the next section, I'd like to mention that one issue should be firmly established: whatever the Jews' reaction will be on the new Christian orientation on the Jewish tradition – accepting, suspicious or rejecting –, after Auschwitz Christianity cannot but acknowledge that in the relation of God and man Judaism holds the oldest rights. The elder son is still the elder son.

7.5 A new perspective

At the end of this book we should ask ourselves what consequences the foregoing has for Christianity in the twenty-first century. It's not my purpose to be exhaustive on this subject. In the preface of this book I already remarked that the reader who wants to engage upon the Jewish way of reading the gospels, will have to get through a lot of work indeed. And this, of course, could and should only be done by the reader involved. Therefore I will finish with a brief sketch of what in my view could be a new perspective for Christians today.

To begin with, a more open view with regard to the concept of "revelation" should be accepted. The New Testament's back-cover is the biggest objection one could have against it. Its end suggests that the revelation has come to an end as well and that nothing essential could be added to or removed from it anymore. And yet the church wasn't satisfied with the New Testament only. As a result of the unavoidable discussions about the correct interpretation of the Bible, councils and synods on the central levels of the churches gave rulings to establish definitely the correct reading and explanation of the Bible. These rulings, especially when they were made in the form of creeds, had in real terms the same or even a bigger authority than the Bible itself. Whoever brings up for discussion the Apostolic Confession can reckon with more resistance than with bringing up for discussion certain parts of the Bible! Arguments borrowed from confessions of faith are often more decisive than arguments borrowed from Scripture. The purpose of such confessions is indeed to lay down once for all the "One and Only Truth" in a number of brief and powerful statements. The consequence is a tremendous narrowing of the Christian faith, a concentration on essentials of which we taste the bitter fruits today: in the eyes of many Christians – theologians and non-practising members of a church alike –, the the wide scope of the Bible has become an inaccessible maze. The ethics lead a marginal life in Christianity and if it is discussed at all, it is often based on obsolete natural philosophy or on scriptural passages taken out of their context.

In Judaism the situation is totally different. As opposed to the dogmatic narrowing of Christianity, a huge exegetical broadening has taken place in the whole of the Jewish tradition. Confessions of faith are really unfamiliar to Judaism. The only statement one could consider as such, is

Deuteronomy 6,4.[a, 311] It's true, the canon of Tanakh is laid down by the rabbis at the end of the first century, but even so the Tanakh is not closed, essentially. If ever a prophet should arise in Israel, his writings could be added to Tanakh.[b] Furthermore, after the fixation of Tanakh the production of books with a generally accepted religious authority didn't stop at all. Firstly, the Mishnah, the core of the later Talmud, was compiled from the Oral Torah. In later centuries, the Mishnah was extensively commented upon in the Gemara. The Mishnah and the Gemara together make up the Talmud which is much more voluminous than Tanakh itself. In the Talmud Tanakh is unclosed as it were. The discussions of the rabbis about the *halakhah*, the system of rules that show how to lead a good life, are found in it. Arguments derived from Tanakh are often decisive in these discussions. Nevertheless not only the conclusions are mentioned. All sorts of viewpoints pro and con are brought forward. Many discussions aren't even rounded off with a conclusion. That's up to the reader. With regard to some points of view it's made clear that they are not valid now, but perhaps will take effect in the future. The entire scope of Jewish life is dealt with in the Talmud. Characteristic for the breadth and openness of the Jewish tradition is the existence of two versions of the Talmud: the Babylonian and the Jerusalem one. The first one, the Babylonian Talmud, is more engrafted onto the urban life of the Jews of Babylon, the second one more onto the rural life in the land of Israel. By and large one is fully aware of the fact that new circumstances of life demand a new orientation on the tradition. In addition to the Talmud, numerous writings were composed from the Oral Torah with an authority almost just as large. However, in this respect Judaism differs completely with Christianity, because this

---

[a] One could consider the thirteen principles of Judaism, Maimonides (1135-1204) laid down, to be a confession of faith (see endnote). They were, however, never generally accepted and bringing them into challenge on good grounds, one doesn't put oneself outside the Jewish tradition.

[b] That's the consequence of the fact one still expects the coming of Elijah and the messiah.

isn't the authority of the "truth" laid down once and for all. It's the authority of an ongoing tradition which renews itself continuously on the base of its principles.

In fact, we not only find this attitude of an open tradition already in Tanakh but also in the gospels. Many books and stories in the Bible have an open end. They invite the readers as it were to continue the story. Anything in Tanakh and in the gospels is in line with an ongoing tradition. The end of Genesis plays in Egypt. In Deuteronomy the Torah ends in the land of Moab. The second book of Kings ends in Babylon. These are all places where, of course, the history of Israel couldn't finish at all. The book of Jonah has such a curious open end as well. The same is true for the gospel of Mark that ends with the open grave (Mark 16,9-20 is a later addition). Even the gospel of Matthew has an open end. In chapter 4 we saw that in this gospel the Ascension isn't mentioned at all. Therefore the question arises: where did Jesus stay after this gospel is ended? The Acts, too, have such a remarkable open end, leaving the reader behind with many questions about its sequel.[312] And just that is what all these open ends are about: the reader or listener himself ought to continue the book by practising its message and possibly by adjusting it to new circumstances. One should never suggest that the "truth" has been found definitively. A living tradition can change essentially at every moment in its history and yet fulfil, or even *better* fulfil, its original principles. That is the situation Christianity has ended up in today.

Another important consideration is that the evangelists wrote their gospels for the greater part against the background of the Torah. This is certainly the case with Matthew and Luke as I have shown in the chapters 4 and 5 and in "Luke the Jew".[313] Therefore, Christians ought to go and read the gospels with the motto: "Reading Torah, the key to the gospels". Just like Jesus, his disciples and the evangelists we should consider the Torah as the centre of the revelation. But not only the Written Torah ought to be restored in the churches as the core of the Scriptures. The Oral Torah as well ought to be rediscovered as an indispensable instrument to open up the New Testament. Only then the reading of the gospels will reach its full growth.

In the Christian church the "Old Testament" has always been read as a historical and prophetical preparation to the New Testament. The writers of the Old Testament looked forward, as it were, and saw the life of Jesus Christ. However, such a way of reading isn't tenable anymore. In reality it was just the other way round: the writers of the New Testament looked "backwards" at Tanakh and asked themselves whether Jesus had fulfilled the principles of faith formulated in it. Therefore, Christians could and should read Tanakh too, as an independent source of instruction with respect to life and faith for all times. The Christian church, however, has no proper tradition, no method, no way of reading available to understand Tanakh in its original Hebrew meaning. That's why Christians today should apprentice themselves to the rabbis to read the Hebrew Bible.

And so I have reached a third point. After Auschwitz, Christianity will be obliged to thoroughly change its attitude towards Judaism. Maybe, this change will not happen at the same pace on all levels. Popes and metropolitans, faith healers and door-to-door preachers will go their own way for a long time yet. It's true, Christianity also has great chances to survive as a kind of folklore without Judaism, because without some faith nobody will feel well after all. Christmas stables, processions and passion plays wouldn't be brushed aside quickly, as little as Father Christmas, Passover fires and Halloween. But as a religion Christianity can't do without a lasting orientation on Judaism any longer. Bit by bit, the lost son will go back home once again. This time, however, not with the conceited attitude of a convert who thinks to be entitled to lay down the rules in his father's house. The new Christian relation with Judaism ought to be like the relation of a younger son to an older son, of a pupil to a teacher. Only then a type of Christianity could emerge that was more or less intended by the evangelists.

Such a Christianity after Auschwitz will lose its dogmatic character. The traditional Christian doctrine, largely developed from Greco-Roman thought – as I have shown in chapter 6 –, will have to abandon the field. New perceptions of faith will be able to develop, based not only on the New Testament, but on Tanakh and the Oral Torah as well. However, these new theological perceptions will never hold the same position as the earlier dogmas. Following Judaism, Christianity will become non-dogmatic. The multiformity, so characteristic for Judaism and found in the New Testament as well, could prevent a new Christian theology from degenerating into a renewed searching after the "only true doctrine". As we have seen, the evangelists thought differently about Jesus. Likewise the Christians, who feel inspired by Judaism, will be allowed to think differently about their teacher Jesus of Nazareth and, in doing so, about their own life in the service of the one and only God.

Instead of questions with respect to an abstract doctrine about grace and salvation, other questions with respect to the way of life will emerge in the centre of Christian contemplation. Then the dynamic Hebrew language is going to play a part in Christian thought again. Then the Hebrew thought, from which I have shown something in chapter 1, will inspire us to a life in Biblical perspective. Grace and salvation will become a daily reality instead of being dogmatic ideas. Then Jesus' word according to Matthew will be fulfilled that says: "Not everyone who says to me: 'Lord, Lord', will enter the kingdom of heaven, but he who will do the will of my father who is in heaven" (Matthew 7,21). And this, of course, requires contemplation with the motto: "Reading Torah, the key to the gospels!"

Notes

1   In Dutch: "Het evangelie uit het leerhuis van Lazarus" (Van 't Riet, 1996).

2   Van 't Riet, 2012 and 2018. In Dutch: "Lukas de Jood" (Van 't Riet, 2009).

3   See NKJV; NEB renders "worldly wealth".

4   Marlowe [found 2009] enumerates 21 different kinds of Semitisms in the Greek of the New Testament.

5   Mussies, 1976, p. 1053.

6   I published a more extended discussion on the subjects of this paragraph in *Lukas de Jood* (Barnard & Van 't Riet, 1984, p. 16 ff.; Van 't Riet, 2009 p. 16 ff.). In that publication references can be found to the studied literature as well.

7   For the difference in Greek-Roman and Jewish thinking see: Zuidema (1977, p. 85-86), who argues that the first is more oriented on space as a static category of consciousness whereas the last is more focused on time as a dynamic category of consciousness.

8   Abram, 1980, p. 129; Prijs, 1980, p. 28. *Gharut* is a form of the stem *Ghet-Resh-Tav*, where *cherut* is derived from *Ghet-Vav-Resh* (Jastrow, 1971, p. 460, 500).

9   Abram, 1980, p. 136-137.

10   Aschkenasy en Whitlau, 1981, p. 35.

11   Breukelmans, 1984, p. 121.

12   Alter, 1981, p. 40.

13   Translations of the Apocrypha can be found in the NEB.

14   Quoted from the NEB.

15   Grundmann, 1971, p. 320.

16   Van der Ploeg, 1970, p. 157-158.

17   Lapide, 1983, p. 7.

18   Baba Metsia 59b. The quotation is from the Epstein Edition of the Babylonian Talmud with some small variations. In the Dutch original I have quoted: Zuidema, 1977, p. 157.

19   Zuidema, 1977, p. 158.

20   For both stories, see: Quispel, 1971, p. 117-118, 122. The English translation of Thomas, Log. 8, is quoted from: Robinson, 1984, p. 118.

21   See e.g.: Guilding, 1960, p. 6 f.

22   E.g., they are part of the NEB.

23   See e.g. Prijs, 1980, p. 22 f.

24   Abram, 1980, p. 78 f.

25 Musaph-Andriesse, 1973, p. 25 f. This book was published in English in 1982 titled: *From Torah to Kabbalah: a basic introduction to the writings of Judaism.* New York, OUP 1982.

26 My definition of *midrash* differs in some way from that of current Biblical scholarship. For a broader discussion about this subject I refer to chapter 4, especially section 4.7.

27 In NKJV vers 24 I have replaced "hurting" by "striping", because in Hebrew the same expression is used as in Exodus 21,25.

28 bT Bava Kamma 83b-84a; Mekhilta of R. Ishmael, Nezikin 8.

29 This is for example the case too with the prophet Elijah and the priest Pinehas, the grandson of Aaron. See: Hengel, 1976, p. 167 f.

30 E.J., Zechariah, column 958.

31 E.J., Zechariah, column 952.

32 In Barnard & Van 't Riet, 1984, p. 141 f. and Van't Riet, 2009, p. 162 f. a more extended discussion of this subject can be found.

33 Ginzberg, 1968, Volume 1, p. 107.

34 E.J., Zechariah, column 952.

35 E.J., Zechariah, column 958.

36 Millgram, 1971, p. 113 f.

37 Deurloo, 1966, p. 529-530.

38 Deurloo, 1966, p. 530.

39 BT Megillah 9a-9b.

40 BT Megillah 9a-9b.

41 E.J., Bible, column 855.

42 Barnard & Van 't Riet, 1984, p. 47-48; Van 't Riet, 2009, p. 55.

43 B.H.W., Aristeas.

44 Roest & Terborgh, 1972.

45 See the last note.

46 De Vries, 1968, p. 16.

47 Vermes, 1983, p. 71; E.J., Torah.

48 C.f. Dodd, 1980, p. 82; Glasson, 1963, p. 24 nt. 2.

49 C.f. De Beus, 1973, p. 116.

50 C.f. my commentary on the prologue of the Fourth Gospel (Van 't Riet, 1996, p. 309 f.).

51 Safrai (2), 1976, p. 798.

52 Safrai (1), 1976, p. 779.

53 Safrai (2), 1976, p. 800.

54 Mekhilta de Rabbi Ishmael, Pischa 1.

55   Safrai (2), 1976, p. 798.
56   E.J., Shema, reading of; and: Nash Papyrus.
57   Lapide, 1983, p. 72 f.
58   Millgram, 1971, p. 86.
59   For the Shema-Yisrael-prayer: see the last section. Today the Amidah-prayer (The "Eighteen Benedictions"; see later) also belongs to the evening-prayer, but this is based on a later extension from the time after the destruction of the temple (Millgram, 1971, p. 160).
60   Hertz, 1976, p. 997 f.
61   Millgram, 1971, p. 107, 160.
62   Millgram, 1971, p. 83 f.
63   De Vries, 1968, p. 16.
64   Van der Sluis e.a., 1978.
65   E.J., Amidah.
66   Safrai (3), 1976, p. 923. For the different versions of this prayer on different liturgical occasions, see: Hertz, 1976, p. 130 f., 895 f.; and: E.J., Amidah.
67   The translation is, in a modernized version, borrowed from: Hertz, 1976, p. 131 f. At the same time I changed in all cases and in accordance with the original Hebrew, the word "thy" into "his".
68   The translation of Hertz (1976) renders: "the strength of salvation". Here I give a more literal translation of the original Hebrew: "the horn of salvation".
69   Neusner, 1975, p. 16-17.
70   The verses 3 and 4 are a later addition to the text.
71   Neusner, 1975, p. 20.
72   Neusner, 1975, p. 16.
73   Flusser, 1968, p. 44.
74   Safrai (2), 1976, p. 802.
75   See also section 3.6.
76   E.J., Grace after meals. Safrai (2), 1976, p. 802.
77   For a brief summary of the argumentation, see: Grundmann, 1971, p. 395 f. Cf. Flusser, 1984, p. 131-132.
78   E.J., Passover.
79   E.J.,Passover.
80   M. Shabbat 7:2.
81   M. Chagiga 1:8.

82 A more extended treatment of the Pharisees can be found in: Van 't Riet, 2009, p. 162-178.

83 Until recently the general opinion of Christian exegetes was that Jesus transgressed the precepts of the Sabbath. The abolishment of the Sabbath as the traditional Jewish holy day is often worded more or less explicitly. Some quotations can illustrate this generally (!) accepted opinion. Geldenhuys, 1950, p. 203: "...Jesus, who rejects all man-made Sabbath-regulations, ..." (on Luke 6,6-11). Caird, 1963, p. 99: "Any threat to the Sabbath was bound to evoke strenuous opposition, yet Jesus not only broke these regulations but often seems to have gone out of his way to break them" (on Luke 6,1-11). Thompson, 1972, p. 105: "Jesus claims an authority overriding the Sabbath regulations" (on Luke 6,1-11). Barclay, 1975, p. 72: "In this incident Jesus openly broke the law" (on Luke 6,6-11). Schlatter, 1975, p. 325: "... dass sich Jesus dem Sabbatgebot nicht unterwarf, wenn aus ihm das Verbot der Hilfe wurde" (on Luke 13,10-17). B.H.W., Sabbat: "Because of the sovereignty of love, Jesus sometimes didn't hesitate to transgress the commandment of the Sabbath in a rather provoking way" (translated from Dutch). Grundmann, 1971, p. 279: "Lukas nimmt die verschiedenen Sabbatheilungen auf, weil er in der Befreiung der Liebe von allen Beschränkungen ein zentrales Anliegen der Christenheit sah" (on Luke 13,10-17, where Grundmann quotes Schlatter in agreement). Creating a contradiction between love and the precepts of the Sabbath, however, is disastrous for the understanding of the gospel-stories about healing on the Sabbath.

84 Flusser, 1968, p. 47.

85 Lapide, 1983, p. 60. In my book "Het evangelie uit het Leerhuis van Lazarus" (*The Gospel from the Study House of Laz'arus*) I have showed that this story deals with the difference of opinion about the question if a blind person's life is permanently in danger (Van 't Riet, 1996, p. 254-255). In that case healing with material means is permitted.

86 I don't agree with the opinion of Flusser (1968, p. 44) that the plucking of the heads of grain is added by the Greek translator of an originally Hebrew or Aramaic story, who had no longer any knowledge of the customs of the people. The three Jewish evangelists are unanimous in mentioning the plucking. Flusser's idea that the original story only mentioned the rubbing in the hands, originates from his opinion that the historical Jesus was in complete agreement with the Oral Torah. His repeated conclusion that the Gospel of Luke is the most original gospel

(see also: Flusser, 1983, passim), is caused by the fact that Luke, of all evangelists, is nearest to the rabbis of the "Liberal"-Pharisaic School of Hillel, who edited the Oral Torah (cf. Van 't Riet, 2009, p. 162-178).

87 Lapide, 1983, p. 55.
88 Van 't Riet, 2009, p. 162 f.
89 Lapide, 1983, p. 56.
90 Lapide, 1983, p. 60.
91 See: E.J., Nazirite.
92 I earlier discussed Luke's attitude to the temple of Jerusalem in "Lukas, de Jood" (*Luke the Jew*) (Van 't Riet, 2009, p. 134 f.).
93 For example the edition of the Dutch Statenvertaling (a translation comparable with the King James Version) published by De Nederlandsche Bijbel-Compagnie in Amsterdam; J. Brandt & Son, Haarlem; Joh. Enschede & Sons, undated.
94 For example in the Dutch translation published by Nederlands Bijbelgenootschap, Amsterdam, 1951.
95 For example in the above-mentioned translation of Nederlands Bijbelgenootschap, Amsterdam, 1951.
96 In the above-mentioned edition of the Statenvertaling.
97 For example the Dutch Petrus Canisius-translation published by Het Spectrum, Utrecht/Antwerpen, undated.
98 B.H.W., Evangeliënharmonie.
99 E.J., New Testament, Canonization.
100 Klijn, 1974, p. 41.
101 Lindijer, 1981, passim; Barnard & Van 't Riet, 1984; Van 't Riet, 2009, section 9.1 and 9.3.b.
102 Included in: Orden van Dienst en Heidelbergse Catechismus voor gebruik in de erediensten van de Gereformeerde Kerken in Nederland, undated. On the 1st of May 2004 these churches were included into the Protestant Church of the Netherlands (PKN).
103 See for the Jewishness of Luke my book "Lukas de Jood" (*Luke the Jew*) (Barnard & Van 't Riet, 1984; Van 't Riet, 2009).
104 See: Barnard en Van 't Riet, 1984; Van 't Riet, 2009, section 5.1.b and 5.1.c (incl. the note in section 5.1.c).
105 E.J., Aggada.
106 E.g. the Revised Standard Version (1971); the NKJV (1982).
107 Smelik, 1979, p. 41.

[108] An extended discussion about the idea of *midrash* can be found in my book "Lukas versus Matteüs" (*Luke versus Matthew*) (Van 't Riet, 2005, chapter 2).

[109] In "Lukas, de Jood" (*Luke the Jew*) (Barnard & Van 't Riet, 1984; Van 't Riet, 2009, par. 4.4) I have shown this for Luke 1. The birth-story of Jesus in Luke 2, I have discussed in "Christendom à la Jezus" (*Christianity in Jesus' way*) (Van 't Riet, 2001, p. 80-85).

[110] Ginzberg, Vol. II, 1968, p. 9.

[111] Boon, 1980, p. 8. Connected to: Den Heyer, 1983, p. 206, the following reconstruction can be made regarding the way in which the idea of the messiah, the son of Joseph, developed in the first and second century CE. In Matthew 1 and 2 we find the oldest known version of this messianic idea: a suffering messiah who acts without the use of violence. In the course of the 2nd century, only a short time after the dramatic end of the Bar-Kochba-revolt in 135 CE, this messianic idea became connected to the destroyed movement of the freedom fighters against the Roman authority. From then on the messiah, the son of Joseph, is presented as the messiah anointed to war, who leads the army in the decisive war against the enemies of Israel and who perishes in it. Thus enabling the coming of the messiah, the son of David. From all this can be concluded that not so much the nonviolence as well the willingness to suffer and to die is the essential element of the idea of the messiah, the son of Joseph. This doesn't alter the fact that different rabbis could have had different opinions about this subject.

[112] E.g. the New English Bible, 1970, the New King James Version, 1985 respectively.

[113] Sandmel, 1974, p. 147 f.

[114] E.g. Kroon, undated; Den Heyer, 1983, p. 139 f., cf. also p. 176 f.; Soetendorp, 1966, p. 85.

[115] Ginzberg, 1968, Vol. II, p. 262.

[116] Ginzberg, 1968, Vol. II, p. 250 f.

[117] Drury, 1976, p. 47.

[118] Deurloo, 1966, p. 530.

[119] Ginzberg, 1968, Vol. I, p. 207.

[120] Ginzberg, 1968, Vol. I, p. 186 f.

[121] A more extended discussion of these features of midrashim in the gospels can be found in: Barnard & Van 't Riet, 1984 or Van 't Riet, 2009, par. 4.6. Also in: Van 't Riet, 2005.

122 Beek, 1959, p. 5.
123 Beek, 1959, p. 6.
124 E.J.: Herod I, column 382.
125 E.g.: Glasson, 1963, p. 20 f.
126 Barnard & Van 't Riet, 1984; Van 't Riet, 2009, section 9.3.c; Van 't Riet, 2005, chapter 5 and 7.
127 Matthew doesn't identify Jesus with Elijah, but John the Baptist. See: Barnard & Van 't Riet, 1984; Van 't Riet, 2009, par. 4.3. Also: Van 't Riet, 2005, chapter 4.
128 Den Heyer, 1983, p. 193.
129 Barnard & Van 't Riet, 1984; Van 't Riet, 2009, section 9.1.
130 Barnard & Van 't Riet, 1984; Van 't Riet, 2009, section 9.2.
131 In the previous discussion all differences of opinions between Matthew and Luke are not completely dealt with. In my book "Lukas versus Matteüs" (*Luke versus Matthew*) (Van 't Riet, 2005) I have gone further into the matter.
132 Cf.. E.B. Mac, Talmud and Midrash.
133 Klijn, 1974, p. 26.
134 Klijn, 1974, p. 27; Baarda, 1969, p. 67 f.
135 Klijn, 1974, p. 28.
136 Baarda, 1969, p. 69.
137 Flusser, 1983, p. 16.
138 Flusser, 1983, passim.
139 Conzelmann, 1964, p. 45.
140 Barnard & Van 't Riet, 1984; Van 't Riet, 2009, section 6.6 en 6.8.d.
141 Drury, 1976, p. 40. Cf.: Schramm, 1971, p. 1, note 3.
142 Moreover, I have shown elsewhere that the Q-hypothesis even leads to contradictions (Van 't Riet, 2005, chapter 9).
143 The Oral Torah also has the notion of the spirit of God like a dove (cf. Rashi, on Genesis 1,2).
144 Ginzberg, 1968, Vol. I, p. 56.
145 E.J., Ru'ah Ha-Kodesh.
146 Both the original texts, the Greek one of Mark as well as the Hebrew one of Isaiah, are ambiguous with respect to the position of the expression "in the wilderness": is it the place where the saying was said, or is it the first word of the saying itself? Both interpretations are linguistically possible and Bible-translations vary largely at this point (cf. e.g. the NKJV and the NEB). But on the bases of the parallelism "the wilderness – the desert" and "the road – the highway" in Isaiah 40,3,

one should choose the second option in my view. After all, parallelism is a characteristic feature of the Hebrew poetry. The problem is that Mark quotes Isaiah 40,3 incompletely. Because he removes "the highway" in the second part of the verse, the parallelism is lost and the impression emerges that with the words "in the wilderness" the place of the saying is meant. This even influenced some translations of Isaiah 40,3 (e.g. the NKJV) where the parallelism is broken. I prefer to translate Mark 1,3 in accordance with Isaiah 40,3, interpreted on the bases of the parallelism in the Hebrew text.

147 Strack-Billerbeck, 1969, Vol. 1, p. 135.
148 Strack-Billerbeck, 1969, Vol. 1, p. 136.
149 E.J., Satan.
150 Ginzberg, 1968, Vol. I, p. 276.
151 E.g. the stories Luke 4,16-30 and 4,31-44 (see Barnard & Van 't Riet, 1984; Van 't Riet, 2009, section. 6.8.b).
152 Exodus Rabba 47:5 (102a).
153 See e.g. NKJV.
154 Cf. the interesting explanation in: Vermes, 1977, p. 192 f.
155 The New English Bible with Apocrypha, Oxford/Cambridge, 1970.
156 Vermes, 1977, p. 197. To be sure, this is a word of a rabbi from the third century, but it exactly summarizes the opinion existing on this point in the Judaism of the previous centuries.
157 Cf. Hester, 1977, p. 54-55.
158 Strack-Billerbeck, 1969, Vol. 1, p. 151.
159 See e.g.: Farmer, 1973, p. 181.
160 Literally: "prostrated themselves before it" (NEB). The NKJV translates mistakenly "worshiped it", losing the connection with "throwing down".
161 See the discussion about Luke 4,16-30 in: Barnard & Van 't Riet, 1984; Van 't Riet, 2009, section 6.8.
162 Barnard & Van 't Riet, 1984; Van 't Riet, 2009, section 7.2.
163 Barnard & Van 't Riet, 1984; Van 't Riet, 2009, section 9.3.c.
164 See the last note but one.
165 Schoon, 1983, p. 29; see also: Lapide, 1983, p. 26.
166 Klijn, 1974, p. 100.
167 E.g. Den Heyer, 1998, p. 22 f.
168 Stemberger, 1978, p. 80.
169 Malingrey, 1972, p. 25.

170 Drury, 1976, p. 28.
171 Dijk, 1980, p. 12.
172 E. B. Mac, Christian Myth and Legend.
173 Stemberger, 1978, p. 49.
174 Stemberger, 1978, p. 55-56.
175 E. B. Mac, Christian Myth and Legend.
176 Malingrey, 1972, p. 43; Fontaine, 1972, p. 130.
177 E.B. Mic, Justin Martyr, Saint.
178 E.B. Mic, Tertullian.
179 Malingrey, 1972, p. 51.
180 Malingrey, 1972, p. 43.
181 Fontaine, 1972, p. 126-127.
182 Smelik, 1979, p. 29.
183 Storig, 1969, Vol. 1, p. 189.
184 Sassen, 1942, p. 12.
185 Stemberger, 1978, p. 56.
186 Meijering, 1974, p. 63.
187 Smelik, 1979, p. 29.
188 Smelik, 1979, p. 29.
189 Fontaine, 1972, p. 129.
190 Storig, 1969, Vol. 1, p. 189.
191 Sassen, 1942, p. 15.
192 Smelik, 1979, p. 46.
193 Sassen, 1942, p. 9-10; Storig, 1969, Vol. 1, p. 207.
194 Fontaine, 1972, p. 131.
195 Smelik, 1979, p. 95; Malingrey, 1972, p. 31.
196 Smelik, 1979, p. 92; Fontaine, 1972, p. 131.
197 Sassen, 1942, p. 11.
198 Malingrey, 1972, p. 36.
199 In this context the expression *logos spermatikos* is used; Sassen, 1942, p. 15, 16.
200 Meijering, 1974, p. 37.
201 Sassen, 1942, p. 15, 16.
202 Sassen, 1942, p. 15-16; E.B. Mic, Justin Martyr, Saint.
203 Malingrey, 1972, p. 37.
204 Malingrey, 1972, p. 48.
205 Sassen, 1942, p. 25.
206 Sassen, 1942, p. 19-20.
207 Sassen, 1942, p. 26.

208 Sassen, 1942, p. 18.
209 Meijering, 1974, p. 30.
210 Fontaine, 1972, p. 138-140.
211 Sassen, 1942, p. 21; Fontaine, 1972, p. 135, 136.
212 Fontaine, 1972, p. 140.
213 Fontaine, 1972, p. 131.
214 Sassen, 1942, p. 22.
215 Malingrey, 1972, p. 31.
216 Sassen, 1942, p. 15.
217 Green, 1979, p. 14.
218 Green, 1979, p. 327, note 17.
219 Sassen, 1942, p. 15.
220 Drury, 1976, p. 23.
221 E.B. Mic., Justin Martyr, Saint.
222 Meijering, 1974, p. 24.
223 Meijering, 1974, p. 53-56.
224 Stemberger, 1978, p. 100.
225 Van 't Riet, 1996. p. 311 f.
226 Stemberger, 1978, p. 102.
227 Meijering, 1974, p. 30-31.
228 Drury, 1976, p. 23.
229 Meijering, 1974, p. 31.
230 Malingrey, 1972, p. 55.
231 Meijering, 1974, p, 33.
232 Smelik, 1979, p. 80.
233 Malingrey, 1972, p. 45.
234 Malingrey, 1972, p. 33.
235 Meijering, 1974, p. 55, 56.
236 E.B. Mic, Allegorical interpretation, biblical.
237 Smelik, 1979, p. 100 f.
238 NKJV gives: "which things are symbolic". The Greek text literary has: 'allegorized'.
239 Jansen, 1981, p. 150.
240 E.g. in Isaiah 5; see also: E.J., Vine.
241 For the spirit of God in the form of a dove, see e.g. Matthews 3,16 and parallelisms; cf. also: Tosefta Hagigah 2.5; Ber. Rabba 2.4 etc. For the dove as a symbol for Israel, see e.g. PRE 28. For other places, see Ginzberg, Deel VII, 1968, by: Dove.

242 E.J., Pig.
243 See e.g. Exodus 15,1 and 4, and many other places in Tanakh.
244 E.g. in Michah 4,4. See for other examples: Lapide, 1983, p. 8 f.
245 Sevenster, 1976, p. 12 f.
246 E.g. Smelik, 1979; Jansen, 1981.
247 Drury, 1976, p. 24.
248 Malingrey, 1972, p. 21.
249 Smelik, 1979, p. 102.
250 Jansen, 1981, p. 68 f. For the formulation of this sentence, see: Oostveen, 1982, p. 44.
251 Jansen, 1981, p. 150.
252 Van Klinken, 2009, p. 16.
253 Van Klinken, 2009, p. 81, nt. 27.
254 Van Klinken, 2009, p. 11-14.
255 Van Klinken, 2009, p. 28.
256 Van Klinken, 2009, p. 115 e.v. In Dutch: *Overlegorgaan voor Joden en Christenen* (OJEC).
257 In the periodical *OJEC-Periodiek* en in the *OJEC-Series* of paperbacks (both since 1984) many subjects that played a part in the relations between Jews and Christians were put on the order-paper.
258 Van Klinken, 2009, p. 28, 37.
259 Standard publications in this area are cf.: Isaac, 1962; Parkes, 1969; Radford Ruether, 1974; Jansen, 1981.
260 Cf. Van Klinken, 2009, p. 129.
261 Van Klinken, 2009, p. 26.
262 Van Klinken, 2009, p. 29.
263 Van Klinken, 2009, p. 120.
264 Van Klinken, 2009, p. 121.
265 Here I mention the leaflets of the ICI distributed in large numbers with the title *Wat ieder van het jodendom moet weten* (*What everyone should know about Judaism*) (Van Klinken, 2009, p. 69), the periodical *Ter Herkenning* (*Recognition*) ('s-Gravenhage/Zoetermeer, 1973-1998) and the essay-series *Verkenning en Bezinning* (*Reconnaissance and Consciousness*) (Kampen, 1967-1989).
266 Van Klinken, 2009, p. 151 e.v.
267 Van Klinken, 2009, p. 53
268 Boon, 1983, passim.

269 In the Netherlands K.H. Miskotte was a representative of them with publications like *Het Wezen der Joodse Religie* (*The Essence of the Jewish religion*) (1932) and *Edda en Thora* (*Edda and Torah*) (1939).

270 E.g. in the *Dutch-Reformed Council on the Church and Israel* and in the so-called *Amsterdam School of Exegesis and Biblical Theology* at the University of Amsterdam (Van Klinken, 2009, p. 22 f., 40).

271 In the Amsterdam School (see the previous note) the Talmud as well was taught (Van Klinken, 2009, p. 40).

272 Van Klinken, 2009, p. 150.

273 In 1990 the *Vereniging tot bevordering van kennis van Hebreeuws* (*Society on the promotion of knowledge of Hebrew*) was erected which still counted 400 members in 2010 [www.hebreeuws.org, September 2010]. See also: Schoon, 1984, p. 16 f.

274 This can be concluded from: Van Klinken, 2009, p. 40-41.

275 At best some song-texts were influenced and the yearly Bible-lectionaries were changed by it.

276 Van Klinken, 2009, p. 120.

277 This is the subtitle of my book *Christendom à la Jezus* (*Christianity à la Jesus*) published in Dutch in 2001 (Van 't Riet, 2001). I would like to remark that the word "faith" is female in Hebrew.

278 See my book *Het mensbeeld van de Tora* (*The concept of man in the Torah*) (Van 't Riet, 2006).

279 Van Praag, 1966, p. 563.

280 The Great-uncle of the Israeli author Amos Oz who described him lovingly in his book *Sipur al ahava wechoshech* (A Story of Love and Darkness) (Oz, 2004).

281 E.J.,: Klausner, Joseph Gedaliah.

282 Flusser, 1968, p. 7.

283 Flusser, 1968, p. 8.

284 Flusser, 1968, p. 11.

285 Lapide, 1983, p. 25.

286 Lapide, 1983, p. 18 f.

287 Flusser, 1968, p. 11; Lapide, 1983, p. 12 f.

288 Lapide, 1983, p. 69.

289 Flusser, 1984, p. 165, explains that work-hypotheses are admittedly needed for the reconstruction of Jesus' words, but that those often deal only with minor matters like the correct formulation of a logion.

290 E.g. Flusser, 1984, p. 155; Lapide, 1983, p. 14, 21, 24, 56, 69, 74.

291 Flusser, 1984, p. 149.

292 Flusser, 1984, p. 164.

293 Flusser, 1984, p. 174.

294 See for Luke: Barnard & Van 't Riet, 1984; Van 't Riet, 2009, passim.

295 Parkes, 1981, p. 42, speaks truly about an "unmistakable increase in hostility", and according to the index this is about the "attitude to Jews" (see under: Mark, Gospel of, en: Matthew, Gospel of, p. 427).

296 See for a more extended discussion on the Pharisees: Barnard & Van 't Riet, 1984, of Van 't Riet, 2009, section 9.1.

297 Barnard & Van 't Riet, 1984; Van 't Riet, 2009, section 9.1.

298 Parkes, 1981, p. 42-43.

299 Barnard & Van 't Riet, 1984; Van 't Riet, 2009, section 6.8. In the discussion about Luke's Nazareth-story found in that section, this aspect isn't explicitly mentioned, because the development of the argument didn't permit me to do so in that place.

300 For John, see my book "Het evangelie uit het leerhuis van Lazarus" (*The gospel from the study-house of Lazarus*) (Van 't Riet, 1996, especially chapter 25).

301 Grimal, 1962, p. 145.

302 Grimal, l962, p. 54.

303 E.J., Pig.

304 Tcherikover, 1975, p. 342; Daniel-Rops, 1965, p. 180; Lapide, 1983, p. 63-64; Zuidema, 1977, p. 102.

305 Barnard en Van 't Riet, 1984; Van 't Riet, 2009, par. 2.2, 9.1.

306 Barnard en Van 't Riet, 1984; Van 't Riet, 2009, par. 9.3.b.

307 This is completely in accordance with my argument in "Luke, the Jew": Luke wrote both his books for a Jewish public (see Barnard & Van 't Riet, 1984; Van 't Riet, 2009, passim).

308 See e.g. Grundmann, 1971, p. 310.

309 Grundmann, 1971, p. 311.

310 Barnard & Van 't Riet, 1984; Van 't Riet, 2009, par. 5.1.e.

311 Dasberg, 1977, p. 384.

312 This open end of the Acts plays an important part in the discussions about the dating of the book (see e.g. Staudinger, 1982, p. 33 f.).

313 Barnard & Van 't Riet, 1984; Van 't Riet, 2009, see especially section 7.1.b.

Literature

English literature

CRIANT I, 2The Jewish people in the first century 2, Compendium Rerum Iudaicarum ad Novum Testamentum, Section I, Vol. 2, S. Safrai, M. Stern (Ed.), Assen, 1976.
E.B. Mac. Encyclopaedia Britannica, Macropaedia, 15th Ed., Chicago, 1979.
E.B. Mic. Encyclopaedia Britannica, Micropaedia, 15th Ed., Chicago, 1979.
E.J. Encyclopaedia Judaica, Jerusalem, 1978.
NKJV New King James Version.
NEB New English Bible.
PRE Pirke de Rabbi Eliezer, G. Friedlander (Ed.), New York, 1970.

Alter, R., *The Art of Biblical Narrative*, New York, 1981.
Dodd, C.H., *The interpretation of the Fourth Gospel*, Cambridge, 1980.
Drury, J., *Tradition and Design in Luke's Gospel, A Study in Early Christian Historiography*, Atlanta, 1977.
Farmer, W.R., *Maccabees, Zealots and Josephus, An Inquiry into Jewish Nationalism in the Greco-Roman Period*, Westport, Connecticut, 1973.
Ginzberg, L., *The legends of the Jews*, 7 Volumes, Philadelphia, 1968-1969.
Glasson, T.F., *Moses in the Fourth Gospel*, London, 1963.
Guilding, A., *The Fourth Gospel and Jewish Worship, A study of the relation of St. John's Gospel to the ancient Jewish lectionary system*, Oxford, 1960.
Hertz, J.H., The *authorised Daily Prayer Book, Hebrew text, English translation with commentary and notes, Revised edition*, London/Jerusalem/New York, 1976.
Hester, D.C., Expository Articles, Luke 4:1-13, in: *Interpretation* 31, 1977, p. 53-59.
Jastrow, M., *A Dictionary of the Targumim, the Talmud Babli and Yerushalmi, and the Midrashic Literature*, New York, 1982.
Lauterbach, J.Z., *Mekilta de-Rabbi Ishmael, Critical edition on the basis of the manuscripts and early editions, English translation, introduction and notes*, 3 Vol., Philadelphia, 1976.
Marlowe, M.D., *The Semitic Style of the New Testament*, op: http://www.bible-researcher.com/hebraisms.html, 2009.
Millgram, A., *Jewish worship*, Philadelphia, USA, 1975, 2nd Edition.
Millgram, A.E., *Sabbath, The day of delight*, Philadelphia, 1971, 7th Edition.

Mussies, G., Greek in Palestine and the Diaspora, in: *CRIANT* 1, 2, 1976, p. 1040-1064.

Neusner, *Invitation to the Talmud, A teaching book*, New York, 1975, 2nd Edition.

Parkes, J., *The Conflict of the Church and the Synagoge, A Study in the Origins of Antsemitism*, New York, 1969.

Radford Ruether, R., *Faith and Fraticide*, New York, 1974.

Riet, P. van 't, *Luke the Jew : An introduction to the Jewish Character of the Gospel of Luke and the Acts of the Apostles*, E-book edition, Zwolle, 2012; Paperback edition, Kampen, 2018.

Safrai, S., The Synagogue, in: *CRIANT* 1, 2, 1976, p. 908-944.

Safrai, S., Religion in everyday life, in: *CRIANT* 1, 2, 1976, p. 793-833.

Safrai, S., Home and Family, in: *CRIANT* 1, 2, 1976, p. 728-792.

Sandmel, S., *A Jewish Understanding of the New Testament*, Augmented Edition, New York, 1974.

Tcherikover, V., *Hellenistic civilization and the Jews*, New York, 1975, 3rd Edition.

Vermes, G., *Jesus the Jew, A historian's reading of the Gospels*, Glasgow, 1977, 2nd Edition.

Vermes, G., *Jesus and the World of Judaism*, London, 1983.

French literature

Isaac, J.M., *L'Enseignement du mépris*, Paris, 1962.

German literature

Conzelmann, H., *Die Mitte der Zeit, Studien zur Theologie des Lukas*, Tübingen, 1964, 5th Edition.

Flusser, D., *Jesus in Selbstzeugnissen und Bilddokumenten*, Reinbek, 1968.

Grundmann, W., *Das Evangelium nach Lukas*, Berlin, 1971.

Hengel, M., *Die Zeloten, Untersuchungen zur Jüdischen Freiheitsbewegung in der Zeit von Herodes I. bis 70 n. Chr.*, Leiden/Köln, 1976, 2nd Edition.

Schramm, T., *Der Markus-Stoff bei Lukas, Eine literarkritische und redaktionsgeschichtliche Untersuchung*, Cambridge, 1971.

Staudinger, H., Überlegungen zur Datierung des Lukasevangeliums und der Apostelgeschichte, in: *Paderborner Studien* 1/2, 1982, p. 31-36.

Strack, H.L., Billerbeck, P., *Kommentar zum Neuen Testament aus Talmud und Midrasch*, 6 Volumes, München, 1969, 5th Edition.

Israelian literature

Oz, A., *Sipur al ahava wechoshech*, Jerusalem, 2004.

Dutch literature

B.H.W. Bijbels-Historisch Woordenboek, Deel 1 t/m 6, B. Reicke, L. Rost (Red.), Utrecht/Antwerpen, 1969-1970.
ZGIO Zoals gezegd is over, Phoenix Bijbelpockets, 30 Volumes, Zeist/Bussum/Antwerpen 1962-1969.

Abram, I.B.H., *Joodse traditie als permanent leren*, Hilversum, 1980.
Aschkenasy, Y., Whitlau, W.A.C., Geliefd is de mens, Over een spreuk van Rabbi Akiba (Avoth III, 14), in: *Aschkenasy e.a.*, 1981, p. 7-24.
Aschkenasy, Y., Whitlau, Tomson, P.J., Uden, D.J. van, W.A.C. (Red.), *Geliefd is de mens*, Hilversum, 1981,
Baarda, Tj., *De betrouwbaarheid van de evangeliën*, Kampen, 1969.
Barnard, W.J., Riet, P. van 't, *Lukas de Jood, Een joodse inleiding op het evangelie van Lukas en de Handelingen der Apostelen*, Kampen, 1984.
Beek, M.A., *Flavius Josefus, Het leven van Herodes*, Amsterdam, 1959.
Beus, Ch. de, *Johannes' getuigenis van het Woord, Over de proloog van het Evangelie van Johannes*, Nijkerk, 1973.
Boon, R., *Hebreeuws Reveil, Wat bracht christen-theologen rond 1500 in de leerschool der rabbijnen?*, Kampen, 1983.
Breukelman, F.H., *Bijbelse Theologie 2, De ouverture van het Evangelie naar Mattheüs*, Kampen, 1984.
Daniel-Rops, H., *Het dagelijks leven in Palestina ten tijde van Jezus*, Utrecht/Antwerpen, 1965.
Dasberg, J. (Vert.), *Siach Jitschak, Gebed van Jitschak, Siddoer, De geordende gebeden voor het gehele jaar*, Jeruzalem/Amsterdam, 1977.
Deurloo, K.A., De midrasj en het Nieuwe Testament, In: *Wending* 21, 9, 1966, p. 524-533.
Dijk, J., *Het begon in Jeruzalem, Joodse achtergronden in de boeken van Lucas*, Ede, 1980.
Flusser, D., *De laatste dagen in Jeruzalem, De Paasweek op de voet gevolgd, Een Joodse visie op de gebeurtenissen rond het proces tegen Jezus*, Kampen, 1983.
Flusser, D., *Tussen oorsprong en schisma, Artikelen over Jezus, het Jodendom en het vroege Christendom*, Hilversum, 1984.

Green, M., *Evangelie-verkondiging in de eerste eeuwen*, Goes/Amsterdam, 1979.

Grimal, P., *Het leven der Romeinen in de Oudheid*, Utrecht/Antwerpen, 1962.

Heyer, C.J. den, *De Messiaanse weg, Deel 1, Messiaanse verwachtingen in het Oude Testament en in de vroeg-joodse traditie*, Kampen, 1983.

Heyer, C.J. den, *Paulus, Man van twee werelden*, Zoetermeer, 1998.

Jansen, H., *Christelijke theologie na Auschwitz 1, Theologische en kerkelijke wortels van het antisemitisme*, 's-Gravenhage, 1981.

Klijn, A.F.J., *De wordingsgeschiedenis van het Nieuwe Testament*, Utrecht/Antwerpen, 1976, 5th Edition.

Klinken, G. van, *Christelijke stemmen over het jodendom, Zestig jaar Interkerkelijk Contact Israël (ICI), 1946-2006*, Delft, 2009.

Kroon, H., *Openbaring, Verklaring van een bijbelgedeelte*, Kampen, undated.

Lapide, P., *Hij leerde in hun synagogen, Een joodse uitleg van de evangeliën*, Baarn, 1983.

Lindijer, C.H., *De armen en de rijken bij Lukas*, 's-Gravenhage, 1981.

Malingrey, A.M., Fontaine, J., *De oud-christelijke literatuur*, Utrecht/Antwerpen, 1972.

Meijering, E.P., *Onmodieuze Theologie, Over de waarde van de theologie van de 'grieks' denkende kerkvaders*, Kampen, 1974.

Miskotte, K.H., *Het Wezen der Joodsche Religie, Bijdrage tot de kennis van het joodsche geestesleven in dezen tijd*, Amsterdam, 1933.

Miskotte, K.H., *Edda en Thora, Een vergelijking van germaanse en israëlitische religie*, Nijkerk, 1939, 2nd Edition.

Musaph-Andriesse, *Wat na de Tora kwam, Rabbijnse literatuur van Tora tot Kabbala*, Baarn, 1973.

Oostveen, T., In Auschwitz ging het christendom failliet, in: *De Tijd*, 19 februari, 1982, p. 44-47.

Oz, A., *Een verhaal van liefde en duisternis*, Amsterdam, 2005.

Ploeg, J.P.M. van der, *Vondsten in de woestijn van Juda*, Utrecht/Antwerpen, 1970.

Praag, H. van, Hoe leest men als Jood het Nieuwe Testament?, in: *Wending* 21, 9, 1966, p. 558-564.

Prijs, L., *Inleiding in de joodse godsdienst*, Kampen, 1980.

Quispel, G., *Het Evangelie van Thomas en de Nederlanden*, Amsterdam/Brussel, 1971.

Riet, P. van 't, *Het evangelie uit het leerhuis van Lazarus, Een speurtocht naar de joodse herkomst van het vierde evangelie*, Baarn, 1996.

Riet, P. van 't, *Christendom à la Jezus, De herziening van het christelijk geloof vanuit haar joodse bronnen*, Kampen, 2001.

Riet, P. van 't, *Lukas versus Matteüs, De terugkeer van de midrasj bij de uitleg van de evangeliën*, Kampen, 2005.

Riet, P. van 't, *Lukas de Jood, Een joodse inleiding op het evangelie van Lukas en de Handelingen der Apostelen*, Zwolle, 2009.

Roest, P., Terborgh, W.F.G., *Rapport van een onderzoek naar kinderbijbels*, NBG/KBS, 1972.

Sassen, F., *Geschiedenis der patristische en middeleeuwse wijsbegeerte*, Nijmegen/Utrecht, 1942, 3rd Edition.

Schoon, S., Nieuwere ontwikkelingen in de joods-christelijke ontmoeting, in: *Verkenning en Bezinning* 18, 3, 1984 (december).

Sevenster, J.N., De wortels van het heidense antisemitisme in de oudheid, in: *Verkenning en Bezinning* 10, 1, 1976.

Sluis, D.J. van der, Tomson, P.J., Uden, D.J. van, Whitlau, W.A.C., *Elke morgen nieuw, Inleiding tot de Joodse gedachtenwereld aan de hand van het Achttiengebed*, B. Folkertsma Stichting voor Talmudica, 1978.

Smelik, K.A.D., *Hagar en Sara, De verhouding tussen jodendom en christendom in de eerste eeuwen*, Baarn, 1979.

Soetendorp, J., Het boek Daniël, De visionaire verzetsliteratuur, in: *ZGIO* 17, 1966, p. 83-96.

Stemberger, G. (Red.), *De Bijbel en het Christendom*, 4 Delen, Haarlem, 1978

Störig, H.J., *Geschiedenis van de filosofie 1*, Utrecht/Antwerpen, 1969.

Vries, S.Ph. de, *Joodse riten en symbolen*, Amsterdam, 1968, 4th Edition.

Zuidema, W., *Gods partner, Ontmoeting met het jodendom*, Baarn, 1977.

About the Author

Dr. S.P. (Peter) van 't Riet (1948) studied studied mathematics and psychology at the Free University of Amsterdam and wrote his thesis on an educational-psychological subject. He was successively a teacher of mathematics at a school for secundary education, teacher of the didactics of mathematics at the Technical University of Delft, manager at the Teacher Training Centre of Zwolle, director and professor at the Windesheim University of Zwolle.

Since the seventies he has studied the Judaism of the first centuries as well as the Jewish exegesis of the Bible, especially the Jewish character of the New Testament. He published the following titles in Dutch (the first four together with his fellow-author Will J. Barnard):

- Luke, the Jew (1984)
- Reading Tora, the Key to the Gospels (1986)
- As a Dove to the Land of Assur (1988)
- Catching the Coat-tail of a Jewish Man (1989)
- The Gospel from the Study-house of Lazarus (1996)
- Luke, the Jew (2ᵉ revised edition, 1997)
- Christianity à la Jesus (2001)
- Luke versus Matthew (2005)
- The Image of Man in the Torah (2006)
- The Philosophy of the Creation-story (2008)
- Luke, the Jew (3ᵉ revised edition, 2009)
- Reading Tora, the Key to the Gospels (2ᵉ revised edition, 2010)

In 2012 two English translation were published as e-books: *Reading Tora, the Key to the Gospels* and *Luke, the Jew*, in 2014 followed by *The Image of Man in the Tora* and in 2018 by *A Dove to the Land of War*. More information about these and other publications of the author can be found on his website: www.petervantriet.nl.